# The Chinese Economy and its Future

# The Chinese Economy and its Future

## Achievements and Problems of Post-Mao Reform

Edited by Peter Nolan and
Dong Fureng

Polity Press

First published 1990 by Polity Press
in association with Basil Blackwell

Editorial office:
Polity Press
65 Bridge Street, Cambridge CB2 1UR, UK

Marketing and production:
Basil Blackwell Ltd
108 Cowley Road, Oxford OX4 1JF, UK

Basil Blackwell Inc.
3 Cambridge Center
Cambridge, MA 02142, USA

ISBN 0 7456 0522 2

*British Library Cataloguing in Publication Data*
A CIP catalogue record for this book is
available from the British Library.

*Library of Congress Cataloging in Publication Data*
A CIP record for this book is available from the Library of Congress.

Typeset in 10 on 11 pt Times by
Wearside Tradespools, Fulwell, Sunderland
Printed in Great Britain by
TJ Press Ltd, Padstow

# Contents

# Contributors

*Chen Dongsheng* is Research Fellow, Institute of Industrial Economics, Chinese Academy of Industrial Economics

*Dong Fureng* is Honorary Director, Economics Research Institute, Chinese Academy of Social Sciences; Vice-Chairman of the Financial and Economics Committee of the National People's Congress of the People's Republic of China

*Du Runsheng* is at the Research Centre for Rural Development, State Council of the People's Republic of China

*Jiang Yiwei* is Former Director of the Institute of Industrial Economics, Chinese Academy of Social Sciences

*Li Yining* is Professor, College of Economics, Peking University

*Liu Hongru* is Vice-Administrative Director, People's Bank of China

*Bruce McFarlane* is formerly Professor of Politics, Adelaide University, South Australia

*Peter Nolan* is Fellow and Director of Studies in Economics, Jesus College; Lecturer in the Faculty of Economics and Politics, Cambridge University

*Carl Riskin* is Professor of Economics, Queens College, City University of New York; Senior Research Scholar, East Asian Institute, Columbia University

*Austin Robinson* is Emeritus Fellow, Sidney Sussex College; Emeritus Professor, Faculty of Economics and Politics, Cambridge University

*Ajit Singh* is Fellow and Director of Studies in Economics, Queen's College; Lecturer, Faculty of Economics and Politics, Cambridge University

*Tian Yuan* is Executive Director, Research Centre for Economic, Technological and Social Development, State Council of the People's Republic of China

*Wang Jiye* is Director, Economics Research Institute, State Planning Commission of the People's Republic of China

*Peter Wiles* is Emeritus Professor, London School of Economics

*Zhao Renwei* is Director, Economics Research Institute, Chinese Academy of Social Sciences

*Zhou Xiaochuan* is Assistant to the Minister of Foreign Economics and Trade, People's Republic of China

# Preface

China's attempt in the 1980s to move away from a Stalinist system of political economy was a process of great importance. In that decade the economic reforms scored many achievements, attracting enormous interest in both the socialist and non-socialist countries. Simultaneously, new problems emerged which raised questions about the future course of the Chinese economy. This volume is a cooperative effort by Chinese and Western scholars to look critically at the first decade of China's post-Mao economic reforms and to assess the path down which the economy might travel in the future. The editors wish to thank Dr Charles Curwen for his translation of the Chinese texts and Dr John Thompson of Polity Press for his considerable contribution to shaping the volume.

This book was completed before the political changes that occurred after June 1989.

# 1

# Introduction

## Peter Nolan

## Background to the Chinese reforms of the 1980s

### The Chinese economy pre-1949

Belief in the Stalinist system is virtually dead throughout the socialist bloc. For most of the socialist countries the question is not whether reform should proceed, but how, and towards what model. Although these countries operated fundamentally similar systems for decades their pre-socialist backgrounds were different, and this will influence the ways the reforms proceed in the different cases. Accordingly, it is useful to begin by briefly examining Chinese political economy pre-1949.

In contrast with other areas of the world of comparable size, for most of the past 2,000 years China's huge territory was united. The basis of political rule was a centralized imperial bureaucracy. However, despite bureaucratic interventions, the peace and unity which this provided permitted enormous long-term economic growth with widespread production for profit in the market, which in most products comprised one enormous free-trade area. By the Song dynasty in the eleventh and twelfth centuries China had a sophisticated network of commercialized cities, relatively high levels of commoditization of agriculture and handicrafts, and advanced merchant capital. One of the great historical questions, still unanswered, is why this system, with such vibrant 'capitalist sprouts' in many parts of China, was able to achieve great technical progress by the late Song dynasty but thereafter, while it grew enormously in quantitative terms, experienced no technological breakthrough comparable with the European Industrial Revolution (the 'Needham question'). On the eve of the Opium Wars (i.e. pre-1839) China was not on the verge of independent industrialization.

For most of the ensuing century after the Opium Wars (i.e. from the 1840s to the 1940s) China's political situation was chaotic. The decline of the Qing dynasty (1644–1911) was accompanied by major rebellions. Moreover, in striking contrast to Meiji Japan's rulers, the Qing resisted modernization for decades, finally fully accepting its necessity only after the defeat by Japan in 1896. The period from the collapse of the Qing in 1911 until the rise to national power of the Guomindang in 1927 was turbulent with a succession of 'warlord' governments ruling different parts of China, no consistent national rule and, indeed, a collapse into banditry in many parts of the country. Even under the Guomindang (1927–36) military struggle was waged persistently against the Chinese Communist Party (CCP). For most of the period from 1911 until the Japanese invasion in 1936, the most stable areas were the Treaty Ports under Western protection. These mostly turbulent conditions greatly handicapped economic development. Successive governments failed to raise more than a tiny fraction of national income for the state budget, a large proportion of which was spent on military and other non-economic activities. From 1900 to 1936 agricultural and handicraft output grew at roughly the same pace as population (i.e. around 0.7–0.8 per cent per annum) (Perkins 1969: 216). The overall rate of gross investment never rose above around 7 per cent of gross domestic product (GDP) and was usually much below this, despite an investible surplus estimated to be 27 per cent of net domestic product in 1933 (Perkins 1975b: 134; Riskin 1975: 72). By the 1930s, China was still a poor underdeveloped economy with the vast bulk of the population working in, and most output contributed by, agriculture. Overall output growth was extremely slow, with gross national product (GNP) per person estimated very roughly to have grown by just 3.3 per cent per decade from 1870 to 1952 (Swamy 1979: 31). However, considerable advance occurred under Japanese control in Manchuria, providing the foundation for China's post-1949 heavy industry. Moreover, under mainly indigenous Chinese ownership, rapid growth (from a non-existent base) occurred in the modern industrial sector: factory output in 15 main industrial sectors grew by 10–11 per cent per annum from 1912 to 1936 (Chang 1969: 71). By the 1920s around 1.5 million people were employed in China as a modern industrial proletariat (Chesneaux 1968: 24). These were highly concentrated geographically, especially in Shanghai and in the network of towns spreading down the Yangtse River. The provision of a reasonably secure framework in the Treaty Ports, each of which was like a 'mini-Hong Kong' in the freedom to enterprise that it provided (Myers 1980: 139–40), was vital to modern industrial growth in such inhospitable overall surroundings.

Under different conditions, notably more effective state action to assist economic development, the Chinese economy could have advanced much more rapidly than it did pre-1949. However, the dynamism displayed by Chinese capitalism under disadvantageous circumstances in response to the 'demonstration effect' provided by modern imports and goods produced in 'foreign' factors in China (see Dernberger 1975) provides evidence of the enormous growth potential of China's economy, especially in well-located areas along the east coast.

# The Chinese economy, 1949–1978

**Structures and policies** For most of the period 1949–78 China was insecure internationally. The Korean War (1950–3) was a terrible trauma for China and solidified the mutual hostility between China and the West. The USSR initially provided China with a degree of international security, but the relationship was fragile and collapsed in the late 1950s. In the 1960s China was more isolated and threatened than even the USSR had been in the 1930s. Under such conditions, policies which maximized national economic and military independence received high priority.

In domestic politics, China followed broadly the same path as the other socialist countries. A 'vanguard' Communist Party, with a long tradition of centralized operation stretching back to the 1920s, monopolized political power. All the main economic policies were decided by a small group of key personnel in the Politburo at the centre of the Party, with Mao Tsetung at its head. Although always a small minority of the total population, the Party penetrated deep into socioeconomic life. This system was able effectively to focus national efforts on key goals, but it produced the same economic problems as in other socialist countries. The high degree of centralization combined with deep Party penetration of the economy meant that it had a much greater capacity than a market-based economy with more dispersed decision-making to make great nationwide policy 'leaps', sometimes with undesirable results. Moreover, while some Party members were both 'Red' and 'expert', many were not, so that at all levels decisions were taken or influenced by technically incompetent Party cadres. Furthermore, monopolistic political control enabled the Party to stifle intellectual discussion. For long periods under Mao economics was reduced to administration and slogans, with most topics condemned as 'bourgeois'.

In the 1950s China rapidly constructed a Soviet-type material balance administrative planning system. A socialist economy was considered to involve replacing the anarchy of the market with a state-administered plan. Almost all the means of production were nationalized or transferred to ownership by 'collectives', which *de facto* operated mostly as state-owned institutions. Planners determined all significant variables directly, including enterprise inputs, output levels, product mix and prices. Competition, entrepreneurship and the pursuit of profit were eliminated: 'No longer will one enterprise compete with another; the factories, workshops, mines, and other productive institutions will all be subdivisions, as it were of one vast people's workshop, which will embrace the entire national economy' (Bukharin and Preobrazhensky 1969: 114).

Such a system has fundamental problems. Plans can only be as good as the information upon which they are based, yet enterprises have a strong incentive to provide false information in order to obtain easily attainable targets, understating true productive potentialities and inflating input needs to make output goals easier to attain. The number of decisions in even a simple plan is astonishingly large because of the feedback effects of one decision upon others. This has many consequences. It produces a tendency towards conservatism in planning ('administration' rather than purposive planning (e.g. Zaleski 1980)), as it is easier to work incrementally from the previous plan than to attempt major changes of direction. To determine centrally all the decisions in the plan is impossible, as China soon found during its First Five Year Plan (1953–7), so that a great deal of detailed planning has to be done at lower administrative levels, with only the simplest of exchanges of major commodities occurring between regions. This reinforces other pressures towards regional and sectoral self-sufficiency, with all the resulting costs in terms of opportunities forgone for trade and specialization. By the late 1970s, around 26 per cent of China's industrial output was produced in a small number of large plants, a mere 18 per cent produced in medium-sized plants and 56 per cent produced in small-scale, mainly urban, state-run plants.[1] This involved considerable costs in forgoing the benefits of economies of scale. The sheer complexity of planning combines with the necessity to construct 'taut' plans (because it is known that enterprises tend to understate production capabilities), so that it is impossible to produce a plan which does indeed balance inputs and outputs; instead there is simultaneously shortage and surplus throughout the system. In China in the early 1980s there were severe shortages of iron ore, non-ferrous metals, construction materials, transport equipment and energy. However, in 1980 the value of stockpiles of machinery and equipment was greater than that year's total capital construction investment, and almost a full year's supply of steel had been produced in unneeded varieties (Riskin 1987: 172). The fact that enterprises are uncertain about receiving inputs creates a tendency to hoard scarce inputs, thereby exacerbating the shortage. Thus the socialist economies have a high level of capital accumulation wastefully tied up in stocks.

If the plan is to balance at all, output (gross value or in physical units) must be the key success indicator by which enterprises are rewarded. Many difficulties result from this. None is more fundamental than that of trying to stimulate enterprises to innovate. The primacy of output targets combines with the unreliability of material supplies (hence the reluctance to have to negotiate new supply lines resulting from product, and perhaps from process, innovation) and state administration of prices (hence, price inflexibility in response to innovation) to produce a powerful anti-innovation bias (Berliner 1976). The cumulative impact of other distortions produced by the primacy of output targets is enormous. For example in a 'sellers market', where output is prized above other criteria of enterprise performances, quality suffers. If machinery is of poor quality and tends to break down frequently, then capacity utilization tends to fall throughout the system and the proportion of capital stock used for repair and maintenance tends to rise.

Even if planners had perfect information, even if the best hopes of computerized planning were realized (which was far from the case in China pre-1976), even if a complete set of 'shadow prices' could be produced, a key dynamic force would be missing. Direct administrative control replacing the market eliminates the 'Schumpeterian' effects of competition, which stimulates entrepreneurs to produce better products more cheaply for fear of bankruptcy and in order to gain the profits derived from market success.

These and other problems resulting from the attempt to replace the market with administrative planning have been written about by a large number of authors in relation to the socialist countries in general (see Ellman 1989, ch. 2, for a summary) and China in particular (e.g. Xue 1986). Such problems appeared in China during the First Five Year Plan (1953–7). In Sun Yefang's words (quoted in Lin 1981), which strongly recall those of Bukharin on the USSR in the 1920s, socialism would encounter severe difficulties without the 'magic whip' of competition. However, China's economists were permitted to debate these issues only briefly at the end of the First Five Year Plan (during the 'Hundred Flowers' campaign of 1957) and again in the early 1960s during China's second brief National Economic Plan (NEP) phase.[2] Changes were, indeed, made to the system of administrative planning, but they involved alterations in the level at which planning work was carried out rather than in the relationship of the enterprise to the market.

Population interrelates deeply with other economic phenomena and stands at the centre of economic development. China's population policies since 1949 exhibit both the failures and successes of Chinese socialism. Through the immense administrative power of the CCP, China established a system which was able to provide basic health care for almost all Chinese people and to provide a minimum guaranteed level of food supply. The guaranteed levels of health care and food supply were not high, but they had an enormous impact on mortality rates, reducing them from pre-1949 figures of 30–34 per 1,000 people (Orleans 1972: 53) to a maximum of 20 per 1,000 in 1957 (Aird 1972: 328–9) and perhaps as low as 11 per 1,000 (SYC 1983: 109). By the mid-1970s death rates had reportedly fallen as low as 6–7 per 1,000 (ZTZ 1986: 21). However, in the 1950s fertility rates remained at around 35–6 per 1,000. At the end of the First Five Year Plan, Ma Yinchu drew attention to the problems posed for China's economic development by a natural population growth rate which had risen to over 23 per 1,000 in 1957 (ZTZ 1986: 21) (see, for example, the account in Walker 1964). However, Ma's views were criticized heavily. Only sporadic attempts were made between 1949 and the late 1960s to reduce fertility rates. The official view for most of the time was that population growth did not threaten economic development. Indeed, Mao himself spoke of birth control as 'a way of killing off the Chinese people without shedding blood' (quoted by Aird 1972). Although in the 1970s serious measures were taken to control fertility, a huge momentum of population growth had built up with a long-term average annual population growth rate of 2.0 per cent from 1952 to 1978, and a population total which had increased from 575 million to 975 million over the same period (ZTZ 1986: 21).

China's pattern of intra-enterprise organization developed closely along Soviet lines during the First Five Year Plan (Schurmann 1968). One-man management, detailed subdivision of work, piece rates, an elaborate bonus system and sizeable wage grade differentials spread quickly through large-scale industry. Collectivization formed the cornerstone of agricultural policy. Mao had enormous confidence in the benefits from economies of scale in agriculture and in the possibilities for collective ownership, work organization and income distribution to release rural productive energies. He argued that collective farms were the only way to avoid class polarization in the villages.

Soviet methods of industrial enterprise management are not strikingly different from those of large-scale Western capitalist enterprises. The main differences between the internal organization of Chinese and Western industrial enterprises in the 1950s were the high degree of job security and the low degree of trade union independence in the former. In agriculture, the situation is strikingly different, and severe problems followed from organizing peasants in collective farms. Agriculture has unusual managerial diseconomies of scale, rendering it possible to obtain diligent labour from collective farm members only under exceptional conditions (Nolan 1988). Those difficulties rapidly became apparent in China in the mid-1950s as the Party wrestled with the intractable problem of trying to develop a remuneration system that would induce peasants to work as diligently for the collective as they had formerly worked on their own farms (e.g. Walker 1968).

China's urban and rural institutions underwent huge upheavals after 1957. Mao used his dominant position to launch two extraordinary mass movements, the Great Leap Forward of 1958–9 and the Cultural Revolution, the most intense phase of which was in 1966–8. These movements were an attempt in certain respects to move away from the Soviet path and push rapidly towards 'communism' through a centrally inspired transformation of 'production relations'. Mao considered that this could be done most easily in a poor country where the people were 'poor and blank'. During the Great Leap Forward the system set up laboriously in industrial enterprises in the First Five Year Plan was overturned. Factory management was taken over by committees of Party members and ordinary workers; managers and experts, often humiliated and disparaged, were forced to spend large amounts of time at ordinary factory work; piece rates were abolished, and earnings differentials were compressed (Schurmann 1968; Richman 1969; Howe 1973). In the countryside, even larger changes occurred. Confident of the benefits of economies of scale in all aspects of agriculture, Mao encouraged a mass movement to amalgamate China's 700,000 collective farms into just 24,000 rural peoples' communes containing an average of over 22,000 peasants, with centralized accounting and work organization. These organizations mobilized huge amounts of rural labour for irrigation work in 1957–8, much of which turned out to be useless since most of the schemes that could usefully be constructed with traditional technology had already been completed (Perkins 1969). Moreover, huge changes took place in all aspects of rural socioeconomic life: the 'private plot' was virtually eliminated; cooking, eating, laundry services and childcare were frequently socialized; income differences between villages within the commune were removed; a large part (in some cases all) of the collective income available for distribution to households was distributed according to the 'communist' principle of 'to each according to their need'. While there was initially considerable popular enthusiasm, a rapid deterioration in work motivation and disintegration of economic planning set in.

The economic collapse of 1959–61 forced a widespread retreat from Great Leap Forward policies. Urban enterprises returned to a situation similar to that of the First Five Year Plan. In the countryside, although the rural peoples' commune remained in name and with certain functions intact, the basis of work organization and accounting returned to the much smaller collective farm – the 'production team'. The private sector was restored and expanded rapidly. The distribution of collective income to team members de-emphasized the 'according to need' criterion in favour of 'according to work' (Walker 1968). Like the Great Leap Forward, the Cultural Revolution was an immensely complex event, involving briefly an attack on the Party itself. In view of the lessons of the Great Leap Forward, nothing as dramatic as that event occurred in the countryside. From 1965 to 1976 the fundamentals of rural institutions remained stable. However, considerable fluctuations occurred in both local and national policy towards such questions as the degree of freedom that peasants were allowed to work on their private plots and sell on free markets, and the degree of emphasis given to distribution 'according to need' and 'according to work' (see Chan et al. 1984 on the fluctuations of policy). At the height of the Cultural Revolution Mao promoted a return in factories to policies similar to those of the Great Leap Forward, with the same problems for enterprise organization, plan coordination and worker motivation (Richman 1969). The economic problems caused by these policies led to a reversion in the early 1970s to policies closer to those of the First Five Year Plan.

Overall the Maoist approach to the internal organization of economic institutions had a core of Stalinist features overlaid with major deviations from that model towards something distinctively Maoist during the Cultural Revolution and particularly the Great Leap Forward.

China's international economic strategy under Mao followed the Soviet path closely. International markets were regarded as economically anarchic systems from which China's domestic economy should be insulated. Accordingly, international trade was monopolized by the state and enterprises were cut off from direct contact with the international economy. The prices confronting domestic exporters and domestic importers were unrelated to world market prices. Whether their products sold well or badly on world markets made no difference to exporting enterprises. Exports were not viwed by the state as a source of demand stimulus but rather as a means to earn the foreign exchange to fill gaps in domestic supply (Mah 1971). Careful state control of China's import structure in the 1950s plus a heavy bias in domestic investment allocation towards the capital goods sector meant that by 1960 China had a high degree of self-sufficiency in capital goods (Raj 1967). Over the whole Maoist period China's share of world trade fell dramatically from around 1.4 per cent in the mid-1950s to just 0.4 per cent in the mid-1970s (Teng 1982: 168). Far from its heavy industry strategy's being justified by a foreign exchange constraint on growth, China missed out on one of the greatest opportunities to expand foreign exchange earnings and benefit from trade that the world economy has seen.[3] While Taiwan, Hong Kong, Singapore and South Korea were benefiting from explosive export growth, their potential competitors in parts of China like the Pearl River Delta and Southern Jiangsu had virtually withdrawn from international competition.

The best way to benefit from international flows of capital, labour and knowledge can be debated. In these areas, as in trade in goods, the free market is rarely the best method. However, a wealth of historical evidence and, indeed, China's own experience pre-1949 demonstrates the enormous contribution that these flows can make to economic growth. China benefited greatly in the 1950s from Soviet loans, from Soviet experts coming to China and from the large number of Chinese experts trained in the USSR. However, this cooperation ended with the Sino–Soviet split in 1960. Moreover, under Mao China was generally reluctant to allow any economic relationships other than trade with the advanced capitalist countries. Mao's confidence that an almost isolated socialist economy could attain rapid technical progress proved illusory. After the huge transfer of foreign technology in the 1950s China's rate of technical progress was abysmal and it could have benefited greatly, even under Stalinist economic planning, from larger flows from the advanced capitalist countries.

**Results**   Over the long term under Mao China's economy performed well in certain respects. Gross material product grew at an annual average rate of over 7 per cent from 1953 to 1978 (table 1.1). The growth rate of net material product was below this, reflecting the increasing amount of material inputs being used to produce a unit of output, but, even so, a growth rate of almost 6 per cent per annum (table 1.1) during the same period was a strong performance compared both with China's past and with most developing countries. The economic structure shifted rapidly away from agriculture towards industry with agriculture's share of gross material product falling from 57 to 28 per cent between 1952 and 1978 (ZTZ 1986: 7). Despite rapid long-term population growth and severe constraints on expansion of the cultivated area (and hence crop output), China attained some long-term growth in consumption: the reported

**Table 1.1** Key economic indicators, all China (output and income data all at comparable prices)

| | Average annual growth rate (%) | |
|---|---|---|
| | *1953–78* | *1978–87* |
| Total social product (gross material product) | 7.4 | 10.8 |
| Gross value of agricultural output | 2.9 | 6.5 |
| Gross value of industrial output[a] | 10.6 | 11.9 |
| Heavy industry | 13.0 | 10.0 |
| Light industry | 8.7 | 14.1 |
| National income (net material product) | 5.7 | 9.0 |
| Agriculture | 1.9 | 6.0 |
| Industry | 10.5 | 10.4 |
| Construction | 5.9 | 12.8 |
| Transport | 6.3 | 9.5 |
| Commerce | 3.2 | 9.9 |
| Population | 2.2 | 1.3 |

[a] Including output produced at village (*cun*) and lower levels.
*Source*: ZGTJNJ 1988: 38, 45, 52, 97

average annual growth rate of real consumption per person from 1952 to 1976 was 2.2 per cent (ZTZ 1988: 43). Various policies ensured a low degree of inequality in the distribution of the wage fund. Personal income distribution was affected by such measures as controls on wage grades in state enterprises, sectoral and regional differentials, rules governing the method of income allocation to rural commune members and ceilings on the distributed income of communes. The Gini coefficient for personal income distribution in China in the late 1970s was estimated to be only 0.33 (Riskin 1987: 250). Moreover, wage goods distribution was affected by price policy (high prices for luxury consumer durables, low prices for basic items of consumption), rationing, compulsory inter-regional grain transfers and regulations governing food distribution in communes. Although not producing complete equality and affecting some inequalities more than other, these measures ensured that China achieved a high degree of poverty relief from the available wage fund.

However, these achievements have to be set against serious shortcomings. The structures of the Stalinist economy as applied in China produced quite rapid overall growth of output in a wasteful fashion, requiring a large and growing amount of capital to produce a unit of output and allowing consumption to grow only slowly at best. Moreover, consumption growth was seriously handicapped by the failure to control population growth until late in the Maoist period.

China needed an extremely high rate of savings and investment to achieve its fairly high long-term growth rate of national output: the 'accumulation' rate[4] rose sharply in the First Five Year Plan to over 24 per cent of national income, increased to 31 per cent in 1957–62 (in 1959 the 'accumulation' rate reached no less than 44 per cent of national income) and, after a sharp decline in the early 1960s (a mere 10 per cent of national income in 1962), rose again in the mid-1960s and stood at 33 per cent in the Fourth Five Year Plan of 1971–5 (SYC 1983: 25). It is difficult for a poor economy to absorb effectively such large infusions of capital. Moreover, to a considerable degree, the high rates of investment reflected microeconomic inefficiency. Furthermore, the long-term trend was for a sharp decline in the productivity of additions to capital stock: the incremental output-to-capital ratio in the First Five Year Plan stood at approximately 0.32; by the Fourth Five Year Plan it had more than halved, to just 0.16 (table 1.2).[5] In an almost closed economy, investment growth is closely related to growth of heavy industry. Although initially pursued as a desirable goal, the microeconomic problems of the administered economy led to sustained long-term priority for this sector. Within total state investment in 'capital construction' between 1952 and 1975, the amount allocated to heavy industry was over three times as great as that for agriculture and light industry combined (ZTZ 1986: 77). Unsurprisingly, the growth rate of heavy industry (13 per cent per annum, 1953–78) greatly outpaced that of light industry (9 per cent per annum, 1952–78) (table 1.1). The so-called 'unproductive' sectors were also sacrificed to the heavy industry drive: by the Third Five Year Plan their share of state 'basic construction investment' had fallen to 16 per cent and housing's share had fallen to just 4 per cent of the total (ZGTJNJ 1986: 449).

Industrial labour productivity expanded quite rapidly over the long term (5.5 per cent per annum growth of real value added per worker) (Riskin 1987: 27), but only through enormous capital inputs so that, in state industry, output per unit of capital fell by no less than 0.7 per cent per annum from 1952 to 1978 (Riskin 1987: 264). In agriculture, rapid increases in capital stock in the 1960s and 1970s were also accompanied by

**Table 1.2**   Increase in national income per 100 yuan of accumulation (in yuan, current prices)

| Year | Increase (yuan) |
| --- | --- |
| 1953–7 | 32 |
| 1958–62 | 1 |
| 1963–5 | 57 |
| 1966–70 | 26 |
| 1971–5 | 16 |
| 1976–80 | 24 |
| 1981–5 | 41 |

*Source*: ZGTJNJ 1988: 69

serious declines in output per unit of capital. Rapid growth of the rural workforce[6] combined with the fundamental shortcomings in rural institutions to produce almost stagnant real agricultural labour productivity between 1952 and 1978 (a rise in real value added per worker of just 5 per cent) (Riskin 1987: 271).

The reported growth rate of average consumption per person in official statistics almost certainly overstates the real growth of consumption. The available data (see table 1.3) show virtually no long-term growth in grain consumption per person and very little in the other main agricultural products. Consumption per person of light industrial products with agricultural raw materials as their main input (especially textiles) was also virtually stagnant. Housing space per person probably did not increase at all. The main improvement occurred in a narrow range of consumer durables, although the initial base was almost zero and the stocks per 100 households in the late 1970s were still extremely low. Moreover, the price of food products in China relative to that of industrial consumer durables was extremely low compared with their relative price on world markets.

**Table 1.3**  Changes in consumption level of the Chinese population

|  | *1957* | *1978* | *1987* |
|---|---|---|---|
| Value of average per capita consumption (index at comparable prices) | | | |
| Whole population | 71 | 100 | 197 |
| Urban residents | 64 | 100 | 176 |
| Rural residents | 74 | 100 | 201 |
| Average per capita consumption | | | |
| Grain (kg) | 203 | 196 | 251 |
| Oil (kg) | 2.4 | 1.6 | 5.4 |
| Pork (kg) | 5.1 | 7.7 | 14.5 |
| Eggs (kg) | 1.3 | 2.0 | 5.6 |
| Sugar (kg) | 1.5 | 3.4 | 6.7 |
| Cloth (m) | 6.8 | 8.0 | 11.3 |
| Aquatic products (kg) | 4.3 | 3.5 | 5.5 |
| Average stocks of consumer durables (per 100 people) | | | |
| Sewing machines | – | 3.5 | 11.0 |
| Watches | – | 8.5 | 42.8 |
| Bicycles | – | 7.7 | 27.1 |
| Radios | – | 7.8 | 24.1 |
| Television sets | – | 0.3 | 10.7 |
| Average amount of housing space per capita (m$^2$) | | | |
| Cities | – | 4.2 | 8.5 |
| Villages | – | 8.1 | 16.0 |

*Source*: ZGTJNJ 1988: 801–3

Valued at world prices, the change in Chinese average consumption per person would probably be less than even the low official figure reported.

Western observers in the 1960s and 1970s generally praised China for its achievements in poverty relief. In the early 1950s China almost certainly achieved a considerable reduction in the proportion of the population in poverty. However, the low rate of growth of average incomes thereafter (the fastest growth of consumption in China under Mao occurred pre-1955) meant that there were very limited possibilities for further reductions in poverty. A wide variety of sources which became available after 1978 shed new light on this issue. Most poverty was rural, and the worst was located away from the economic stimulus provided by the main urban areas. Using a poverty line based on food intake requirements of 2,185 kcal per day, the World Bank estimates that in 1979 no less than 31 per cent of China's rural population lived in absolute poverty (World Bank 1986: 30). It is unlikely that the proportion in the mid-1950s was above this. With good reason China's post-Mao leadership characterized their own economy pre-1978 as one with 'equality in poverty'.

The long-term picture conceals major short-term fluctuations in China's economic performance under Mao. The Cultural Revolution in the mid-1960s had a major impact on the urban areas and temporarily halted industrial expansion. However, it had much less impact in the villages, so that its effects in agriculture were not as severe as those of the Great Leap Forward. The decade from 1965 to 1975 exhibited all the problems discussed above, but the overall growth indicators performed quite well, with real GNP estimated to have grown at about 6.5 per cent per annum over the decade (Riskin 1987: 185). The impact of the Great Leap Forward was much more dramatic. A major reason for this was its massive effect upon the rural economy, which in turn affected the industrial economy via shortfalls in food supply, industrial input and exports. Agricultural output collapsed between 1959 and 1961. The gross value of agricultural output in 1961 stood at just 75 per cent of its 1957 level (SYC 1983). China's net material product (at constant prices) fell sharply, and the 1959 level was only approximately regained as late as 1965 (SYC 1983).

However, it is not for its impact on overall indicators that the collapse of the Great Leap Forward is so important. Rather, its main significance lies in its impact on food availability and death rates. Output of grain per person fell from 306 kg in 1957 to 215 kg in 1960, while that of other agricultural products fell even more drastically (SYC 1983). The average daily availability of food energy per person is estimated to have fallen from 2,164 kcal in 1957 to just 1,535 kcal in 1960 (Riskin 1987: 128), a desperately low average figure. The overall impact on China's population was devastating. China's total population fell by 10.0 million in 1959–60 and by a further 3.5 million in 1960–1 (ZGTJNJ 1988), while reported national death rates rose from 12 per 1,000 in 1958 to over 25 per 1,000 in 1959 (ZGTJNJ 1988). Moreover, certain areas suffered especially severely. If local (especially provincial) leaders had openly admitted the real extent of the disaster, less lives would have been lost. In Sichuan province alone, the total population fell by 6.2 million, from 70.8 million in 1958 to 64.6 million in 1961, yet Sichuan continued to export grain to other areas while its population was falling, and in Anhui province the population fell by 4.4 million, from 34.3 million in 1959 to 29.9 million in 1961 (ZRN 1985). In Sichuan death rates rose from a reported figure of 9 per 1,000 in 1955 to 54 per 1,000 in 1960, while in Anhui the reported death rates rose from 12 per 1,000 in 1955 to 69 per 1,000 in 1960 (ZRN 1985). The three provinces of Sichuan, Anhui and Shandong contained 24 per cent of China's population in the late 1950s, but accounted for 85 per cent of the fall in population in the worst disaster year, 1959–60 (ZRN 1985). Establishing the exact magnitudes of deaths from famine is impossible: current estimates for China in 1958–61 range from 15 million to almost 30 million (Riskin 1987: 136). Whatever the precise figure, it is clear that a demographic catastrophe occurred amidst the largest famine of the twentieth century.

Under Mao the Chinese version of the Stalinist system did well in meeting 'basic needs' in normal times. Among other results this contributed in normal times to low mortality rates and high life expectancy compared with other developing countries. However, because of its highly centralized nature, the same system was capable of launching mass movements which could have disastrous results. In the case of the Cultural Revolution, the relative insulation of the countryside meant that a disaster did not occur, but in the Great Leap Forward it did. The great reduction in mortality which the system achieved in normal times, including extraordinarily rapid falls in infant mortality, has to be set against the huge excess mortality which the system produced in 1959–61.

# The economic reforms since the death of Mao

## An outline of the main reforms

Mao Tsetung's death in 1976 radically altered the balance of political forces in China. It opened up the possibility for a much wider range of economic analysis and for a more honest assessment of the Chinese post-1949 record. Mao's personal influence had been enormous, and he was heavily responsible for the disaster of the Great Leap Forward and the economic difficulties of the Cultural Revolution. However, after his death there was wide agreement that there were fundamental defects with the overcentralized economic system which China had adopted under Soviet influence. The following view is reasonably representative: 'Such a structure put the national economy in a straitjacket, discouraging initiative in all quarters, causing serious waste of manpower, materials and capital, and greatly hampering the growth of the productive forces. For many years, this was a major cause of the slow pace of the growth of the Chinese economy and the improvement of the living standards of the Chinese people' (Liu and Wang 1984). However, admitting the defects of the Stalinist system and having a clear programme of reform are different matters. Serious reform of the post-Mao Chinese economy can be dated from the historic Third Plenum of the Eleventh Central Committee of the CCP in December 1978. Between then and the late 1980s substantial changes occurred. However, there was not a clear programme. Indeed, China's reforms in the 1980s have been likened to a person crossing a river who moves forward from stone to stone without a clear idea of where the next one is since it is hidden under the water ahead. The main unifying theme to the reforms was the move away from the Stalinist economy, to which it seems inconceivable that China will return.

Tentative reforms began in all sectors in the late 1970s, but in the early stages the pace of advance was much the fastest in agriculture. The leadership appreciated the fundamental importance of agriculture in a poor economy like that of China. Moreover, peasants responded enthusiastically to each step in the rural reform, feeling that they could only gain by it (Watson 1983). In part also, the agricultural reforms were relatively simple. They began tentatively contracting land out to groups within the production team, but progressed rapidly by 1983 to full-scale contracting out of collective farmland to individual households. This was, in effect, the largest and most egalitarian land reform in history, since land was mainly divided among China's 200 million rural households on a locally equal per person basis. 'Decollectivization' did not apply to many types of large agricultural means of production nor to some important collective activities. However, the rural labour process underwent a revolution. Peasants were now working for themselves, and could retain any surplus produce or income after meeting compulsory state quotas. A further potential stimulus to peasant incentives was provided by a sharp improvement in the intersectoral terms of trade for peasants in the late 1970s, although the improvement in the 1980s was much slower. The far-reaching changes in rural economic organization provided a breakthrough in people's thinking about the Stalinist system of economic administration.

A considerable contribution to development can be made in labour-surplus countries by small-scale labour-intensive enterprises, as has been demonstrated by the experience of Japan and the newly industrializing countries (NICs) of East Asia (Ishikawa 1967; Hoselitz 1968; Ranis 1979). Even without state intervention such enterprises can grow rapidly, subcontracting for large enterprises, selling finished goods directly for local needs or even selling such products directly to outside markets. They benefit from low land costs, from low wages and hard work from a non-unionized workforce prepared to put up with arduous, dangerous conditions, from low transport costs when producing for local markets and from a flexible structure of production (neither capital nor labour is usually as specialized as in a large modern enterprise). Moreover, there may be social benefits to such activities (e.g. reduced costs of urbanization and rapid increase in labour absorption in the short-term tending to reduce the birth rate by bringing more women into the non-farm labour force) justifying state support. Under Mao, in rural areas in particular, growth of these activities was confined to only a few types of products (mainly inputs for agriculture), with absolute priority in labour allocation accorded to agriculture. In urban areas growth of the small-scale labour-intensive sector was held in check by tight controls over collective enterprises, including stigmatization as 'bourgeois' of many of the service activities in which these enterprises could compete (e.g. petty trading, photograph parlours, tea houses and beauty salons). In both town and countryside the slow growth of real incomes also held back this sector, since the products it is able to produce most efficiently are usually wage goods.

This sector underwent a revolution in the 1980s. Firstly, the enormous rise in agricultural labour productivity greatly increased the availability of rural surplus labour. Secondly, the controls on the collective non-farm sector were relaxed in the early 1980s. Enterprises obtained greatly increased entrepreneurial freedom, and within a short time collective non-farm enterprises operated in a competitive environment. The private sector was legally permitted and from early in the 1980s a relaxed official attitude was adopted towards private labour hiring. As early as 1983 private enterprises with several hundred employees existed. Indeed, in formerly less prosperous parts of China such as Wenzhou, the private enterprise became the dominant form of rural non-farm business organization by the mid-1980s (Nolan and Dong 1989). While the collective enterprise remained dominant in the more advanced areas, such as Southern Jiangsu, a wide variety of new subcontracting arrangements was introduced. In the small-scale non-farm sector, as in agriculture, there was tremendous popular support for the increased operation of market forces, which people perceived could for some time only mean an increase in employment opportunities and family income.

In some respects, the greatest single change in China's political economy after Mao's death was in the attitude towards the international economy. The shift towards an open policy away from Maoist isolationism took a big step forward with the 1979 law on Chinese Foreign Joint Ventures. This was the first of numerous laws intended to encourage foreign investment. Initially, foreign investment was isolated from the rest of the economy in four 'special economic zones', but the way was quickly opened for wider access of foreign investment to China, in which the most important measure was the establishment in 1984 of 14 'open coastal cities'. In 1980 China resumed its membership of the International Monetary Fund and the World Bank. These steps were important in terms of both access to capital and also the considerable weight of policy advice that subsequently flowed from those institutions to the Chinese government.

A radical shift also occurred in the 1980s in China's attitude towards foreign trade, involving fundamental rethinking of its role in economic development. Instead of being regarded as a sphere for the exploitation of poor countries, China's leadership shifted to an explicit recognition of the enormous contribution that international trade can make to economic advance. China has an abundance of certain natural resources, a large pool of low-wage surplus labour and many areas with strong commercial and manufacturing traditions. Moreover, some potential trade competitors from East Asia were moving into more sophisticated exports with higher value-added per worker as labour costs rose. China's leaders were acutely aware that they had missed out on a great historic opportunity to expand exports rapidly in the 1960s and 1970s. Given the right set of policies there were considerably opportunities to expand export earnings, and hence the capacity to import, even in the more slowly growing world economy of the 1980s. A number of measures were taken to enliven the over-centralized administration of international trade so that more direct contacts could be established between domestic enterprises and international buyers and suppliers. Alongside some decentralization of the organization of foreign trade went a considerable devaluation of the yuan, and exporting enterprises were even permitted to retain a proportion of the foreign exchange earned from exports. The extent of the 'airlock' between the domestic and the world economy was much reduced compared with the Maoist period. Moreover, the increased role of market forces within the domestic economy meant that domestic enterprises were keener to take advantage of opportunities to profit from international trade.

In the late 1970s over 80 per cent of the value of industrial output was still produced in state enterprises, so that improving their effectiveness was of central importance to the long-term success of the reform. However, their reform proved more difficult to accomplish than that of the collective and private sectors. Nevertheless, considerable changes did occur in the first decade of the post-Mao reforms. The overall objective of the reforms was to increase enterprise autonomy, raising the efficiency of enterprises through new incentives to compete in the marketplace. The attempts to do this can be divided into two phases with the turning point being the 'Decision of the Central Committee on Reform of the Economic Structure' in 1984. In the first cautious phase the principal changes were in internal enterprise organization, with a return to Taylorist methods of work organization and remuneration. Some adjustment also occurred in industrial relative prices, with the state attempting to bring prices closer in line with costs of production in different industrial sectors. However, the main method with which it was hoped to increase the vitality of enterprises was increased rights to retain profits, which spread rapidly to most state enterprises in the early 1980s. However, this did little to increase enterprise incentivies. Given the still fundamentally unreformed nature of the Chinese industrial price system, profits were a poor indicator of enterprise performance, and profit retention became the subject of protracted bargaining between the enterprise and its superior planning authorities. Rather than work to cut costs to raise profits the system placed a premium on cultivating connections to obtain through bargaining a better contracted profit retention share. Beginning in 1983, an attempt was made to circumvent these difficulties by substituting a series of taxes for profit sharing. However, because enterprises and sectors faced unequal market conditions, particularly in the form of prices that were more or less divorced from enterprises' costs of production, the crucial tax was the 'adjustment tax' which itself became the subject of protracted bargaining.

By the mid-1980s it was obvious that attempts to reform industrial enterprises would be unsuccessful under the existing price system, and in October 1984 the Central Committee announced that price reform was 'the key to reform of the entire economic structure'. A considerable reduction in state price control occurred in 1985. However, overnight elimination of price control in a system where prices bore little relationship to supply and demand would have produced chaos. Accordingly, the decision was taken to introduce a 'dual track' system, with part of the enterprise output sold at state fixed prices and part at either free-market or 'floating' prices (with the state determining the boundaries of the 'float'). By 1987, the proportion of non-agricultural consumer goods and industrial means of production sold at state fixed prices had fallen to around 50 per cent and 65 per cent respectively.

In the mid-1980s just 2,300 large state enterprises produced 27 per cent of industrial output (ZTZ 1986: 47–8). However, there were well over 90,000 small and medium-sized state industrial enterprises (ZTZ 1986: 47). There were major difficulties in administering the new system for so many enterprises. Moreover, these enterprises were able to adjust more flexibly to market changes than were large enterprises. From the mid-1980s onwards an increasing number of small state enterprises were either contracted out or leased to collectives or individuals, so that the conditions of operation in part of this sector came to resemble more closely those in the small-scale collective sector.

## The main achievements of the economic reforms

The sharp alteration in China's economic institutions greatly increased competition, shifted resource allocation and considerably increased labour intensity of much of the workforce. Although still far from a free-market economy the role of the market in China by the late 1980s had vastly increased compared with pre-1976. This change was reflected in an accelerated growth rate and a much altered growth pattern in the first decade of reform. The average annual growth rate of net material product rose from its long-term trend of under 6 per cent per annum to around 9 per cent (table 1.1). Moreover, this acceleration in output growth occurred simultaneously with a decline in the annual growth rate of population to only around 1.3 per cent in the 1980s (table 1.1). Owing to the relatively large number of people entering the reproductive age groups from the mid-1980s to the mid-1990s (an 'echo-effect' from the post-Great Leap baby boom) and the many difficulties, both short- and long-term, associated with trying to implement too harsh a population control policy in the early 1980s, China's natural growth rate of population was rising in the late

1980s (from a low point of 1.08 per cent in 1984 to 1.44 per cent in 1987) (ZTZ 1988: 14), but was still much below the long-term trend rate of the Maoist period.

At least as important as the overall acceleration in the growth rate was the striking change in the balance of growth. Agricultural growth exploded in the early 1980s as the rural reforms unfolded. In the early 1980s the average real annual growth rate of agricultural output was close to 10 per cent (ZTZ 1988: 22), an extraordinarily high figure for a country as large as China with limited possibilities to export farm produce. Even over the whole decade the growth rate of net agricultural output was almost three times the long-term growth rate of the Maoist period (table 1.1). These figures shed light upon the defects of the commune system. The overall industrial growth rate changed little after 1978. However, major changes occurred in the balance of industrial growth, of which the most striking was the reversal in the growth rates of heavy and light industry, reflecting China's move away from a Stalinist economy. During the reform decade the gross value of light industrial output accelerated to a real annual average growth rate of over 14 per cent, while that of heavy industry declined to around 10 per cent (table 1.1). A number of factors contributed to this. On the demand side urban and rural purchasing power grew rapidly, and the income elasticity of demand for light industrial output was mostly higher for light industry's products than for the direct consumption of food. On the supply side, the production of light industrial inputs (e.g. cotton, leather and timber) from agriculture grew rapidly, and much capacity shifted from heavy to light industrial production. Moreover, the overall productivity of capital almost certainly increased (table 1.2) so that less output was required of the capital goods industries to produce a unit of final product. The main contribution to improved capital productivity came from agriculture in which the acceleration in real output growth was achieved with stagnant total fixed capital stock (Nolan 1988). The second important contribution to increased capital productivity came from the rapid expansion of output and employment in labour-intensive non-farm activities. The rapid shift in employment towards the tertiary sector (its share of total employment rose from 11.0 per cent in 1978 to 17.4 per cent in 1987 (ZTZ 1988: 17)) helped increase the efficiency of resource use through widening markets and better provision of information. Moreover, rapid growth occurred in output and employment in labour-intensive industry, much of which produced light industrial products and often used capital relatively efficiently. In the villages the number of workers in 'township enterprises' rose from 28 million to 88 million between 1978 and 1987 (ZGTJNJ 1988: 292–4), while the number employed in urban collective enterprises rose from 24 million in 1980 to 35 million in 1987 (ZTZ 1988: 15). The share of the non-state sector in the total gross value of industrial output (at current prices) rose from just 19 per cent in 1978 (ZTZ 1986: 48) to over 40 per cent in 1987 (ZTZ 1988: 36).

Enormous changes occurred in China's international trade after Mao's death. Following a long period of slow export growth and a steadily falling share of world trade, China's export performance improved markedly in the 1980s. In volume terms, China's export growth rate rose from 6 per cent per annum in 1968–80 to 12 per cent in 1980–6 (World Bank 1988: 242–3), despite the fact that this was a period of great difficulties in world trade. China's share of world trade rose from 0.8 per cent in 1978 to 1.7 per cent in 1987, and the ratio of its exports to GNP rose from just 5 per cent in 1978 to 13 per cent in 1987 (Wang Bingqian 1989), a turnaround which both assisted domestic growth and was a reflection of improved domestic supply conditions.

Few nations, let alone those of China's size, have experienced such an improvement in living standards in such a short space of time as that which occurred in China in the 1980s. Chinese data show a doubling of average real material consumption per person between 1978 and 1987 (table 1.3). Because of problems with the relative prices used to make the estimates, it is possible that these data somewhat overstate the degree of advance. Nevertheless, the less problematic data in physical units confirm remarkable progress (table 1.3). The smallest increase was in grain consumption, but an annual level of over 200 kg per person is high relative to other developing countries, and it would be surprising if levels of direct consumption rose much above this. Moreover, the share of 'fine grain' (principally rice and wheat) in peasants' grain consumption rose sharply from 50 per cent in 1978 to around 80 per cent in the mid-1980s (ZTZ 1988: 103). The average consumption per person of the principal subsidiary foodstuffs rose extremely rapidly after, at best, stagnation over a long period. For centuries China's average daily calorie intake per person had probably fluctuated around 2,000 cal.[7] As population expanded arable area per person declined while labour input and yield per hectare increased, leaving output per person more or less constant; in Ishikawa's (1967) graphic phrase China simply moved along the 'subsistence parabola'. In the 1980s China moved sharply away from the parabola, with the average daily calorie intake per person rising to over 2,700 in the mid-1980s (Nolan 1988). A considerable advance in average cloth consumption per person occurred in the 1980s (table 1.3). Even more impressive was the doubling in housing space per person (table 1.3). Such an advance in housing provision has rarely been seen in any country and certainly not in any of the centrally planned economies, in which housing has been systematically squeezed.

However, the most remarkable increases were in consumer durables, produced by better-motivated state enterprises, heavy industry reallocating some of its capacity and the rapid expansion of small-scale, mainly collective, enterprises. Average stocks per 100 households of such items as sewing machines, watches, bicycles, radios and television sets rose rapidly in the 1980s (table 1.3). The absolute increases in output were extremely large (table 1.4).

Many aspects of great importance to people's quality of life are

**Table 1.4** Output of selected consumer durables in China, 1978 and 1987 (millions)

|  | 1978 | 1987 |
| --- | --- | --- |
| Bicycles | 8.5 | 40.9 |
| Sewing machines | 4.9 | 9.6 |
| Watches | 13.5 | 61.4 |
| Television sets | 0.5 | 19.4 |
| Colour | Negligible | 6.7 |
| Radios | 11.7 | 16.1 |
| Cameras | 0.2 | 2.4 |
| Washing machines | Negligible | 9.9 |
| Refrigerators | 0.0 | 4.0 |
| Electric fans | 1.4 | 35.1 |

*Source*: ZTZ 1988: 40

impossible to quantify. Enormous changes in these areas occurred in the 1980s, mostly in a direction that improved the quality of life. Although the CCP still exercised strong control over social and cultural life, the boundaries of individual freedom widened greatly. A vast array of new cultural possibilities appeared, including access to non-Chinese culture, especially through television. Almost as important as the expansion of cultural freedom was the great increase in freedom of movement in the 1980s. Increased incomes and the availability of food outside state rations tied to place of residence released Chinese people to move about their country, an activity which was strictly limited pre-1976.

It can be argued that changes in the average living standard is a less important indicator of development than changes in the number and proportion of people in poverty. A wide variety of sources suggests that the Chinese post-1978 reforms were accompanied by a rapid reduction in absolute poverty, partially through the release of production potential in poor areas which the rural reforms made directly possible, partly through 'trickle-down' effects to poor people from richer strata and areas, and partly through state policies to use some of the benefits of growth to help disadvantaged areas. The World Bank concludes: 'Using a poverty line based on food intake requirements of 2185 kilocalories per day it is estimated that the proportion of the rural population in poverty declined from 31% in 1979 to 13% in 1982 . . .; *the speed and scale of the improvement is probably unprecedented in human history*' (World Bank 1986: 30) (emphasis added). Detailed analysis of an individual province such as Anhui shows that every single *xian* in the province obtained some increase in real average income per person between 1978 and the mid-1980s (Nolan 1988). Data from, arguably, China's poorest province Gansu show that, even here, a significant increase in real consumption occurred in the 1980s (table 1.5).

**Table 1.5** Consumption and income of peasants in Gansu province

|  | *1980* | *1986* |
| --- | --- | --- |
| Average per capita net income of peasants (current yuan) | | |
| All China | 191 | 424 |
| Gansu province | 153 | 269 |
| Average per capita consumption of Gansu's peasants | | |
| Grain (kg) | 238 | 237 |
| 'fine' grain (kg) | 120 | 199 |
| Vegetables (kg) | 44 | 45 |
| Edible oil (kg) | 1.5 | 2.5 |
| Pork, beef, mutton (kg) | 8.8 | 7.7 |
| Eggs (kg) | 0.6 | 0.9 |
| Sugar (kg) | 0.5 | 0.5 |
| Alcoholic drink (kg) | 0.6 | 1.0 |
| Cotton cloth (m) | 5.1 | 2.9 |
| Synthetic cloth (m) | 0.6 | 1.7 |
| Consumer durable ownership per 100 peasant households in Gansu | | |
| Bicycles | 41 | 71 |
| Sewing machines | 19 | 44 |
| Radios | 16 | 50 |
| Watches | 24 | 145 |
| Television sets | 1.3 | 9.4 |
| Tape recorders | 0.4 | 4.8 |
| Washing machines | Negligible | 1.6 |
| Housing space per person ($m^2$) | 13.9 | 13.4 |

*Source*: ZNTN 1987: section 7

# Problems and debates

**Two stages of reform** Overall the first decade of China's economic reform since Mao's death was outstandingly successful. However, by 1988 the reforms were far from complete and many problems had emerged. The purposes of the essays in this book is to analyse the main economic issues in China in the late 1980s and to identify those that are likely to be at the centre of policy debate in the 1990s.

China's economic reform can be divided into two stages, although there is no neat boundary between them. The first stage was characterized mainly by relatively simple institutional changes in which reform was widely welcomed by the producers who were directly affected. This, broadly speaking, applied to the agricultural reforms and the reform of the small-scale non-farm sector. Mainly because of irrationalities in the previous institutional arrangements which had suppressed the growth and greatly reduced the efficiency of capital and labour in these sectors, institutional reform in the labour process and in market relationships produced outstanding results. This underpinned the great improvement in living standards in the 1980s. However, many of these were one-off gains and could not be expected to produce the same rates of growth over a long period. Moreover, in the second phase of reform attention switched to large and medium-sized state-run enterprises. These enterprises are much less flexible than agriculture and small non-farm enterprises, and their workers and managers form a privileged elite for whom the reforms increase uncertainty. Moreover, in the second stage of the reform it became increasingly clear that a partially reformed economy was associated with a wide range of economic and social problems. Indeed, by 1988 most Chinese economists felt China to be in an acute crisis, which was in sharp contrast with the heady successes of the early and mid-1980s. This sense of crisis related to a number of issues which will now be examined in turn.

**Absence of clear model**   Few people in China advocated a return to the Stalinist system practised under Mao. However, a determination not to take one path still leaves a wide range of possibilities open. The leadership in the late 1980s spoke of China as being in the 'primary stage of socialism' and of the need to build 'socialism with Chinese characteristics', but these characterizations had little concrete meaning for economic institutions and policies. Some commentators felt that China would end up as a capitalist country with a minimal role for the state, looking in institutional terms not too dissimilar from Hong Kong or Mrs Thatcher's blueprint for Britain. Such speculations were based on a belief that this is the most effective way to grow and that capitalism, albeit of the petty commodity type, has been a powerful force in China over many centuries and is hard to suppress. The depth of popular dissatisfaction with Stalinism and its vestiges in China in the late 1980s was so deep that a rapid lurch towards unrestrained capitalism cannot be ruled out.

Many Chinese economists consider that a desirable model towards which the Chinese economy should move is one in which the planners regulate markets through macroeconomic levers such as taxation, subsidies and the rate of interest, and leave the market to regulate the enterprise. The Swedish economy provides an example of such a system, and is increasingly studied in China. Indeed, Sweden combines a small amount of direct state ownership of industrial assets with a high degree of overall social control of the economy, and is a socialist country in fundamental senses. The main issue is whether it would be possible to establish effective control simply through indirect levers in a vast poor country such as China.

China's policymakers have shown great interest in the 'developmental state' model of the East Asian NICs of Singapore, Taiwan and South Korea.[8] In this model the state plays a much more interventionist role using both direct and indirect levers to make up for the different ways in which markets fail in respect to growth. Each of these countries is small and until recently was extremely vulnerable politically, so that it was vital for national survival that the government and bureaucracy worked single-mindedly to achieve successful growth. The key question is whether it is possible in less threatening settings and in much larger countries with more complex political pressures to construct a 'developmental state' which works in a relatively uncorrupt fashion via both direct and indirect levers to stimulate growth.

The term 'market socialism' is not often used in China nor is there much explicit discussion of the USSR's NEP of the 1920s, which informs much of the Soviet reform discussion, providing a useful popular conception of the system towards which Gorbachev would like to see the Soviet Union move. However, many Chinese economists implicitly have an 'NEP-type' model as their concept of the most suitable institutional set-up for China. Such an economy would attempt to combine the virtues of plan and market in stimulating growth in a fashion close to that of the 'developmental state', but would also have a commitment to socialist values.

In the end the path that China takes will not be determined by China's leaders selecting a model with the advice of economists, but will be the outcome of complex historical forces. It is possible that the outcome may be a sort of 'bureaucratic market muddle' in which the bureaucracy retains great powers to intervene through direct and indirect levers, but uses these powers mainly to further its own interests and is preoccupied with its own internal struggles rather than single-mindedly pursuing growth. Such a scenario would be closer to post-1947 India than to the East Asian NICs. Chinese decision-makers and advisers have been more interested in East Asian than in South Asian development, although the latter may in many ways be more relevant to them.

The chapters by McFarlane, Riskin and Nolan all, to different degrees, analyse the ambiguities of the new Chinese development model. Riskin stresses the absence of a clear overall model to guide China's economy into the 1990s, considering that this constitutes a serious barrier to sustaining popular support for the reform process in which considerable social tension is generated by the differential impact of the reforms on different social groups. McFarlane also finds it hard to identify a coherent reference point towards which the Chinese reforms are evolving, beyond the undoubted dynamism generated by the release of the forces of petty commodity production. McFarlane argues that the Yugoslav experience should serve as a salutary reminder to the Chinese leadership of the problems of a reform based on commodity production but lacking an overall conception of the appropriate role of central planning in stimulating growth. Yugoslavia provides a warning to Chinese leaders of the problems for central planning posed by strong forces for regional autonomy. McFarlane also warns of the dangers that exist if the leadership lacks a clear and popularly appealing conception of the socialism it claims to be constructing. At least the Stalinist–Maoist conception was clear and, at certain points, had considerable popular appeal. Nolan's chapter is entirely concerned with the issue of the type of system towards which China is evolving. He argues that China needs some form of market socialism, and identifies the key issue as the capacity of the Chinese state to turn itself from a mainly self-serving state into a developmental state with socialist values. He is more confident than McFarlane or Riskin that this is what China's political economy is evolving towards, but acknowledges the immense difficulties involved in accomplishing this. He admits that it is possible that China might instead take a different path, of which he considers the most likely alternative to be some form of 'bureaucratic market muddle'.

**The politics of reform**   China has a large body of Party and government bureaucrats who have for decades provided direct instructions to enterprises. A radical change in their role was called for under the reforms. Zhao Ziyang declared in 1986: 'Economic departments of the government at all levels should no longer devote their energy to assigning quotas, approving construction projects and allotting funds and materials. Instead, they should do overall planning, implement policies, organise co-ordination, provide services, use economic means of regulation and exercise effective inspection and supervision . . . *All personnel of government should fully understand the necessity and historic significance of this transformation'* (emphasis added). However, the old habits proved extremely hard to break. In the late 1980s central and, increasingly, local authorities still exercised considerable control over state enterprises, subsidizing loss-making enterprises, heavily taxing profitable enterprises and setting up new administrative bodies to take over many of the functions formally devolved to enterprises. Only about a fifth of large and medium-sized state enterprises had gained real freedom from administrative authorities by 1986–7.

China's economic reform of the 1980s destabilized its politics. The reforms had a massive impact on popular consciousness. After decades of stability in basic values tremendous psychological disorientation was caused by a sudden shift away from those values towards an unclear new set of values. On the one hand China's population was told that the old values of 'self-reliance' and 'serve the people' were to be replaced by new values such as 'take the lead in getting rich' and an 'open door' to the outside world. However, simultaneously the people were urged to guard against 'decadent bourgeois ideas' and reject 'capitalist filth'. There is a strong analogy with the nineteenth-century *ti-yong* debate about Western technology (Levenson 1968): China's rulers hoped then, as they did in the 1980s, to benefit from Western technology (*yong*) without absorbing the values (*ti*) that go with it. Moreover, the erosion of traditional values in the 1980s was occurring in the course of a reform which was having a differential impact on different sectors, regions and social strata, causing jealousies and tensions. Li Yining's chapter has as its central theme the degree of 'social tolerance' that the Chinese population has for reform. Implicit in his analysis is the concern that China might be thrown into chaos (*da luan*), the age-old fear of China's rulers, if the reforms proceed too fast. A crucial issue, to which it is difficult to gauge the answer, is the strength of popular feelings which the reforms released for great political democracy and even an end to the leading role for the CCP.

**Agriculture**   Agriculture is still the foundation of the Chinese economy, and problems in this sector have wide ramifications for the whole economy. After explosive growth in the early 1980s, China's agricultural growth rate slowed down to around 4 per cent per annum from 1984 to 1987 (ZTZ 1988: 23). Given that the population was growing at only around 1.5 per cent per annum, this was far from disastrous. In a poor country of China's size we would not expect a long-term growth rate of farm output per person of much more than 2–3 per cent per annum. However, the most worrying aspect was the failure of grain output to grow beyond its peak of 1984 (ZTZ 1988: 26). Riskin devotes much attention to the agricultural problems of the late 1980s. Indeed, he considers that it is here that the fate of the whole reform programme will be decided. He believes that a considerable increase in state investment in agriculture is needed. Du Runsheng also addresses the problem of lagging agricultural growth. He and Riskin are in agreement that not only is increased state investment needed but also it is vitally necessary to maintain and strengthen cooperation among farm households in respect to a wide range of activities outside direct cultivation of the soil. Poor areas in particular experienced a breakdown of village cooperative activities in the late 1980s. However, no issue was more important than that of price in analysing the slowdown in agricultural growth and the stagnation in farm output. As Du Runsheng notes soberly: 'when farmers feel that growing grain is not worthwile, they will turn to production that gives higher returns. The state should implement an appropriate price protection policy for grain production'. In the late 1980s the state shied away from allowing a sufficiently large increase in farm purchase prices in general, and grain purchase prices in particular, to stimulate an acceleration in the growth rate of farm output and marketing. The 'social tolerance' of urban workers to the consequential increase in food prices was felt to be low. The 'Polish problem' was never far from the minds of China's leaders. Food subsidies, a small relative increase in farm purchase prices and slow growth of farm output were chosen in preference to a more radical, but politically dangerous, alternative.

**Loss of control over investment**   In order to encourage lower levels to have a greater interest in raising revenue and using it well the 1980s saw a major decentralization of budgetary control: the share of 'basic construction investment' (investment in fixed assets by state-owned units) falling outside the central budget rose from 18 per cent in the early 1980s to over 50 per cent in 1981–5 (ZTZ 1986: 73). This involved some decentralization to the enterprise, but it consisted mainly of decentralization to the local authorities. Moreover, an increased proportion of total investment in fixed assets was carried out by collectives and individuals (their share rose from 30 per cent in 1981 to 36 per cent in 1987) (ZTZ 1988: 56). Wang Jiye analyses this process and the problems that stemmed from it. Both enterprises and local authorities had long operated in an environment of 'investment hunger' in which there were no penalties for poor returns on investment and many gains to obtaining as much new investment as possible, since prestige and future streams of employment, income and materials flowed from this. In China's partially reformed economy of the 1980s, in which market principles were not fully operational, relaxation of central budgetary control led to a continued rapid expansion of capital construction with little attention to rates of return and in directions not consistent with central priorities. The structural forces leading to 'overinvestment' were strong and were avoided only during the brief periods when tight direct central control operated.

The sharp decline in the proportion of state capital construction allocated to agriculture has already been noted: the national social returns to such investment were high but this did not sufficiently enter the calculations of local authorities whose concerns were too parochial. The social returns from power and transport investment were also high. These sectors constituted major bottlenecks in the 1980s, with large amounts of fixed capital left idle because of power shortages and stocks of goods remaining idle because of shortage of transport space. In the late 1970s and early 1980s state investment in both energy and transport was permitted, alarmingly, to fall in absolute terms (at current prices) (ZTZ 1988: 63). Although the position was remedied somewhat in the mid-1980s, their share of state 'basic construction investment' (23 per cent and 15 per cent respectively in 1987 (ZTZ 1988: 63)) was still low given their crucial importance and previous relative neglect. Robinson focuses on energy, examining China's output and energy production plans in the light of his wide experience with energy planning in developing countries. He argues that Chinese plans are based on an unrealistically low 'energy elasticity' (the ratio of the growth rate of use of primary energy to the growth rate of GDP). He believes that unless policy alters radically China's growth plans will be severely impeded by inadequate energy supply.

If China is, indeed, to shift to a decentralized system of resource allocation in which enterprises and local authorities have permanently increased independence, then the banking system will be vital in guiding their actions in desired directions via credit policy and interest rates. Liu Hongru examines the recent evolution of China's banking system and concludes that it is still far from operating mainly on market principles. Even increases in the rate of interest in the 1980s did little to restrain the demands of enterprises and local authorities for credit since the banks themselves did not operate on a commercial basis and were happy to increase credit to their clients (nor were real interest rates always positive). However, it would not be sufficient for the banking system merely to impose tougher conditions on local authorities so that they and industrial enterprises paid more attention to the rate of return on projects. In a poor country at China's stage of development, what is required for many types of investment (e.g. transport and communications, agriculture and power supply) is not short-term commercial criteria but, rather, consideration of long-term social benefits. This needs more state authority over investment allocation than existed in China in the late 1980s. Moreover, such investments often are 'lumpy' and straddle regions, so that leaving the construction to local agencies is rarely the best way of producing optimal social results.

**Reform of large-scale industrial enterprises**  In the mid-1980s, less than 6,000 state-owned large and medium-sized industrial enterprises (2 per cent of the total number) accounted for around two-thirds of the total value of industrial fixed assets and of industrial taxes and profits handed to the state. Their reform was central to the improved operation of the whole economy. In contrast with small-scale industries and agriculture the operators of enterprises (workers and managers) were apprehensive about the implications for themselves of making their enterprises more competitive. Moreover, their administrative superiors, especially the local authorities, clung tenaciously to control of the enterprises throughout the 1980s. Dong Fureng advocates the joint-stock company as a way of increasing the interest of enterprise employers in reform and reducing outside interference by administrators whose main concern is not enterprise efficiency. There is a wide range of possibilities for share ownership, from non-tradeable shares issued only to enterprise employees to freely tradeable shares available to any individual or institution. A strong school of thought in China believes that a 'capital market' in the form of a stock exchange is a necessary corollary of joint-stock companies. While only tentative moves had been made in this direction by the late 1980s, the implications of this proposal are enormous.

China will be beginning from scratch. Experience with setting up stock markets in other developing countries suggests that there will be huge problems in obtaining effective corporate disclosure and reporting in the absence of either the necessary tradition or accounting skills, in preventing insider dealing, in avoiding penetration of an embryo market by international organized crime and in establishing a viable legal framework (Rider and Fung 1989). On the narrower economic front it is not self-evident that share ownership via a stock market, as opposed to the various possibilities for non-tradeable share ownership, is the best route to proceed. Singh argues that the evidence from the advanced capitalist economies does not support the proposition that stock markets make a useful contribution to growth through gathering together savings or channelling savings to companies with the best investment prospects or encouraging efficient use of past savings. Indeed, he considers that non-stock-market economies such as Japan and the Federal Republic of Germany have performed better than stock-market economies such as the United States or the United Kingdom. He argues that the hitherto non-stock-market economies 'are more likely to be harmed rather than helped by the globalization and liberalization of financial markets which is currently taking place'. Singh implies that, in so far as share ownership can help invigorate China's large-scale state enterprises, it should be confined to those methods that do not involve public trading of company shares.

In the view of many people, part of the reason for the rapid economic growth in the non-stock-exchange economies of Japan and the Federal Republic of Germany is the nature of the internal organization of their large-scale enterprises which, allegedly, reduce conflict between workers and managers. Jiang Yiwei argues that China should investigate carefully the possibility that a system of mainly worker-owned shares might improve the operation of China's large-scale state enterprises by providing greater intra-enterprise democracy: 'In most enterprises management rights should be handed over to the labour force as a collective, and should be based on democratic decision-making and a highly collective system of manager responsibility'. In fact, China in the 1980s moved in a rather different direction from the one suggested by Jiang, with the Central Committee of the CCP calling in 1984 for Chinese enterprises to adopt 'centralised and unified leadership and direction of production and strict labour discipline' (Liu and Wu 1986: 680). However, the situation is fluid, and a single central decision could change the way that China's state enterprises are organized. While China moved away from Maoist policies in enterprise organization in the 1980s, it is far from clear which method will eventually dominate.

It is doubtful whether any major change in the internal organization of enterprises can produce a great improvement in the performance of large-scale industry without a fundamental change in their external setting. Despite the passage of a Bankruptcy Law in 1987 (after long argument) there appeared virtually no chance of a large state enterprise's being declared bankrupt in the late 1980s. Indeed, around 15 per cent of state industrial enterprises made losses but carried on business through state subsidies. Moreover, state administrators, especially local authorities, still removed a substantial portion of the profits from profitable enterprises. Accordingly, both the 'sticks' and the 'carrots' characteristic of capitalist markets were greatly weakened. As several of the chapters by Chinese economists in this book stress, the budget constraint on state enterprises remained 'soft'. A major reason for this was that the price system was still heavily administered and bore little relationship to supply and demand in either factor or product markets. Accordingly, relying on profits as the criterion of enterprise performance would have produced irrational and unfair results. Tian Yuan analyses these issues and argues that a radical transformation of the ownership structure of state industry is necessary, but that it must proceed in tandem with price reform. Unfortunately, as virtually all Chinese economists admit, reforming prices gradually produces its own set of problems. The most feasible way to do this is to permit 'dual-track' pricing for any given commodity, as China has done, gradually raising the proportion sold at free-market prices. However, this provides great opportunities for bargaining and corruption in respect of the proportions of output sold at fixed and non-fixed prices and permits those in possession of rights over goods in short supply to benefit from the price differential between parallel markets. Dong Fureng and Tian Yuan both argue strongly for the eventual elimination of the system, but recognize that to eliminate it at a stroke would cause even greater problems than its gradual phasing out.

Few issues in the reform of China's state-run industries are as sensitive as employment policy. The 'stick' of potential unemployment for poor work performance hardly existed even in the late 1980s, and the intensity of work was widely acknowledged to be low. Putting market forces fully into practice in the 1990s might lead, initially at least, to a decline in state industrial employment. Wiles argues that employment should not be examined simply in economic terms. Rather, employment should be acknowledged as desirable for the psychological benefits it provides. While he considers that narrowly economic criteria must be taken into account, Wiles believes that the desirability of employment for its own sake might justify China's choosing technologies which are more labour absorbing than those which maximize growth over a given time period. In fact, China's growth in the 1980s was very 'Wilesian', with rapid expansion in those non-agricultural sectors which absorb labour most rapidly in the short term. The main employment debate for the 1990s is about the degree to which market forces should determine the level and nature of employment in the large-scale state sector.

**Destabilization from the international economy**  Zhou Xiaochuan examines the revolution in China's approach towards the international economy which occurred after Mao's death. This had far-reaching consequences for Chinese politics and culture as well as narrower economic effects. The changes produced economic problems as well as benefits. Although China's exports in the 1980s grew rapidly, the yuan remained overvalued and the quality of foreign capital and consumer goods was generally superior to that of comparable domestic products. Furthermore, the free-market price of domestic goods in short supply was extremely high compared with the state fixed price, so that profits could often be made by importing goods in order to re-sell them at free-market domestic prices. Moreover, benefits could frequently be obtained through the supply of goods more cheaply and quicker by directly importing rather than buying from domestic suppliers. The decentralization of a certain amount of control over international trade interacted with these influences to produce an unplanned explosion of imports: the rate of growth of imports (in current dollars) averaged no less than 21 per cent per annum from 1978 to

1985, opening up a yawning trade deficit amounting to 54 per cent of export earnings in 1985 (ZTZ 1988: 85). For a country used to extreme conservatism in its international economic dealings, this was a shocking outcome. Rather than sink deep into debt, the government responded by recentralizing controls and strictly limited imports, which remained roughly constant (in current dollars) from 1985 to 1987, while exports continued to rise, bringing the trade account rapidly back into balance. Zhou Ziaochuan argues that China must proceed cautiously in its reform of its relations with the international economy. The experience of the mid-1980s shows that reforms need to be carefully synchronized. When reform in the international sphere leaps ahead of domestic reform serious problems arise.

**Inflation**   For the first time since 1949, China in the 1980s experienced serious open inflation, causing intense debate and great concern among China's economists and policy-makers. Many people recall that it was hyperinflation which helped bring about the downfall of the Guomindang in 1949. China's inflation was, in fact, quite moderate compared with that in most Latin American countries. Indeed, many Latin American countries would be pleased to have as their *annual* rate of inflation the reported figure of a 56 per cent increase in China's 'staff and workers' cost of living index' for the whole period from 1978 to 1987 (ZTZ 1988). It is true that the rate of inflation in retail prices in 1988 was exceptionally large by Chinese standards – perhaps over 30 per cent in major cities – but it was still well below the rates in most Latin American countries. However, China's population was not used to inflation and it was in relation to their 'social tolerance', to use Li Yining's phrase, that China's inflation rate was high.

A number of factors combined to produce the acceleration in China's inflation rate compared with the Maoist period. To some degree the problem was cost push. Tian Yuan points out that the attempt to increase the relative price of some heavy industrial inputs did not lead to efforts by state enterprises to behave more efficiently and economize on the use of these inputs. When goods were in short supply and/or where there was a local monopoly in supply, enterprises were able to simply to pass on the increases in input prices as increases in final product prices, particularly for that portion of their output sold at free-market prices.

However, it is not obvious why, in the absence of demand (in the shape of the money supply), a change in relative prices should necessarily result in an overall rise in the general price level unless there is an exceptional change in the velocity of circulation. As the World Bank forcefully puts it: 'In a properly functioning economy, excess demand in one sector would imply excess supply in others, and such imbalances would be corrected through relative price changes induced by market forces. Generalised excess demand and supply would in principle only arise if there were macroeconomic mismanagement. The solution to such problems would thus lie not in price control, but in more restrictive macroeconomic policies' (World Bank 1986: 176). In fact, China did not on the whole follow a restrictive macroeconomic policy in the 1980s. From 1952 to 1978 the money supply (M1) grew at an average annual rate of less than 10 per cent, while in the post-1978 period (1979–86) the rate of growth of M1 accelerated to an average annual rate of around 19 per cent, compared with real national income growth of around 9 per cent (Hua et al. 1988).[9] A number of factors combined to produce this result, none of which was narrowly economic. Because the state considered it politically impossible to permit urban food prices to rise fully to free-market levels it incurred large losses on sales of food, particularly grain, to the urban areas. Moreover, those increases that did occur were partially compensated for by state subsidies. Further, a relatively large share of state enterprises were running at a loss and were subsidized by the state either nationally or locally. By 1988, subsidies to loss-making enterprises and subsidies to compensate consumers for price rises together totalled an amount equal to over 28 per cent of state budgetary outlays (Wang Bingqian 1989). Before 1978 the state budget had mostly been in surplus, but in the 1980s there was a series of budget deficits (ZTZ 1988: 75), with the deficit standing at around 10 per cent of total budgetary expenditure in the mid-1980s (Riskin 1987: 326) and reaching around 13 per cent by 1988 (Wang Bingqian 1989). Moreover, as has been seen, in the absence of full commercial principles for the banking system, decentralization of control over banking, with banks coming under intense pressure from local authorities to grant loans, allowed a rapid rise in the supply of bank credit. The demand for funds was insatiable. Even the increased rate of interest in the 1980s made little difference in a soft budget environment where more loans were easily available and where bankruptcy for state enterprises was almost unthinkable. From 1980 to 1987 commercial credit (of all sorts) expanded by an average annual rate of around 23 per cent (ZTZ 1988: 76). A final element in the story is the volatility introduced by the large increase in personal savings (in different institutions) in the 1980s, from 2.1 billion yuan in 1978 to 30.8 billion yuan in 1987 (ZTZ 1988: 104). An important reason for the sharp increase in the rate of inflation in 1988 was a vicious circle of panic about an erosion in the real value of these savings by inflation leading to their rapid depletion and a further temporary upward twist to the inflationary spiral.

**Inequality**    That China is a large country is a truism so important that it bears repetition. The problems of dealing with powerful regional interests are special for countries the size of India or China and produce the need for political compromises that do not arise in smaller countries such as Taiwan or South Korea, let alone city states like Hong Kong or Singapore. Moreover, growth in such huge economies, embracing an amalgam of well and poorly located areas, can never hope to be as rapid as in small well-located countries. Few economies, even small ones, have grown in a spatially balanced fashion. Capital and labour are attracted to well-located areas, even though these areas are crowded. This happened in China prior to the impact of Western imperialism as well as under its impact. Despite serious attempts under Mao to control regional inequality, large differences in levels of development existed even in the 1970s. After that, much wider regional differences opened up, with extremely rapid rates of advance in favourably placed areas along the eastern seaboard. Although the real output and incomes of poor areas certainly grew under the impact of the reforms, their growth could not match that of eastern seaboard provinces like Jiangsu (table 1.6). Chen Dongsheng argues that China should accept the advantages to the whole economy of allowing the rapid advance of these areas, but should ensure that some of the resources generated there are devoted to helping backward areas. China's policies in this respect in the late 1980s already compared favourably with other large developing countries. However, as Chen points out, helping poorly located areas is a complex process, without an easy or obvious solution. The vicious circle of poverty in backward areas is extremely hard to break even with plentiful state assistance (Wang and Bai 1990).

Under Mao, income differentials in China were low compared with other developing countries. Zhao Renwei reports a Gini coefficient for all-China in the 1970s below that of most comparable countries. However, major changes to income distribution occurred in the 1980s. Moreover, McFarlane argues that new forms of rent-related income inequalities began to emerge with the possibility for the consolidation of inequalities via a system of interlocking factor markets. Zhao points out that the changes in

**Table 1.6**   Key economic indicators for Jiangsu province (all data at 1980 prices)

|  | Average annual growth rate (%) | |
|---|---|---|
|  | *1953–87* | *1979–87* |
| Total social product (gross material product) | 9.3 | 15.2 |
| National income (net material product) | 7.2 | 12.0 |
| Gross value of agricultural output | 6.6 | 14.5 |
| Industrial output at village (*cun*) or lower level | – | 32.2 |
| Gross value of industrial output | 12.4 | 15.7 |
| Heavy industry | 18.9 | 14.4 |
| Light industry | 10.8 | 16.8 |
| All-people owned | – | 10.4 |
| Collectively owned | – | 22.0 |
| National income per person | 8.0[a] | 10.7 |

[a] 1952–87.
*Source*: JSJJNJ 1988: section III

income distribution were extremely complex. The major change was a reduction in the gap in average income between peasants and urban workers. Zhao shows that the numbers of people in absolute poverty in the countryside fell sharply. Alongside this went relatively fast rates of growth of peasant income in well-located areas. In such areas, the benefits of growth, especially of non-farm employment, increased the income of most village strata. According to Zhao, the overall result for some was an increase, but not an 'excessive' one, in rural income inequality as measured by the Gini coefficient. In the urban areas the persistence of fairly egalitarian remuneration policies in state enterprises led, according to Zhao, to a reduction in the reported Gini coefficient in the mid-1980s. Much more difficult is the problem of those who obtain high incomes from what Zhao calls 'the contradictions and frictions arising from the transition from one economic system to another'. The opportunities for well-placed people in the Party and government to take advantage of the dual-track system to earn high quasi-legal or illegal incomes little related to personal work ability or effort multiplied following the halfway house of economic reform in the 1980s. These caused great dissatisfaction among the mass of the Chinese population, contributing greatly to the 'social tension' analysed by Li Yining.

China still lacks a clear convincing ethic concerning inequality. Under Mao the system was at least reasonably clear: income from capital was not permitted and income inequality from labour was tolerated up to a point in the interests of promoting incentives, but the goal was gradually to raise the proportion of income distributed 'according to need'. In the 1980s the main slogan affecting income distribution was 'take the lead in getting rich', and much official literature argued that 'income according to work' (an ambiguous concept) was justified because it conformed to the 'Marxist truth' that it promoted the development of the productive forces:

Eliminating exploitation ... has created the conditions for the realization of genuine equality, i.e. equal labour rights. ... When we say only distribution according to work brings about genuine equality, we mean that equality lies in using the same yardstick, labour, to measure labourers. Distribution according to work recognises differences in individuals' labour capacity and contribution, and therefore also differences in their income derived from payment. Because of this, it has nothing in common with egalitarianism. Socialism promotes the development of the productive forces, whereas egalitarianism hinders them. (Peking Univeristy Economics College 1988: 120)

In fact, as Mao correctly pointed out, following Marx's comments in the *Critique of the Gotha Programme*, while such a distribution principle might be pragmatically necessary, it embodied a right of inequality, a 'bourgeois right', which should not form the final basis of socialist distribution. Purely market-determined income distribution produces persistent class, regional, sexual and racial structures affecting people's capacities to compete in the marketplace. While pragmatism might dictate that this is a necessary expedient it has little to do with principles of socialist equality. In practice, Nolan argues, the Chinese state in the 1980s did a great deal to intervene with the market to increase the opportunities for poorly placed social groups to improve their capacities to be fulfilled and to earn income. This distinguished China sharply from other developing countries, and gave its policies a genuinely socialist flavour, but the government found it difficult to provide an overall ethical justification for this which made sense to ordinary people.

## Notes

1   In 1978, just 9 per cent of industrial output was produced in *xiang* (village) enterprises (ZTZ 1986: 48).
2   On China's second NEP see Schurmann (1964); the first NEP period was in 1952–3 immediately after the completion of land reform.
3   The degree to which China's trade possibilities were limited by Western political hostility is extremely complex and does not permit an easy summary.
4   In Chinese terminology 'accumulation' is defined as 'newly-added fixed assets of material and non-material sectors (less depreciation) and newly acquired circulating funds in kind by the material sectors during the year' (SYC 1983: 29).
5   The incremental output-to-capital ratio is here taken to be the increase in national income per 100 yuan of accumulation.
6   The total number of rural workers rose from 182 million in 1952 to 313 million in 1978 (ZTZ 1986: 27).
7   Perkins (1969) argues that over the long term China's output of grain per person varied little.
8   On the 'developmental state' concept see, especially, Johnson (1987).
9   M3 grew at around 21 per cent per annum from 1981 to 1987 (Study Group on Inflation 1989).

## Bibliography

Aird, J. S. (1972) Population policy and demographic prospects in the People's Republic of China. In Joint Economic Committee, US Congress, *People's Republic of China: An Economic Assessment*. Washington, DC: US Government Printing Office.
Berliner, J. (1976) *The Innovation Decision in Soviet Industry*. Cambridge, MA: MIT Press.
Bukharin, N. and Preobrazhensky, E. (1969) *The ABC of Communism*. Harmondsworth: Penguin.
Chang, J. K. (1969) *Industrial Development in Pre-Communist China*. Edinburgh: Edinburgh University Press.
Chan, A., Madsen, R. and Unger, J. (1984) *Chen Village*. London: University of California Press.
Chesneaux, J. (1968) *The Chinese Labour Movement, 1919–1927*. Stanford, CA: Stanford University Press.

Cowan, C. D. (ed.) (1964) *The Economic Development of China and Japan.* London: Allen and Unwin.

Dernberger, R. E. (1975) The role of the foreigner in China's economic development. In D. H. Perkins (ed.), *China's Modern Economy in Historical Perspective.* Stanford, CA: Stanford University Press.

Deyo, F. C. (ed.) (1987) *The Political Economy of the New Asian Industrialism.* London: Cornell University Press.

Eckstein, A., Galenson, W. and Liu, T. C. (eds) (1968) *Economic Trends in Communist China.* Edinburgh: Edinburgh University Press.

Ellman, M. (1989) *Socialist Planning.* Cambridge: Cambridge University Press.

Feinstein, C. H. (ed.) (1967) *Socialism, Capitalism and Economic Growth.* Cambridge: Cambridge University Press.

Galenson, W. (ed.) (1979) *Economic Growth and Structural Change in Taiwan.* London: Cornell University Press.

Hoselitz, B. (ed.) (1968) *The Role of Small Industry in the Process of Economic Growth.* The Hague: Mouton.

Howe, C. (1973) Labour organisation and incentives in industry, before and after the Cultural Revolution. In S. Schram (ed.), *Authority, Participation and Cultural Change in China.* Cambridge: Cambridge University Press.

Hua Sheng, Zhang Xuejun and Luo Xiaopeng (1988) Ten years in China's reforms: looking back, reflection and prospect. *Economic Research (Jingji Yanjiu)*, September, no. 9.

Ishikawa, S. (1967) *Economic Development in Asian Perspective.* Tokyo: Kinokuniya.

Johnson, C. (1987) Political institutions and economic performance: the government–business relationship in Japan, South Korea, and Taiwan. In F. C. Deyo (ed.), *The Political Economy of the New Asian Industrialism.* London: Cornell University Press.

Joint Economic Committee, US Congress (1972) *People's Republic of China: An Economic Assessment.* Washington, DC: US Government Printing Office.

JSJJNJ [*Jiangsu Economic Yearbook (Jiangsu Jingji Nianjian)*] (1988). Nanjing: Nanjing Daxue Chubanshe.

Kornai, J. (1980) *Economics of Shortage.* Amsterdam: North-Holland.

Levenson, J. R. (1968) *Confucian China and its Modern Fate.* Berkeley, CA: University of California Press.

Lin, C. (1981) The reinstatement of economics in China to-day. *China Quarterly*, March, no. 85, 1–48.

Liu Guoguang and Wang Ruisun (1984) Restructuring of the economy. In Yu Guangyuan (ed.), *China's Socialist Modernisation.* Beijing: Foreign Languages Press.

Liu Suinian and Wu Qungan (1986) *China's Socialist Economy: An Outline History (1949–1984).* Beijing: Beijing Review.

Mah, F. H. (1971) *The Foreign Trade of Mainland China.* Edinburgh: Edinburgh University Press.

Myers, R. H. (1980) *The Chinese Economy Past and Present.* Belmont, CA: Wadsworth.

Nolan, P. (1988) *The Political Economy of Collective Farms.* Cambridge: Polity Press.

—— and Dong Fureng (eds) (1989) *Market Forces in China.* London: Zed Books.

Orleans, L. (1972) *Every Fifth Child.* London: Methuen.

## 36   Peter Nolan

Peking University Economics College (1988) *Selected Materials on China's Economic Reform*. Beijing: Beijing Daxue Jingji Xueyuan.

Perkins, D. H. (1969) *Agricultural Development in China, 1368–1968*. Edinburgh: Edinburgh University Press.

—— (ed.) (1975a) *China's Modern Economy in Historical Perspective*. Stanford, CA: Stanford University Press.

—— (1975b) Growth and changing structure of China's twentieth century economy. In D. H. Perkins (ed.), *China's Modern Economy in Historical Perspective*. Stanford, CA: Stanford University Press.

Raj, K. N. (1967) Role of the 'machine-tools sector' in economic growth. In C. H. Feinstein (ed.), *Socialism, Capitalism and Economic Growth*. Cambridge: Cambridge University Press.

Ranis, G. (1979) Industrial development. In W. Galenson (ed.), *Economic Growth and Structural Change in Taiwan*. London: Cornell University Press.

Richman, B. (1969) *Industrial Society in Communist China*. New York: Vintage Books.

Rider, B. A. K. and Fung, S. (1989) The stock market – a question of confidence, to be published.

Riskin, C. (1975) Surplus and stagnation in modern China. In D. H. Perkins (ed.), *China's Modern Economy in Historical Perspective*. Stanford, CA: Stanford University Press.

—— (1987) *China's Political Economy*. Oxford: Oxford University Press.

Schram, S. (ed.) (1973) *Authority, Participation and Cultural Change in China*. Cambridge: Cambridge University Press.

Schurmann, F. (1964) China's 'New Economic Policy' – transition or beginning? *China Quarterly*, January–March, no. 17, 65–91.

—— (1968) *Ideology and Organisation in Communist China*. Berkeley, CA: University of California Press.

Study Group on Inflation (1989) On harnessing China's inflation. *Economic Research (Jingji Yanjiu)*, March, no. 3.

Swamy, S. (1979) The response to economic challenge: a comparative economic history of China and India, 1870–1952. *Quarterly Journal of Economics*, February, 25–46.

SYC [*Statistical Yearbook of China*] (1983). Hong Kong: Economic Information Agency.

Teng Weizao (1982) Socialist modernization and the pattern of foreign trade. In Xu Dixin et al. (eds), *China's Search for Economic Growth*. Beijing: New World Press.

Walker, K. R. (1964) A Chinese discussion on planning for balanced growth: a summary of the views of Ma Yin-Ch'u and his critics. In C. D. Cowan (ed.), *The Economic Development of China and Japan*. London: Allen and Unwin.

—— (1968) Organisation for agricultural production. In A. Eckstein, W. Galenson and T. C. Liu (eds), *Economic Trends in Communist China*. Edinburgh: Edinburgh University Press.

Wang Bingqian (1989) Report on the implementation of the state budget for 1988 and on the draft state budget for 1989. *Beijing Review*, 32 (18).

Wang Hong (1989) China's export performance in the 1980s. Cambridge University, unpublished manuscript.

Wang Xiaoqiang and Bai Nanfeng (1990) *The Poverty of Plenty*. London: Macmillan.

Watson, A. (1983) Agriculture looks for 'shoes that fit': the production responsibility system and its implications. *World Development*, 11 (8), 709–730.

World Bank (1986) *China: Long-term Development Issues and Options*. Washington, DC: World Bank.

Xue Muqiao (1986) *China's Socialist Economy* (2nd edn). Beijing: Foreign Languages Press.

Yu Guangyuan (ed.) (1984) *China's Socialist Modernisation*. Beijing: Foreign Languages Press.

Xu Dixin et al. (eds) (1982) *China's Search for Economic Growth*. Beijing: New World Press.

Zaleski, E. (1980) *Stalinist Planning for Economic Growth, 1933–1952*. London: Macmillan.

ZGTJNJ [*Chinese Statistical Yearbook (Zhongguo Tongji Nianjian)*] (1986). Beijing: Zhongguo Tongji Chubanshe.

—— (1988). Beijing: Zhongguo Tongji Chubanshe.

ZNTN [*Chinese Rural Statistical Yearbook (Zhongguo Nongcun Tongji Nianjian)*] (1987). Beijing: Zhongguo Tongji Chubanshe.

ZRN [*Chinese Population Yearbook (Zhongguo Renkou Nianjian)*] (1985). Beijing: Zhongguo Shehui Kexue Chubanshe.

ZTZ [*Chinese Statistical Outline (Zhongguo Tongji Zhaiyao)*] (1986). Beijing: Zhongguo Tongji Chubanshe.

—— (1988). Beijing: Zhongguo Tongji Chubanshe.

# Part I

## Overviews

# 2

# Where is China Going?

## Carl Riskin

## Introduction

The first decade of the era of economic reform in China (1978–87) divides roughly in half. The first five years were marked by dynamic growth in agriculture and rural small-scale industry, the resurrection of the private sector and the opening up to the world economy. At the same time, reform efforts faltered badly in the core urban industrial sector. However, during this period experiment in the intransigent urban economy was cushioned by growing surpluses of food and raw materials of agricultural origin.

The second five years witnessed a heating up of the reform effort in the urban economy but a faltering of farm progress. Agriculture's long-term problems, swept under the rug when institutional change alone was productively re-allocating resources and releasing energies, now re-asserted themselves. Within the rural economy, energies and resources gravitated to the dynamic village and township industries, while farming, particularly grain production, stagnated. Consequently, the environment for reform of the core economy changed and became more problematic.

The road ahead for reform is thus 'tortuous and winding'. It should not have been expected to be anything else. Let us follow the necessary logical steps backwards from the ultimate goal of making enterprises innovative, efficient, economical and responsive to demand – a goal that speaks to changing enterprise *behaviour*. Its behaviour is dictated by the economic, political and social milieu in which the enterprise finds itself. Chinese reformers understand that to change behaviour requires transforming this milieu – hence the policy of making enterprises 'autonomous' entities, with substantial control over their resources and responsibility for their own profits and losses. But enterprise autonomy without price reform would allocate resources irrationally and reward performance arbitrarily. Therefore, by extension of the chain of reasoning, desired enterprise behaviour

The author expresses gratitude to Keith Griffin, Peter Nolan and Marilyn Young for helpful comments on earlier drafts of this paper, which was completed in mid-1988, before the political changes that occurred after June 1989.

requires price reform and mobility of resources, including factors of production such as labour, i.e. freedom for resources to move over space and time in response to changes in relative prices.

Moreover it is not enough to adjust relative prices occasionally. There are millions of different prices, and demand and supply conditions change continuously. No deliberate policy of setting prices in accordance with these shifting conditions is feasible. Price reform must therefore mean allowing most prices to fluctuate according to market conditions.

There are branches outward from this chain of economic logic. Let us return to enterprise autonomy: if it is to be real, it must imply (in Kornai's celebrated phrase) hardening of the 'soft budget constraint', making the firm unable to avoid the consequences of either bad management or bad luck.[1] Why then should enterprise managements willingly accept a truly hard budget constraint?[2] The answer must be that they will do so only if there is a carrot to balance the stick – a sufficiently high probability that successful management or innovation and/or good luck (see note 1) will bring great reward.

In a well-developed capitalist economy these conditions, along with the instability and insecurity that is their opposite side, tend to exist automatically. How can firms be made to behave as they would in a well-developed capitalist economy? This problem is sometimes referred to in China as 'solving the ownership question'. In agriculture, the ownership question was solved by making farmers quasi-owners of their farms. In industry, therefore, managements must be similarly treated via leasing or other contractual arrangements.[3] However, autonomous managements will be led by the market to take risks, innovate and strive for efficient operation only if they stand to make large gains from success and suffer large losses from failure. The quasi-rents earned from skill or luck would be quite indistinguishable from returns to property ownership. Moreover, management must be able to buy and sell the resources over which they have usufruct rights. Thus their non-ownership would become largely fictitious.

To spell out the logic of reform is thus to make explicit the vast change in China's political economy that it implies. Substantial control over resources would pass to independent managements, the state and party would lose direct control of the economy,[4] private fortunes would have to be allowed to accumulate, bankruptcies would be an everyday occurrence and unemployment a consequence of rational cost-cutting labour-saving measures. Speculations can be made about the political economy of such a regime. For instance, we might expect intensifying labour–management conflicts as management develops a keen interest in profit maximization. Further, the establishment of concentrations of economic wealth would threaten to produce a melding of economic with political power, and consequently to distort policy towards serving particularistic economic interests.

These tendencies are of course only suggested by the direction of change being advocated by reform elements of the leadership and intelligentsia, and are by no means fully embodied in current policies and institutions. Moreover, they might well be regarded as prices necessarily paid and risks willingly taken for a political economy *capable of generating very rapid economic growth*. However, the inherent logic sketched above, although fraught with consequences for all Chinese, has not really been faced publicly in Chinese debates. Rather, the question of ultimate consequences has been avoided by approaching the reform programme incrementally (the only politically feasible approach). Unfortunately, it is in the nature of the programme that half-steps breed trouble. For example, 'price reform without enterprise reform would intensify inflationary pressure. Enterprise reform without price reform would distribute rewards arbitrarily' (Garnaud 1988).[5] The contradictions created by each half-step force the leadership to decide whether to go forwards or backwards. The most committed reformers have hoped that such recurring contradictions would keep up the pressure for further change. They continue to advocate change as, in mid-1988, accelerating inflation, widespread corruption and new agricultural difficulties have combined to generate formidable political obstacles.

## Structural change

Fundamental to the prospects for reform is a healthy agriculture. A glance at the broad structure of total product and labour force reveals some interesting trends (table 2.1). During the entire period from 1952 until the late 1970s, agriculture's share of combined industrial and agricultural output fell steadily, going from 64 per cent of the total to 26 per cent, while industry's rose concomitantly from 36 per cent to 74 per cent. However, very little change in labour force structure accompanied this marked shift in sectoral product shares. In 1979 almost three-quarters of all Chinese were still farming, although they were producing only a quarter of the gross national product (GNP). An arithmetical result of the widening gap between product structure and labour force disposition was a widening productivity gap: whereas in 1952, an industrial worker produced 6.5 times as much gross output value as a farmer, by 1979 this difference had grown to a factor of 14.[6]

One of the driving impulses of Chinese economic policy during the last decades of Mao Tsetung's leadership was the perception that inequality threatened to grow: without constant vigilance, it was argued repeatedly, 'polarization' would surely occur.[7] It might be surmised that the growing structural inequality in sectoral productivities provided an objective basis for this concern. With urban workers on average producing an output value many times that of the farming majority of the population, only extraordinary measures could prevent sectoral personal incomes from similarly polarizing. The policy of keeping urban wages virtually unchanged for some two decades was such an extraordinary measure. Yet it

**Table 2.1** Distribution of gross product and labour force among primary, secondary and tertiary sectors in China and low-income countries (selected years)

|  | 1952 | 1965 | 1978 | 1986 |
|---|---|---|---|---|
| Percentage of GNP (current prices) | | | | |
| China | | | | |
| Primary sector | – | – | 29 | 29 |
| Secondary sector | – | – | 48 | 46 |
| Tertiary sector | – | – | 23 | 25 |
| Low-income countries | | | | |
| Primary sector | | 41 | | 32[a] |
| Secondary sector | | 28 | | 33[a] |
| Tertiary sector | | 32 | | 35[a] |
| Percentage of China's gross industrial and agricultural output (1970 prices) | | | | |
| Agriculture | 64 | 42 | 26[b] | 26 |
| Industry | 36 | 58 | 74[b] | 74 |
| Percentage of labour force | | | | |
| China | | | | |
| Primary sector | 84 | 82 | 74 | 61 |
| Secondary sector | 7 | 8 | 15 | 22 |
| Tertiary sector | 9 | 10 | 11 | 17 |
| Low-income countries | | | | |
| Primary sector | | 77[c] | | 72[d] |
| Secondary sector | | 9[c] | | 13[d] |
| Tertiary sector | | 14[c] | | 15[d] |

Only since 1985 have estimates of GNP (*guomin shengchan zongzhi*) been released in China along with the more traditional macroeconomic measures. Therefore the breakdown of total product into primary, secondary and tertiary sectors, which is based on this concept, is not available for earlier years, even though such a breakdown is available for labour force distribution. The shares of industry and agriculture in their combined gross output value gives an alternative view of trends during those years. It should be kept in mind that this method double counts intermediate goods and therefore exaggerates the relative share of industry, which uses more intermediate goods than agriculture.

[a] 1985.
[b] 1979.
[c] 1965.
[d] 1980.

*Sources*: For China, *Hongqi*, 16 August 1987: 24–5; *Beijing Review*, 50, 14 December 1987; Riskin 1987: 270; ZTN 1986: 167, 274; ZTZ 1987: 4–5. For low-income countries, World Bank 1987: 206, 264

could not stop but only slow down the widening of the urban–rural gap, for a rising rate of participation in the labour force lifted urban per capita income despite the wage freeze. It was certainly an unpopular policy, both because of the freeze itself and because of the intergenerational and other inequities to which it gave rise. It no doubt helped to discredit the particular brand of egalitarianism – now derided as 'everyone eating from the same pot' – promoted during the period in question and to give equality a bad name in post-Mao China.

Now consider what happened between 1978 and 1986. As table 2.1 shows, the output structure ceased its previously relentless change and remained almost the same for eight years.[8] In both 1978 and 1986 agriculture produced 26 per cent of GNP, while industry's share actually *declined* by two percentage points – a remarkable and superficially counter-developmental phenomenon in a developing country.[9] In contrast, labour force structure, which had shifted so reluctantly before, now moved dramatically, with the share of primary production (agriculture) falling from 74 to 61 per cent, that of secondary production (industry) rising by almost a half (from 15 to 22 per cent) and that of services rising even faster (from 11 to 17 per cent).

In sum, the previous pattern of rapidly changing production structure and stagnant labour force structure was exactly reversed after 1978, with the production structure standing still while the labour force substantially re-allocated itself. One marked result of this reversal was a similar turnabout in the structural basis of urban–rural inequality. The productivity gap between industry and agriculture, expressed in terms of GNP per worker, declined from 8.2 in 1978 to 4.4 in 1986.[10] There was a widespread opinion in urban China in the early 1980s that the peasants (meaning those commercialized suburban farmers visible to the city dwellers) were markedly improving their relative position. Whatever conscious policy might have been doing to the urban–rural gap, its structural basis was diminishing.

The many changes in China's economy since the reform efforts began were not all produced by those efforts. Some were the results of changes in plan priorities and development strategy rather than of reform *per se*. This is certainly true of the higher growth rates of consumer goods industries, which came about through a deliberate planned shift in resources from heavy to light industrial sectors. Similarly, the new availability to some sections of the population of previously unavailable consumer durables, such as colour television sets, video cassette recorders etc., came about because the state decided to permit the import and manufacture of such goods. Even the rapid growth of agricultural production after 1977 owed much to initial improvements in farm prices, sharply increased chemical fertilizer supplies, relaxation of state dictation to the farmers and replacement of the policy of local food-grain self-sufficiency with one of encouraging diversification – all matters of deliberate plan strategy rather than reform as it is usually understood. When price changes began to hurt agriculture (because of low state purchase prices and rising industrial prices) and the planners neglected to channel investment resources to it or otherwise support its continued growth, agriculture ran into difficulties, even though household contracting, the most important reform, persisted. Thus in agriculture, as in other sectors, successes and failures have had much to do with the *nature* of state intervention and not just with the amount of it.

The trends depicted in table 2.1 and discussed above, however, were to a significant degree the results of reform. Prior to the reforms a huge amount of surplus labour was kept in agriculture in a state of disguised unemployment.[11] Claude Aubert (1987: 12) has estimated that the actual number of labour days devoted to a hectare of wheat or rice in the mid-1970s was *several times* the required number.[12] Although peasants were not banned from taking non-agricultural jobs (in fact, rural indus-trialization was one of the hallmarks of the late Maoist strategy), the state restricted off-farm opportunities in a number of ways:

1   private entrepreneurship was essentially eliminated, making local de-velopment depend almost entirely on the initiative, talent and political connections of the local cadres;
2   population movement to towns and cities was largely banned;
3   commune and brigade investment was limited to a narrow range of mostly heavy industries;
4   there was a strong ideological bias against anyone earning an income significantly higher than the local average, which weakened the impulse to develop new forms of production;
5   a similar bias operated against trade and services as wasteful, even capitalistic, 'non-productive' activities.

The reforms effectively removed these constraints, allowing some 50 million people to leave farming for rural industry, trade, construction, transport and services between 1980 and 1986.[13] Family private enterprises alone absorbed over 13 million people between 1981 and 1986, notably in trade (6 million), industry (2.5 million) and transport (1.4 million) (ZNTN 1987: 12). Between 1980 and 1985 there was a *net* reduction of 14.2 million, or 5.5 per cent, in the crop-farming labour force (ZNTN 1986: 228–9),[14] while grain output was rising by over 18 per cent (ZNTN 1986: 180).[15] Within the rural economy the proportion of total output made up of industry and services rose to *over half* in 1987, although it was produced by only 20 per cent of the rural labour force. It was this exodus from agriculture that was largely responsible for the anomaly of that other unexpected structural change implied by table 2.1, i.e. the decline in the productivity gap between industrial and agricultural labour. Peasants poured out of farming into relatively low productivity industrial, trade and service activities. Their departure subtracted nothing from farm output, and added little (per worker) to non-farm output but a great deal to non-farm employment.

Had the late Mao era never occurred, had a pro-industrialization strategy similar to that of the First Five Year Plan (1953–7) been followed and had the labour force been more freely mobile after the late 1950s, then China might well have arrived close to the 1985 structure of labour force and total product. Yet it would not be correct to say that the structural reforms and changes in development strategy have led China back towards an economic structure more common to developing countries.

As table 2.1 indicates, the broad structure of total output is somewhat closer in 1986 than it was in 1978 to that of the World Bank's category of 'low-income countries' (LICs).[16] However, China's secondary sector remains much larger, at the expense of a much smaller service sector. Moreover, when we examine labour force structure it is apparent that between 1978 and 1986 China moved sharply *away* from the pattern typical of LICs. China's secondary sector has grown much larger, but now at the expense of its primary sector rather than of the tertiary, which is similar in relative size to that of LICs generally.

One result of these changes can be seen in table 2.2. It is evident that, as far as the relation between labour productivity in the three broad sectors of the economy is concerned, China more closely resembled LICs before the reform than in 1986. The rapid realignment of the labour force, as peasants moved out of agriculture and into low-productivity industry and services, drove down the relative outputs per worker in both the latter sectors while raising it in agriculture. In addition, of course, China has not (yet) permitted the proliferation of professional and financial service positions with very high salaries that enable services to boast the highest value added per worker in the national accounts of market economies. Thus an average service worker in China in 1986 produced less than one-third as high a fraction of GNP as his or her counterpart in LICs generally. The Chinese farmer advanced to rough parity with the LIC farmer, while the Chinese industrial worker lost substantial ground.

The above results seem puzzling at first, given the still very low prices

**Table 2.2** China's relative sectoral outputs per worker as a multiple of those of low-income countries, 1978 and 1986

| Sector | 1978 | 1986 |
|---|---|---|
| Agriculture | 0.88 | 1.06 |
| Industry | 1.26 | 0.82 |
| Services | 0.90 | 0.30 |

This table gives China's relative output per worker for each sector as a multiple of the corresponding figure for LICs generally. For instance, the first entry is derived by first dividing Chinese agriculture's share of total output by its share of the labour force, and then dividing the result by the corresponding figure for LICs. The low income group's sectoral outputs of the latter are from 1985, and their sectoral labour force distribution is that of 1980.

received by Chinese farmers for their products in comparison with relative farm prices elsewhere in the world. Despite this price disadvantage, the proportion of GDP produced by Chinese farmers appears to be as high or higher than that produced by their counterparts in LICs. The explanation must lie in the greater average *physical* productivity of intensively cultivating Chinese farmers compensating for their output's lower exchange value.

Can farm labour productivity be maintained and improved in a more market-dominated environment in the face of disadvantageous relative prices? Unfortunately, publicly available data for physical output per worker appear to be flawed (ZNTN 1986: 169).[17] We know that grain output grew at a healthy rate from 1978 to 1984 while the grain-growing labour force was diminishing; thus labour productivity was rising rapidly. But what happened to it after 1984, when grain output fell and remained below its 1984 level through 1988, is unclear. Land productivity is quite different, of course, but it does represent an indirect way of finding the output per worker under suitable circumstances.[18] Table 2.3 shows the average annual rate of increase of output per acre of major farm products between 1980 and 1985. These healthy growth rates, in conjunction with what was happening to sown acreage (declining by about 0.5 per cent per year) and to the crop-farming labour force (shrinking), suggest that output per worker probably rose at significant rates during this period.

**Table 2.3**   Average annual growth rate of land yields for major farm products, 1980–1985

|  | Percentage increase in output per unit sown area |
|---|---|
| Grain | 5 |
| Cotton | 10 |
| Edible oil | 5 |
| Sugar | 4 |

*Source*: ZNTN 1986: 169

# The farm problem

However, there were already various straws in the wind presaging coming difficulties. For one thing, farmers had trouble selling the surplus from their bumper harvest of 1984, and the state abandoned its practice of guaranteeing purchase of all surplus. For another, relative prices began moving against agriculture as inflation hit major industrial farm inputs and consumer goods while farm staple prices remained controlled. As a result, from 1982 onwards input costs loomed larger and larger in relation to gross farm income, forcing net income lower (see table 2.4). A peculiar result of

**Table 2.4** Decline in farm net-to-gross income ratio

|  | *1980* | *1982* | *1983* | *1984* | *1985* | *1986* |
|---|---|---|---|---|---|---|
| Proportion of gross rural income taken by various expenses | 39.1 | 34.7 | 35.8 | 36.6 | 42.3 | 44.9 |
| Ratio of net to gross rural income | 60.9 | 65.3 | 64.2 | 63.4 | 57.7 | 55.1 |

*Source*: ZNTN 1987: 152

the various pressures on agriculture was that the rate of commercialization declined after 1982 for all major crops except grain, and even for grain it fell after 1984 (see table 2.5). In the meantime, the state, having engineered a six-year agricultural boom chiefly by means of institutional reforms that restored long-absent incentives, reneged on its promise of increased investment in that sector.

The forces causing stagnation in grain output after 1984 led the Minister of Agriculture to describe the farm situation as 'grim' and the *China Food Journal* to call it a 'crisis' (FBIS 88-012:13; 88-030:40). In part, the problems illustrate the tendency in China's reform to put old wine in new bottles. In 1985, following the bumper harvest of the previous year, the old system of assigned quotas for grain sales to the state was replaced by one of negotiated sales 'contracts' (Oi 1986). A prime motive on the part of the state seems to have been to unburden itself of the obligation to purchase all grain surplus available, which it had been unable to do in 1984. A new single-price formula was adopted to replace the old formula under which farmers were paid increasingly high prices for above-quota sales. The new formula caused grain farmers' net income to fall (He 1988). Moreover, when the subsequent harvests failed to reach the level of 1984, the state apparently began treating contracts as fixed obligations, just as they had

**Table 2.5** Rate of commercialization of major crops (percentage sold of total physical output)

|  | *1980* | *1982* | *1983* | *1984* | *1985* |
|---|---|---|---|---|---|
| Grain | 22.8 | 25.9 | 30.9 | 34.8 | 25.9 |
| Cotton | 99.1 | 97.2 | 96.6 | 95.3 | 84.4 |
| Edible oil | 71.2 | 71.9 | 65.4 | 67.4 | 66.0 |
| Meat | 71.7 | 72.1 | 69.3 | 69.1 | 67.1 |
| Aquatic products | 62.3 | 65.3 | 58.0 | 58.2 | 55.4 |

*Source*: ZNTN 1986: 170

quotas. One writer states that under the new system, 'the quantities covered by the contracts were greater than under unified procurement and the demands on agricultural varieties were stricter' and farmers complained that 'contracts are more unified than unified procurement' (*Fazhan Yanjiu Suo* 1987). In fact, the term 'quota' is still used to refer to the grain sales obligation, and contract purchase quotas are a good deal higher for some grain-producing provinces than they were in the past. Hubei's former quota of 1.75 billion kilograms, for instance, has risen to 2.9 billion kilograms plus additional obligations added on at various local levels. Many non-grain crops, such as hemp, sugar, tea, silkworm cocoons, pork and eggs, are also partially or totally controlled. 'When there is no market for principal farm and sideline products, and some goods haven't even the slightest access to the market, how can it be a commodity economy?' (Xiao and Huang 1988).

In addition to the problem of output prices, rapid inflation in agricultural inputs and producer goods prices has further squeezed farm incomes, while lagging investment has weakened the agricultural infrastructure and the accelerated shrinkage of farm acreage in the face of housing and industrial construction booms have eroded the productive base.[19]

The state posture towards agriculture, despite the significant reforms in that sector, has continued in one basic way to resemble that of the past, i.e. the state still hopes that, with the right institutions, agriculture will develop on its own and not be a burden on the national budget. The proportion of capital construction investment devoted to agriculture and the food-grain growth rate for the various subperiods of the years since 1952 are plotted in figure 2.1. In the 1950s also the Party thought that institutional change – at that time collectivization and the communes – would provide a growing farm output and surplus without the need for diversion of major state investment resources to agriculture. As a result, only 7+ per cent of the capital construction budget was devoted to agriculture (and the related sectors of forestry, fisheries and water conservancy).

The emergency conditions occasioned by the famine of the early 1960s[20] brought just such a temporary diversion, with agriculture's share climbing to almost 18 per cent during the years of recovery from the crisis, 1962–5. However, with the return to relative normality the state again backed away from its increased role. Despite the governing slogan of 'agriculture as the foundation' and the nominal 'priority' given to that sector in development strategy of the 1960s and 1970s, its actual priority in claiming state investment resources was low, hovering at around 10 per cent, while the long-term growth rate of grain production drifted slowly downwards. The reforms of the late 1970s brought fast growth, and as a result investment was allowed to fall continuously and precipitously to a mere 3.4 per cent of total capital construction investment by 1986. In absolute terms, the state invested 20 per cent less in agriculture during 1981–5 than it had during 1976–80. As a result, the total irrigated area declined by 2.5 million acres during the Sixth Five Year Plan, with most of the decline occurring in the mechanically irrigated area (ZTN 1987: 139), and 'a substantial number' of reservoirs were left 'in disrepair and dangerous' (Shi 1987).[21] As figure 2.1 suggests, the fact that the growth of grain production rose sharply between 1976–80 and 1981–4 because of institutional change, and despite the absolute drop in agricultural investment, gave the government an excuse to continue and even intensify its policy of benign neglect.

The result is that there has now been a decade of deteriorating infrastructure whose rectification may well require larger expenditures than the sum total of reasonable levels of investment maintained throughout the period. One can question whether all the infrastructure built up during the collective era was rational and economically worthy of maintenance. That period was one in which economic criteria for evaluating investments were often ignored and immediate returns to investment were low. However, such investments were a precondition for the large increases in farm output that occurred after 1977[22] when policies changed and incentives improved, and it is quite likely, given China's demographic

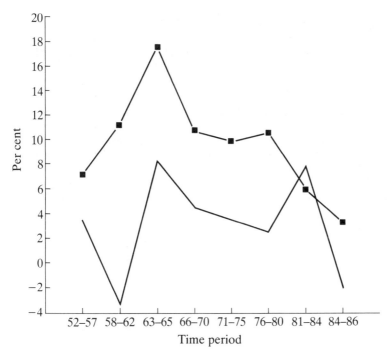

**Figure 2.1** Agricultural investment (—■—) and growth (—).
*Sources*: Riskin 1987; ZTN 1986

conditions and shortage of cultivated land per capita, that social returns to farmland capital construction investment are substantially higher than private returns – i.e. it is more important to China to produce something close to its total food needs than it is profitable to its farmers to do so – especially under the distorted relative price regime that has existed continuously both before and during the reform period. Without vouching for the importance of each piece of infrastructure that has deteriorated or been abandoned in recent years, one can still question the general neglect of agricultural investment, and this is indeed what Chinese commentators have been doing.

The problems of agriculture have been discussed in some detail because it is here as much as anywhere that the fate of China's reform programme will be determined. The luxury of experiment, of room to make mistakes like the many that have been made in the last decade, can be afforded only in conditions of thriving agriculture. If food supply becomes a serious problem again, the outlook for industrial and commercial reform in turn becomes gloomier.

# Reform and Chinese socialism

The reformers themselves regard the urban reform process as one of trial and error or, in their words, 'groping for stones to cross the river'. Many stones have been negotiated and China's forward motion, if not its progress toward a discernible goal, is not in doubt. While successful management of the farm problem would provide a more favourable environment for this groping process, it does not of course ensure its success. The problem of transforming a state-managed economy into a competitive profit-oriented market-driven one has no easy and obvious solution, and the difficulties already encountered are legion.[23] However, I wish to step back and address the broader question of how reform proposes to transform China's socioeconomic system and what its implications are for socialism in China. It will help to begin with a solid appreciation of the gains of this first decade.

First and foremost, the latitude for free expression of ideas has widened enormously. No longer must all publicly expressed thoughts spring directly from a small opus of Marxist classics, let alone a single collection of quotations. Along with this weighty gain has come a widening domain of personal expression in other arenas, from dress to religion to music and other cultural activities.

Second, the majority of China's working people – the farmers – are much freer (but not free) of arbitrary domination by state and Party officials. Whereas, as we have seen above, the contract system can still be as onerous as the old quota system, at least the daily work activities of farmers are no longer dictated from above. People manage their own time, and while the seasons, the weather and the technical demands of agriculture are also stern task masters, an additional layer of human authoritarianism has been stripped away. For a small minority of farmers paths of upward mobility have been created to reward entrepreneurial ability.

Third, personal income has increased rapidly. Impressive gains have been made in farm incomes generally, and while these gains are distributed unequally over the country, bringing more advantage to suburban and developed commercialized regions, they are nevertheless distributed very widely so that virtually all regions have benefited. For the entire period since 1978 rural incomes grew faster than urban, although because of their larger base urban residents enjoyed a greater absolute increase in their incomes.

Fourth, and related to the above, the incidence of poverty has markedly declined. Chinese commentaries suggest that the number of rural residents below the poverty line (200 yuan in 1986 prices) fell from over 200 million in 1979 to 70 million in 1986, and World Bank estimates based on official income data agree in general with this picture. A reduction of over 100 million in the number of absolutely poor people in only seven years must be celebrated as a feat of major importance that accomplishes exactly what economic development is supposed to but often does not: improve the condition of the most disadvantaged members of society. Although rural reform may well have given rise to new forms of poverty on the part of those without the means to take advantage of the new market conditions or dependent upon weakened social welfare services, the numbers thus affected so far appear to be small relative to the numbers who have benefited.

Fifth, the opening of free markets for private production, trade and services has significantly improved people's lives. A large number of goods and services that had been unavailable or hard to find since the mid-1950s because of the impossibility of handling them through central planning can now be found in the private market.

Sixth, a shift in plan priorities has also made many more consumer goods available to both urban and rural dwellers. Not only have more resources been channelled by the planners into light industry, but foreign exchange has been allocated to the import of modern consumer durables, as part of a major increase in 'openness' towards the world market. Similarly, investment has been poured into housing in the cities, finally reversing a long-term trend toward deterioration of housing standards for the urban population. In the countryside, farmers have put a very large share of their income increments into housing and the rural construction boom can be seen everywhere. Plan priorities as well as reforms are responsible there also, in the sense that the centre has allowed a devolution of control over material resources to occur that has in turn permitted a much higher construction rate than the government wanted. This gain, together with the greater supplies of goods and services made available by the market, can be regarded as the real goods counterpart of the income gains mentioned above as the third item of this list.

Seventh, China has successfully used foreign capital both to supplement domestic savings and to introduce advanced technologies and foreign management systems.

Note that the high industrial growth rates of the reform period, often proudly cited as a product of reform, are *not* included in the above list. Such growth rates are not new to China and are mainly the product of the devolution of control over investment to local governments and now (to a limited extent) enterprises, both of which have a hunger for investment that is relatively uncurbed by budget constraints. An important lesson drawn by reformers from pre-reform history is that nominal growth in GNP is a poor indicator of economic health in China. In fact rapid growth is quite undesirable if achieved by increased production of unwanted goods at high cost. Unfortunately, one cannot say that such a phenomenon is unlikely under the system of plan and market now in place.

Despite this proviso the gains listed above are significant, indeed monumental, in that together they represent both a major advance in human welfare and a breakthrough in the transformation of a rigid system and the attitudes surrounding it. They are the joint product of reform and the use of the state's command over resources to support reform by improving living standards and nursing the political constituency for change. They need to be seen against the backdrop of the evolution of China's political economy over the previous three decades. This history, I have argued elsewhere (Riskin 1987), was characterized by a struggle, led by Mao Tsetung, to escape from the rigid institutions and social malformations created by the inherited central planning and management system without moving closer to practices associated with capitalism. Under the reform regime, however, the struggle has been to escape from both the central planning regime, so deeply embedded in China's political economy, and the additional deformations brought about by Mao's assault on central planning. But practices associated with capitalism are no longer anathema; indeed, they are the treatment of choice.

While the gains are impressive if one remembers China as it looked a decade ago, they are more problematic when viewed as advances towards some kind of coherent and reproducible socioeconomic system. Much of the noticeable gain comes from (a) what we have seen was a one-time improvement in agriculture, (b) the change in the periphery of the economy – the private markets for petty trade and production, and the supplementary market for state enterprise above-quota production – and (c) strictly non-reform policies such as the expansion of light industry and the decision to produce and import consumer durables. Not only has the core of the state industrial economy not been much changed, but the changes that have occurred, e.g. in management systems, wage structure etc., have brought little general improvement in economic performance. In fact, losses in urban enterprises increased by 16 per cent in 1985, 65 per cent in 1986 and another 14 per cent in 1987 (Yan 1988). As for productivity, the results so far are ambiguous, as can be seen in table 2.6.

**Table 2.6** 1985 indexes (1978 = 100) of output, employment and fixed assets in state industrial enterprises (1980 prices)

| | |
|---|---|
| Year-end net fixed assets | |
|   Official estimates | 179 |
|   Chen et al. estimates | 141 |
| Gross output | 172 |
| Employment | 125 |
| Gross output per worker | 138 |
| Gross output/fixed assets | |
|   Official estimates | 96 |
|   Chen et al. estimates | 122 |

*Source*: Chen et al. 1988: 257, 264–5; ZTN 1987: 120–1, 257

Gross output per worker in state industry rose by 38 per cent between 1978 and 1985. On the basis of the official estimates of fixed capital stock, output per unit of fixed assets declined slightly over the same period. This would imply that all or most of the increase in labour productivity was due to increasing amounts of capital per worker. However, the use of a different estimate of fixed assets (Chen et al. 1988) that radically reduces their rate of growth accordingly raises the 1985 index of output per unit of fixed assets to a level 22 per cent above 1978. This result implies some growth in productivity due to factors (such as skill or motivation) other than pure capital accumulation. Without further cross-sectional analysis, however, it is impossible to say whether such improvement, if it occurred, resulted from reforms *per se* or from other factors such as improvements in the planning system after 1978.[24]

By breaking the integrity of the old system without yet putting into place a new one, reform has given rise to a whole set of contradictions to which all possible resolutions are costly. Reform has brought China to the point at which the interests of some large constituencies must be threatened. The question is: which ones? A case in point is the dilemma that the government faces with respect to farm policy: if it moves vigorously to redress the urban–rural terms of trade in agriculture's favour while investing substantially in the farm infrastructure, it will then have to choose between burgeoning deficits and sharply rising urban food prices with the attendant danger of social instability. If, however, it leaves the terms of trade essentially unchanged, the likely result will be a continuing slowdown by farmers and lagging farm output, which in turn will exacerbate urban shortages, retard economic growth and complicate reform.[25]

In a dilemma of this kind, political and social factors come to the fore: the farm population's reaction to unfavourable prices is passive, whereas, in the words of one analyst, sharply rising urban prices could 'easily trigger widespread discontent' and 'lead to social unrest' (Chen 1987). In mid-May

1988, the prices of eggs, vegetables, sugar and pork were raised by 30–60 per cent in state stores in China's cities, occasioning anxiety and angry protests in the urban population (*New York Times*, 19 May 1988). A 10 yuan subsidy was added to monthly wages to help offset the increase, but many urban residents felt that their living standards were declining. Indeed, the urban population as a whole appears to have suffered a decline in real income after 1986.[26]

Because the structure of prices is closely related to the distribution of income, changing it is difficult and risky. However, price control has its own dangers in addition to the irrational allocation of resources it encourages (e.g. the underpricing of urban grain stimulates the development of luxury uses, such as distilling alcohol, while restricting supply). For instance, bribery is a common by-product of constrained markets, as those in possession of underpriced goods and services find illegal ways to extract their full scarcity value from the public. When the state remains in control of most economic institutions, the people who find themselves in such a position are public officials. The spread of this kind of corruption in China has been very rapid, and the giving of expensive gifts and other under-the-table transactions has become commonplace. This is just one means by which political position is used to achieve economic gain; perhaps more than anything else, the parcelling out of profitable sinecures to the offspring of high officials has contributed to the political alienation of ordinary people.

Inflation, bribery and corruption are serious problems, but they can be put in perspective as more or less inevitable derivatives of systemic flux. More serious is the uncertain ideology that emanates from the Chinese political and intellectual establishment – a strange mixture of residual socialist rhetoric and Chicago School values. The former seems designed to safeguard legitimacy and the latter to express direction, but the marriage is unstable.

Official propaganda repeatedly stresses appeal to individual interests as the effective motivator of human energy. Luxury consumer goods are dangled on television before a population with an average per capita income of $450 and tales of the emerging wealthy fill the media. Semi-official publications express open contempt for 'ordinary farmers' and glorify 'entrepreneurs' and 'leading cadres'.[27] 'Developing the forces of production' is treated as the sole criterion for choosing social policies. Public accounts of the way that markets work in capitalist economies are marked by considerable naiveté, confusing the real world with an elementary textbook account of pure and frictionless competition. One need not join Meisner's (1982) lament about the disappearance of utopianism from China's official world view in order to question the apparent evaporation from the reformist enterprise of such values as solidarity, security, cooperation and equality. The teachings that now dominate generally oppose and discredit these values, although the latter continue to be reflected, atavistically as it were, in many policies and practices.

It seems to me that China's reformist leaders have still to find a new model and a new vocabulary to describe what they seek to create. 'Socialism with Chinese characteristics' is essentially a catch-all concept, and the Chinese sardonically dub everything from the much derided dual-currency system to the notorious national airline a 'Chinese characteristic'. Similarly, Su Shaozhi's concept of the 'primary stage of socialism', which the leadership has used to lend Marxist legitimacy to reform policies, does not seriously confront the issue of preserving the core of the socialist enterprise through a long historical detour.

The increasingly common assumption that human beings respond only to personal profit may be intended to correct the past practices of the 'iron rice bowl' and 'everyone eating from the same pot'. But the effect must be to legitimize the well-known indifference of the still bloated and ubiquitous bureaucracies which have come to personify 'socialism' for many Chinese. After all, these organs still operate by the old rules, which include little or no material incentive. If response to material incentive is now celebrated as the universal human virtue, can the growing habit of parlaying official position into material gain be seriously challenged?[28]

In this paper China's reform experience to date has been treated as a set of policy decisions with economic and social effects. The social forces behind reform which are providing its real impetus have been ignored. But reform is not just an intellectual process thought up by dedicated and disinterested patriots. It is also a contest of interests, a reshaping of the institutions ordering resource allocation, income distribution and possibly political access in ways that benefit some and hurt others. China must find a way to integrate the principles that underlie the claim to socialist identity with the breathtaking gains brought by reform. These principles tend to express the interests of the poorer members of society, those at risk of being left behind by reform processes.

At the start of the reforms, observers (e.g. World Bank 1985) generally agree that poverty and inequality in China were markedly less severe than in most other developing countries of similar income level. China before the reforms had some important accomplishments to its credit, including a functioning rural relief programme, an impressive level of public health care and sanitation, and an average life expectancy that was extraordinarily high for China's per capita income level.[29] Although all segments of Chinese society, including the poorest, seem to have benefited from the burst of economic energy that attended the inauguration of rural reform, the long-run sustainability under current conditions of improvement across the board is open to question. In the end, the degree to which it proves possible to blend newly released market forces with core socialist values will be determined not by formulations about 'the primary stage of socialism', but by the responses and demands of groups of people, particularly workers and farmers, but also government officials at various levels, intellectuals and others. However, the study of the political economy of China's reform programme[30] has only just begun.

## Notes

1    The argument that natural selection operates efficiently through the market to weed out the incompetent and allow the fittest to survive is a widely accepted myth that many Chinese reformers seem to believe. Even under fictional perfectly competitive conditions, unanticipated fluctuations in supply and demand can wipe out the best-managed firms and reward the worst with riches and success. In real-world conditions, with uncertainty, imperfect information, concentrated and otherwise imperfect markets, political intervention in the economy etc., there is all the more reason to anticipate a vague fit at best between a firm's performance and its economic fate. In any case, we can infer from the practical impossibility of determining the exact mix of reasons for failure of the myriad firms that go bankrupt each day in a market economy that a hard budget constraint requires institutionally ruling out rescue even where it might have been called for in individual cases.

2    To put the question somewhat differently: why should talented people not migrate to other forms of endeavour?

3    Chinese reformers point out that separation of ownership and management is a common practice in market economies. But the neglected condition in their discourse is diversity of ownerships in market economies, whereas in the Chinese case the state would remain the common owner of large and medium-sized enterprises.

4    Whether they could successfully guide resource allocation indirectly is, it seems, a question without an a priori answer. I am as unconvinced by the argument that it is done well in Sweden as by the counter-argument that it has largely failed in Yugoslavia.

5    Ross Garnaud is an economist who served as Australian ambassador to China. The quotation is taken from the original English version of an interview with him that was published in Chinese in the *World Economic Herald* of Shanghai.

6    This calculation was carried out in terms of 1970 prices, and so should not be affected by changing relative prices. However, it is affected by the use of gross values, which causes industry's share to be exaggerated in general (see note to table 2.1).

7    See Riskin (1987: ch. 10) for a discussion of Maoist policy on income distribution.

8    This remains true whether we use gross values in constant prices or GNP (net values gross of depreciation) in current prices.

9    Superficially and not actually counter-developmental because the phenomenon reflects a temporary and eminently developmental structural adjustment caused by dynamic agricultural advance.

10   The main reason that industry's 1978–9 productivity advantage in GNP terms is less than in gross output value terms (eightfold compared with 14-fold) is that the double counting that swells industry's gross output is eliminated from its contribution to the GNP (see note to table 2.1).

11  'Disguised unemployment' is defined to mean a state in which a given output both could and would be produced by fewer workers, other inputs remaining the same. Neither institutions nor prices are assumed to be constant.

12  Aubert's estimates of requirements are based on interviews with peasants, and are deliberately made high (often double those of Taiwan). His estimates of actual labour input are based on work-days paid for under the collective distribution system then in effect. These are nominal and exaggerated, but the very large gap he finds between requirements and labour supply is still significant.

13  This is a gross number and is not net of new entrants to agriculture.

14  This figure refers to workers engaged in raising crops (*zhongzhiye*) *per se*, and excludes forestry, fisheries, animal husbandry, rural industry etc. The percentage decline in the grain-farming labour force must have been even greater, since many farmers switched from growing grain to growing more profitable crops.

15  Grain output actually rose by 27 per cent between 1980 and the record year 1984, but it then fell in 1985.

16  The *World Development Report* (World Bank 1987) groups 37 countries, including China, in the 'low-income economies' category. Moreover, the LIC's gross domestic product (GDP) and labour force structures are weighted averages using national GDPs and labour force sizes as the weights. The inclusion of China as a giant member of the group with which it is being compared of course works to minimize differences and makes those differences that remain all the more significant.

17  The grain-farming labour force implied by the figures given here is larger than the total cropping labour force given in ZNTN (1986: 228). It appears that the productivity figures were derived by dividing total grain output by total *rural* labour force (including industrial workers); they are therefore of no use in examining productivity trends for specific crops and products.

18  It is inconceivable under Chinese conditions that labour productivity could grow if land yields are falling, but it is quite possible for labour productivity to stagnate or even decline in the face of rising land yields. Indeed, the latter happened during the two decades preceding the reforms of the late 1970s. Thus rising land yields are a necessary but not sufficient condition for rising labour productivity.

19  Total cultivated land shrank by 600,000 hectares in 1986 alone.

20  For more information about the causes and consequences of this famine, see Ashton et al. (1984), Bernstein (1984) and Riskin (1987: ch. 6; 1989; 1990).

21  Peter Nolan has reminded me that such deterioration may not be new to the reform era, about which more information is available than for the past. However, it is reasonable to assume that maintenance of irrigation works is correlated with gross investment, the decline of which may well indicate that the problem of deterioration has been greater recently than before. The decline in total and mechanically irrigated areas suggests the same conclusion.

22  See Shi (1987) for an argument that the high growth rates of the early reform period resulted largely from past investment in chemical fertilizer plants, research on improved varieties and water control.

23  See Riskin (1987: ch. 14) for a discussion of the record of urban reform through 1986; see also Naughton (1985, 1986) and Walder (1986).

24  Various possible problems with the new estimates of fixed capital cited in table

2.6 are discussed by Chen et al. (1988). Also, value added in constant prices ought to be used rather than gross output. A value-added series, not used here because its methodology could not be checked (it is based upon an unpublished paper), is given by Chen et al. It increases slightly faster than the gross-value series used here. Finally, regarding the question of causation of a possible improvement in productivity between 1978 and 1985, the resurrection of a semblance of system and order in the planning and management system, the return of veteran management and economic cadres to their duties, and various measures to strengthen planning and materials allocation may have had as much or more to do with productivity as reforms did. See the annual issues of ZTN for data on labour productivity of selected industries, as well as other technical and financial indicators; for monthly data, see *China Statistics Monthly*.

25    This dilemma is suggested by Chinese economists themselves in a running debate over the causes and solutions of the farm problem. For a summary, see FBIS 143, FBIS Trends, 8 April 1988 – China, 'China's agricultural policy debate'.

26    The average monthly disposable income per capita of urban housholds rose by 10.6 per cent in 1987 compared with 1986, while the official cost-of-living index in January 1988 was 11.2 per cent above that of the previous January (*China Statistics Monthly*, April 1988: 70, 111). Taken together, these figures imply a decline in real per capita income. Many observers believe that the official price indexes understate the rate of inflation, some putting it as high as 50 per cent per annum in major cities in 1988. See *New York Times*, 19 September 1988.

27    The quotes are from a remarkable article entitled 'Rural society composed of five forces' in *Nongye Jingji Congkan* (*Journal of Agricultural Economics*), 21 March 1988. This piece seeks to define the 'social structure of rural China' by 'taking social position as the main factor and combining it with psychological factors, professional status and personal income'. The result is to write off 'the great majority of ordinary farmers' as not having 'change[d] and remould[ed] their ways of thinking', to celebrate craftspeople, small business people and rural enterprise owners and managers as 'full of vigour and vitality . . . receptive to innovations . . . hav[ing] a strong desire to get rich . . .', 'well-informed, experienced and knowledgeable', 'dar[ing] to take risks'. As for rural workers, although their income makes them 'the envy of ordinary farmers', 'their role is far inferior to that of rural tradesmen and enterprise owners and managers'.

28    In commenting on an earlier draft of this paper Peter Nolan argued that, while corruption involving money may have increased, the use of state or party position to control individuals has probably declined. This may indeed be true in the countryside; in the cities, Walder (1986) has found that patron–client relations continue to dominate industry even during the reform period. But however true, the argument serves as a reminder that other forms of corruption existed in the past.

29    Since 1978, with the weakening of this collective infrastructure, the mortality rate (and especially infant mortality) has risen and life expectancy may have fallen; see Banister (1987: 116) and Dreze and Sen (1990: ch. 11).

30    See Perry and Wong (1985) for a useful and informative attempt to deal with some of thse issues. Despite the title, however, only a few of the contributions in their book adopt a political economy framework in the classic sense of analysing the interactions of the forces and relations of production.

# References

Ashton, B., Hill, K., Piazza, A. and Zeitz, R. (1984) Famine in China, 1958–61. *Population and Development Review*, 10, 4.

Aubert, C. (1987) Rural capitalism vs. socialist economics? Unpublished paper.

Banister, J. (1987) *China's Changing Population*. Stanford, CA: Stanford University Press.

Bernstein, T. P. (1984) Stalinism, famine, and Chinese peasants. *Theory and Society*, 13.

Chen Kuan, Jefferson, G. H., Rawski, T. G., Hongchang Wang and Yuxin Zheng (1988) New estimates of fixed investment and capital stock for Chinese state industry. *China Quarterly*, June, no. 114, 243–66.

Chen Xiwen, *Jingji Yanjiu*, 20 December 1987, excerpted in FBIS 147.

*China Statistics Monthly*, China Statistics Archives, University of Illinois at Chicago.

Dreze, J. and Sen, A. (1990) *Hunger and Public Action*. Oxford: Clarendon Press.

Fazhan Yanjiu Suo Zonghe Keti Zu (Comprehensive Problems Group, Development Institute) (1987) Nongmin, shichang he zhidu chuangxin (Peasants, markets and institutional innovation). *Jingji Yanjiu*, 20 January, no. 1.

FBIS [Foreign Broadcast Information Service], China, Various issues.

He Kang (1988) Minister of Agriculture, Briefing to the NPC Standing Committee, summarized in FBIS 88-012, 20 January.

Meisner, M. (1982) *Marxism, Maoism and Utopianism: Eight Essays*. Madison, WI: University of Wisconsin Press.

Naughton, B. (1985) False starts and second wind: financial reforms in China's industrial system. In E. J. Perry and C. Wong (eds), *The Political Economy of Reform in Post-Mao China*. Cambridge, MA: Harvard University Press.

—— Finance and planning reforms in industry. In US Congress, Joint Economic Committee, *China's Economy Looks Toward the Year 2000*. Washington, DC: US Government Printing Office.

Oi, J. C. (1986) Peasant grain marketing and state procurement: China's grain contracting system. *China Quarterly*, no. 106, 272–90.

Perry, E. J. and Wong, C. (1985) *The Political Economy of Reform in Post-Mao China*. Cambridge, MA: Harvard University Press.

Riskin, C. (1987) *China's Political Economy: the Quest for Development since 1949*. Oxford: Oxford University Press.

—— (1989) Food, poverty and development strategy in the People's Republic of China. In R. Kates and L. Newman (eds), *Hunger in History: Food Shortage, Poverty and Deprivation*. New York: Blackwell.

—— (1990) Feeding China: the experience since 1949. In J. Dreze and A. Sen (eds), *Hunger and Public Action*. Oxford: Clarendon Press.

Rural society composed of five forces (1987) *Nongye Jingji Congkan*, no. 6, excerpted in *Beijing Review*, 21 March 1988, p. 31.

Shi Bing (1987) Guanyu nongye xuyao zengjia touru wenti de tantao (The question of increasing inputs needed by agriculture). *Nongye Jingji Wenti*, January.

Walder, A. G. (1986) The informal dimension of enterprise financial reforms. In US Congress, Joint Economic Committee, *China's Economy Looks Towards the Year 2000*. Washington, DC: US Government Printing Office.

World Bank (1985) *China: Long-Term Development Issues and Options*. Baltimore, MD: Johns Hopkins University Press.

—— (1987) *World Development Report.* Washington, DC: World Bank.

Xiao Junzhao and Huang Caizhong (1988) Yi huo qiu wen tuidong nongye xin fazhan (Seek stability through vitality, promote new agricultural development). *Renmin Ribao*, 6 February, 1–2.

Yan Kalin (1988) Perspective view of the phenomenon of the closing down of 1 million town and township enterprises. *Jingji Ribao*, 6 January, translated in FBIS-CHI-88-015, 25 January 1988.

ZNTN [*Rural Statistical Yearbook of China (Zhongguo Nongcun Tongji Nianjian)*] (1986). Beijing: China Statistical Publishing House.

—— (1987) Beijing, China Statistical Publishing House.

ZTN [*Statistical Yearbook of China (Zhongguo Tongji Nianjian)*]. Beijing: China Statistical Publishing House, various years.

ZTZ [*Chinese Statistical Outline (Zhongguo Tongji Zhaiyao)*] (1987) Beijing: China Statistical Publishing House.

# 3

# Reform of the Economic Operating Mechanism and Reform of Ownership

## Dong Fureng

Reform of China's economic system encompasses both reform of the economic operating mechanism and reform of ownership forms and structure.

## Reform of the economic operating mechanism

All socialist countries pursuing structural economic reform recognize that the aim is reform of the economic operating mechanism. In Hungary and the USSR economic reform is referred to as reform of the economic mechanism. This topic is also widely discussed in China. In the Soviet-type economic structure the operating mechanism created serious problems with economic performance mainly dependent on mandatory planning: the economic mechanism was one of administrative dictat. Mandatory planning directly controlled the activity of every department, locality and enterprise, the production and distribution of innumerable commodities, and in China even determined personal employment and the distribution of certain consumer goods. Each planning target had the force of law, to be obeyed by all departments and enterprises. An administrative structure was established to implement the plan and the operation of the economy was controlled by a dual interlocking management system. A vertical structure consisting of supervisory organs was set up for different industries in government departments at all levels. There was also a horizontal structure according to region, again with administrative organs at all levels of government. In the hierarchical structures each level controlled the level below, right down to individual enterprises, each of which was subordinate to administrative organizations at one level or another which directly controlled their everyday activity. The market mechanism was excluded as alien to a socialist economy, or was permitted to function in an extremely narrow sphere outside the control of planning directives. In general productive resources did not enter the market, and although consumer goods did so on their way to the consumer, their production was controlled by mandatory planning. Consumers had a very restricted choice within limits set by the plan. Therefore the market was not a market in the true sense. Money had merely a passive role, as virtually no more than an accounting convenience, and only a minute function as an economic stimulator. This economic mechanism contributed to socialist economic development, especially in the early stages of industrialization. In the USSR during the Second World War, when there were severe shortages of raw materials, it ensured the needs of the military and of heavy industry. However, serious shortcomings of this system were increasingly revealed as the economy developed. The initiative and creativity of both individuals and enterprises were suppressed, economic performance stagnated, becoming inflexible and inefficient, there was a serious waste of resources, resulting in shortages and overstocking at the same time, and increasing failure to meet the needs of the people. Therefore reform of the operating mechanism of the economy became an objective necessity. The abuses of the old system made people understand that a socialist economy needs the market mechanism, and so in China a socialist economy came to be defined as a planned commodity economy – a new economic system linking planning with the market.

Although most people agree on the necessity of reforming the method of economic operation and introducing the market mechanism, ideas about how precisely to do this vary considerably. Three models have been proposed which are described in broad outline below.

1   Primary regulation by planning and secondary regulation by the market: in this model, the operation of the economy is basically regulated by mandatory planning, while the market plays a supplementary role, only operating as a regulator for unimportant products such as surplus agricultural output, low-priced multivariety goods or industrial goods which play an unimportant role in people's lives. Because the economic operating mechanism remains substantially unchanged in this model, the old abuses cannot be corrected. Few people in China now advocate this approach.

2   The dual-track model: in this model economic activity is divided into three sectors. One sector is subject to mandatory planning and includes the main economic activities, such as major construction projects and the production and distribution of important products, another sector is also subject to mandatory planning but is mainly regulated by means of economic levers and a third sector is entirely regulated by the market, chiefly comprising certain agricultural products, daily necessities, small commodities and labour in the service and repair trades. The first sector will shrink to some extent, while the second expands. The difference between the second and third sectors is that in the former the market mechanism is subject to planning regulation and control. This is a dual-track model in which mandatory

planning and the market mechanism together regulate the economy. This is not only applied across the whole economy, but is often applicable to the production and exchange of the same product. For instance, part of the production and exchange of a particular steel product may be regulated by planning, while another part is market regulated: once the steel industry has met the quotas for production and sale to the state it can sell the surplus on the market. Under this system prices are either unified state prices, negotiated prices determined by supply and demand or free-market prices.

3   The regulated (or planned) market model: mandatory planning is abolished, and the economy is operated by a regulated or planned market mechanism. The state regulates and controls the market, while the market, in turn, regulates and guides the economic activities of enterprises and individuals.

At the moment China is operating the dual-track model, and various opinions are held about it. Some regard it as the goal of economic reform, believing that mandatory planning should be decreased but not abolished and the market mechanism should be employed but limited to areas outside the plan. They consider that mandatory planning is the hallmark of a socialist economy, and its abolition is a negation of socialism. This view is wrong. Hungary's experiments have shown that mandatory planning can be abolished. Of course, the market is not omnipotent and cannot in the last analysis guarantee optimal resource allocation; moreover, it can cause economic fluctuations and waste resources. Market regulation often produces conflict between the profit-seeking behaviour of the enterprise and long-term social goals, necessitating planning, regulation and control of the market. However, planning should not be by directive, because this is incompatible with the market mechanism. It is inevitable that there will be problems under the dual-track system, and there may also be dualism in the economic behaviour of enterprises. For instance, enterprises sometimes welcome mandatory production quotas because this guarantees them inputs at low official prices, allows them to obtain bank loans, ensures guaranteed sale of products to the state and means that they are not at the mercy of the money market. However, enterprises dislike the restraints which mandatory planning imposes upon them. They want the autonomy to sell their own products at market prices and to retain some of their profit. Consequently, some enterprises try to conceal their real productive capacity so that the state quotas are as low as possible, allowing them to produce more goods outside the plan and make more profit by selling them at prices higher than those paid by the state, even for superior products. There are several other problems. For example, the dual-price system inherent in the dual-track system causes chaos in enterprise accounting and encourages speculation. Therefore the dual-track system can only be transitional, and not the goal of reform itself. The longer it survives the greater will be the friction and dislocation. Reform should gradually lead

China's economy from the second model to the third.

In the third model the state regulates and controls the market via the economic parameters, and uses the market to provide signals to enterprises and individuals which guide their behaviour so that the goal of profit maximization can be harmonized with long-term social aims. This attenuates the shocks and fluctuations associated with the market economy, and decreases the haphazard behaviour of enterprises and the resulting waste. Naturally, the third model does not exclude the possibility that under certain circumstances administrative methods of regulation may be used.

Three kinds of reform are needed so that China's method of economic operation can move towards a regulated or planned market system.

1   A complete integrated market system does not yet exist in China; many factors of production are not allocated by the market, and those markets which do exist are far from being developed and integrated. However, it cannot be created overnight; related systems and organizations have to be set up gradually or adapted by appropriate reforms in commerce, finance, prices, information, labour and so on. The realization of a market system is impeded by the inadequate development of the social division of labour and the forces of production, by the fact that the vestiges of the self-sufficient natural and semi-natural economy still survive, and because transport and communications are backward. This task is far more difficult than was anticipated. For example, price reform has encountered great difficulties and serious distortion in relative prices has built up over several years, frequently giving rise to distorted signals to enterprises, leading to serious dislocation between supply and demand. If the price structure is not reformed the market mechanism will not be able to regulate economic performance, but price reform, because it impinges upon different economic interests, is particularly difficult.

2   The transformation from mainly direct to mainly indirect methods of regulating and controlling the economy is in progress at present, but certain difficulties have been encountered. State administration has not been correspondingly reformed, and those bodies set up under the old economic system still survive, performing their old function and interfering directly with the everyday running of enterprises. State economic personnel are accustomed to the old work methods and are unfamiliar with the indirect method of economic regulation, so that when problems arise (such as an excessive increase in borrowing), they frequently resort to direct methods. Because of the gradual nature of reform, the old operating mechanism still functions and can obstruct the change in methods of regulation and control. For instance, in the last few years the number of products to which the State Planning Commission applies mandatory planning has been reduced from 120 to 60 – from 40 per cent to 20 per cent of industrial products. However, administrative departments at different levels and local authorities have all

increased the number of their mandatory quotas, and in some enterprises the entire production is subject to directives and the market hardly functions at all. Only 18 per cent Shanghai's industrial output value is subject to state planning quotas, but in several industries, especially metallurgy, textiles and engineering, almost 100 per cent of their main products are sometimes subject to mandatory planning, and even products in excess of the plan have been retrospectively included (*Peoples' Daily*, 14 May 1987). Unless the replacement of direct by indirect methods is continued, market regulation of the economy will be difficult to achieve.

3  State-owned industry should be reformed so that it operates according to the laws of the market and participates actively in market exchange. At present state-owned industries are unable to do this because they cannot react promptly to market changes; they do not behave competitively or respond to indirect state regulation. In 1986 state-owned industries produced 68.7 per cent of industrial output value, and, if they fail to become the main field of market activity, market regulation of the economy will be fundamentally impossible.

# Ownership reform

The idea that economic reform requires reform of the economic operating mechanism has been widely accepted, but the notion that structural reform involves a change in the form of ownership has not. This question either has not been raised at all (as in the USSR) or else has been opposed (as in China). However, the experience of both Hungary and China shows that, in the process of economic reform, the question of ownership reform inevitably comes up. Indeed, ownership reform is essential if the shortcomings of state-owned enterprises are to be eliminated. It is also necessary in order to establish an integrated market system which will become the socialist economy's operating mechanism.

The old economic system had many such shortcomings associated with low efficiency, low economic returns (many enterprises made a loss in fact), slow technological progress, poor quality, products unchanged for years, disjuncture between production and demand etc. Under the planned commodity economy it was intended to avoid such defects in state-owned industries by transforming them into independently managed commodity-producing enterprises, responsible for their own profit and loss. In the last few years this course has been followed in economic reform: increasing the autonomy of enterprises, allowing them to retain part of their profits, increasing economic stimuli, experimenting with a 'bankruptcy law' to encourage them to run themselves better and reduce losses, introducing the market mechanism so that inputs and ouputs are both linked with the market, encouraging competition between enterprises and so on. However, state-owned enterprises have still not become self-managed commodity producers responsible for their own profit and loss.

The autonomy of such enterprises has increased, but they are still subordinate to administrative organizations which interfere with their everyday activities. The powers delegated by central government often do not arrive at the enterprises themselves but are retained by administration at other levels, and the profits which the central government decided to leave in their hands are often creamed off in one way or another by various departments. The situation is even less satisfactory in respect of the responsibility of enterprises for their own profit and loss. Even today no one is responsible for state property; what has changed is that enterprises can retain part of their profits, but loss is still borne by the state, and enterprises use all sorts of methods to distribute large sums of money and goods to their employees. The passage of a 'bankruptcy law' is not a very strong restraint, and enterprises are not generally worried by the threat of bankruptcy.

Without management autonomy and responsibility for profit and loss enterprises cannot become commodity producers subject to market forces. Enterprises which are not responsible for their own profit and loss cannot actively compete. They feel no pressure from market competition; they are unable and do not need to respond flexibly to market changes. For example, when supply exceeds demand for a certain product, enterprises sometimes continue to increase output, and despite an increase in the interest rate some continue to scramble for bank loans.

Under these circumstances, when the state adopts indirect methods of regulation and control, the results are disappointing. This is why direct methods often have to be employed. For example, although the state imposed a tax on bonuses in order to curb their excessive issue, enterprises continued to distribute large sums of money and goods under other names. This obstructs the regulatory function of the market mechanism.

Whatever efforts are made, reform will be disappointing unless state-owned industries become autonomous and subject to market forces, the microeconomic base through which the state exercises indirect regulation and control. At present we are experimenting widely with reforms to separate ownership from management, while maintaining state ownership, in order to correct shortcomings in these enterprises and improve their response to the market mechanism. The state continues to own the overall assets, while the right of management is handed over, in different ways, to the enterprise and its operators. We are now widely promoting systems of renting and various froms of contracting. It is hoped that, through contracts entered into with the state, enterprises or those who run them (leasees, contractors) will acquire adequate self-management rights, the duty to hand over the prescribed proportion of profits and the responsibility to make up deficits. A detailed assessment of these reforms is not possible here, but, judging from the experiments which hae been made, they are effective: enterprises are more independent, more responsible and more efficient, and are more like genuine commodity producers. However, several problems remain. For example, budget constraints are not very hard, and although enterprises and their operators are able to take a share of the profits, any large deficit has to be borne by the state since the enterprises are in no position to do so; enterprises haggle with the state for better terms and sometimes raise the prices of their products while they are fulfilling contracts in order to extract the maximum profits. Some enterprises under lease or contract consider only short-term profit. The 'investment shortage syndrome' and the lavish distribution of bonuses have changed little. If conditions change while the contract is being fulfilled and input prices rise, the enterprise can request revision of the contract; state administrative organs can change or annul contracts at will. Thus, although the separation of ownership and management has a role in transforming enterprises and in turning the market mechanism into the operating mechanism of the socialist economy, this role may be limited.

The obstructions which state-owned enterprises encounter on the road to independence are related to the fact that reform is partial and uncoordinated as well as to the state-ownership form of public ownership. When the state owns the assets of an enterprise, its administrative organs act as proprietors and intervene in its day-to-day running, making it difficult for the enterprise to escape from its subordinate position and run its own affairs. In Hungary, although reform has continued for almost 20 years and mandatory planning was abolished at the outset, nationalized enterprises, as the Hungarian economist Janos Kornai put it, depend on the market but are even more dependent on state administrative organs which still interfere with their activity, issuing orders and directives which they usually cannot disobey. Such dependence is even greater in China. As long as the assets of an enterprise are owned by the state, budgetary constraints will be soft, and various administrative bodies will have the right to interfere in enterprise affairs but will not be responsible for their decisions, and therefore will not be responsible for profit and loss. The enterprises themselves, having no management autonomy, cannot bear responsibility for profit and loss either, and will always be bailed out by the state anyway. Soft budget constraints prevent state-owned enterprises from operating as genuine commodity producers, and indeed make it unnecessary for them to do so. They are unwilling to engage in competition, which therefore exercises no pressure upon them; the market means little to them and they rarely react to its movements.

Therefore, as well as pushing forward with reforms which separate ownership and management, we must explore the question of ownership reform. Some experiments are already under way. First, some small state-owned enterprises are being privatized (a process which had already started in the case of some small commercial and service enterprises); mainly owned by individuals, they are subject to very tight restraints with respect to their property relations, but they naturally become autonomous and responsible for their own profit and loss, and have to operate according to market principles, participate in competition and submit to market regulation. Second, some state-owned enterprises have been transferred to collective ownership. Genuine enterprises of this kind are self-managing, budget constraints are stronger than in state-owned enterprises and they are necessarily responsible for their own performance. However, these reforms are more suitable for small state enterprises than for large and medium ones. Third, some state-owned enterprises have been transformed into joint-stock companies, whose stock may belong to the state, to other enterprises or to individuals. Their assets (including those of state-controlled joint-stock companies) do not belong entirely to the state, which can participate in decision-making only as a stock holder. This releases the enterprise from appendage status and enables it to be self-managing. Their asset relations are unambiguous, and ultimately every shareholder is responsible for profit and loss. Budget constraints are hard or nearly as hard as in privately owned enterprises. Consequently, these enterprises can become subject to market forces and the market system can expand. This is a hopeful experiment.

Reform of the ownership structure will mean abandoning the traditional single form of public ownership, in which state ownership was predominant, and adopting diversified forms of ownership, in which different forms of public ownership have the dominant role. This will help turn state-owned enterprises into genuine commodity producers. Every form of ownership has its advantages and disadvantages: public ownership is in general more in harmony with our social aims; an economy in which public ownership is dominant enables the realization of social aims, and is more conducive to social justice; it prevents conflicts of interest, disparities of wealth and poverty, and ensures the development of the economy in the direction of socialism. However, the soft budget constraint is difficult to eradicate and leads to economic inefficiency and waste. An individual ownership economy, particularly individual capitalist ownership, in which economic interests are strongly stimulated and restricted, can compete in the market and be regulated by the market. At the microeconomic level productivity and economic returns are usually high, but because its interests are difficult to reconcile with social aims, the operation of this economy can easily damage social justice and cause wide differences in income and unequal distribution of property. Without a flourishing dominant public sector, without guidance and essential restraints, the individual economy leads towards capitalism. Many of the economic problems attributable to the deficiencies in state-owned enterprises could be solved by the retention of state ownership only in areas which affect the political and economic lifeblood of the country, which ensure the public good and in which profit-making is not the primary consideration. Other state-owned enterprises can be transformed into collective or individual or, in the case of small enterprises, private capitalist ownership. While maintaining the leading role of public ownership, different forms of non-public ownership (individual, private capitalist or mixed forms) should be developed.

Although friction and contradictions may continue to exist, a multiform ownership structure in which multiform public ownership is dominant offers a better solution to the problems of balancing efficiency and social justice, general enrichment and desirable income differentials, planning and flexibility, social and private interests, and macroeconomic and microeconomic benefits. Under a multiform system of ownership with public ownership dominant and with the breaking up of the state-ownership monopoly, enterprises under different forms of ownership can compete with each other and the stimulus of competition will lead those state-owned enterprises which have been preserved to become independent responsible commodity producers. They will participate more actively in market competition and respond to market changes. Reforms which encourage separation of ownership and management will be more effective. Consequently, the reform of ownership and the establishment and development of a multiform ownership structure dominated by public ownership will promote the creation of a full market system and the transformation of direct into indirect state regulation and control. All this will, in turn, assist the reform of the economic operating mechanism.

In sum, reform of the economic operating mechanism must be combined with reform of the ownership structure: both are essential and inseparable elements in the reform of the economic system.

# 4

# Market Socialism and Democracy

## Bruce McFarlane

## Introduction

The events in the world's most populous country spanning the period 1950–78 were of earth-shaking significance. This is often forgotten in the hurly-burly of reports in the Western economic press about Chinese innovations in economic reform and China's rediscovery of problems well known to East European economic planners. These events led to a giant step forward in the abolition of class exploitation, and opened up new perspectives and horizons for the lowly in society. All the attempts to denigrate most of what had been achieved in social and economic policy before the December Party decisions launching the reform cannot alter that basic fact.

The blow struck in China on behalf of the working people and the sorely tried peasantry was one of this century's momentous occurrences. On the economic front, the first decade of socialist experiment, which combined classical ideas about economic planning, most fully developed in the USSR (Kovalevsky 1928; Strumilin 1928), with local Chinese features, has been positively evaluated by critics in this field. This was because of the assistance given to economic development by such policies as good working relations between village cadres and the peasant masses or Chinese adaptation of techniques of production in a highly effective way (Dobb 1960: 46–7). Skilful diffusion of such features has been seen, with good reason, as efficiently building a base for a modern economy (Adler 1957: chs 1–4; Ishikawa 1983, 1984). These authors stressed the need to link the sociopolitical goals set in a period of planning with the plan itself. The gap in their analysis (McFarlane 1984a) was the lack of detail about how to connect the sociopolitical goals embodying the socialist project with the mechanisms for plan fulfilment such as manipulation of interest rates on state and collective capital, taxes and Ricardian rents ('indirect economic levers' in the language of today's Chinese reform literature). The value of such mechanisms has been advocated many times since 1908 by such Western socialist economists as H. D. Dickinson (1939) or engineer–

economists such as E. Barone (1908), while in Yugoslavia they were tried out with mixed success between 1950 and 1970 (McFarlane 1988: chs 9–11).

In the earlier phase of planned economy state planning attempted to wrest control over the production of economic surplus (or surplus labour time) from exploiting groups and to replace the whole system in which they thrived by a new one. This was to be a socialist system, not only in the sense of state ownership of the means of production, but a new society – one in which much more weight would be given to the interest and the views of ordinary people concerning the utilization of the economic surplus.

Today economic reformers emphasize exchange value, markets, labour productivity and the effectiveness of investment. Efficiency is heavily promoted. That is all to the good. But in discussing economic reform we should remember that at this phase of China's political cycle (Maruyama 1983: 10–23), the intention of the leading political forces has been to find new mechanisms for obtaining the economic surplus of society and for using this surplus in ways that bring more wealth to more people in the shortest time. This objective forms the social aspect of planning goals rather than any conscious decision to allow coalitions of private groups to pursue their own material interest at the expense of wider 'civil society'. If this is not the case it is very difficult to explain the behaviour of policy-makers during different phases of the Reform such as the 1987–8 postponement of drastic alterations in relative prices. However, linked to this overriding perspective has been the perceived need to change the class relations that developed in the period 1949–78, the class aspects of the labour process, in a number of sectors.

The consensus among reform-minded Chinese economists and officials seems to be that a clear socialist 'push' had been justified in the past to clear out corruption of the previous Guomindang regime, to stabilize international trade links with the outside world (e.g. through bilateral trade with the socialist countries) and to mobilize rural labour to build rural infrastructure (the so-called 'labour-accumulation projects'). However, after these objectives were basically achieved petty-commodity production should have been encouraged (Liu Shaoqi, quoted by FitzGerald 1968: 125–9). It should have been recognized that market forces could not generally be abolished without deleterious effects on individual and collective material incentives and hence on the rate of economic growth. By 1978 the system was overripe for a change of this type, whatever the solid economic achievements of the earlier period.

It is argued in this chapter that something more than a renewed tolerance of petty-commodity production or even a drive to market socialism is required in the reform period; to give a sense of direction to society as a whole there must be a socialist reference point.

Much has been written in the Chinese Academy of Social Sciences about China's being a society in transition, but very little has been said about what it is in transition to. Is it in transition to a new system of modified social relations of production allowing revival of petty-commodity production, with its attendant rent-taking and subcontracting in small-scale enterprises? Or is it merely a transition from a form of economic planning and socialist economy which had outlived its usefulness and produced a stagnant economy to one moved by a series of pragmatic changes in economic instruments and policy? The distinction between these two has not always been clearly made. The reasons for this can be conjectured with a fair measure of confidence. First, the 'new responsibility system' was not a well-thought-out change of Party policy implemented from the top down, but rather one in which some courageous local officials supported peasant initiatives against scepticism and downright obstruction in the political machine. The true origins of 'workers' control' and market socialism in Yugoslavia are to be found in the attempts of Djilas and Kardelj to revive Marx and Lenin on the Paris Commune and workers' control and suggestions by Kidric to develop a competitive economy, which were initially resisted by Tito (see Djilas 1969: 158; McFarlane 1988: ch. 6). Similarly, it has not suited China's leaders to admit that the shape of the new concepts has not been wholly due to the Party's initiative. Second, the Party and the government have wisely been at pains to avoid the horrors which flowed from attempting to give practical expression to the thesis about 'the struggle between the two roads' and for that reason have themselves only sketchily discussed the issue of coexistence of socialist and petty-commodity modes of production.[1]

There has been little discussion of the deep implications of a revival of petty-commodity production and of social relations of production in which considerable numbers of people are connected, through a plethora of rent and interest payments, with state and collective bodies as well as with other families. These features make 'socialism with Chinese characteristics' a system which contains, apart from its extensive state and collective sectors, some economic relationships which are similar to the social system in areas of the Philippines and Thailand (Bobek 1962; McLennan 1980; Fegan 1983). This point is analysed further below.

Only a few economists have analysed the probable accompaniments of a wider use of market forces in a socialist setting. One such attempt was that of Peter Wiles (1961: 83–96) in the period when economic reforms were getting under way in socialist countries at the beginning of the 1960s. Some of the key areas of analysis which he identified are as follows:

1   changes in the relationship between the output of capital goods and the overall volume of investment and its rate of growth (it is necessary to know how these relationships are moving as part of the steps planners must take when they estimate current sacrifices of total consumption);
2   the connection between the growth of a cash economy ('increased commodity turnover' in present Chinese terminology) and the need for more labour markets;
3   a clearer recognition of the maximand to which economic and commer-

cial units are to respond, be it profit, the rate of return to family capital and labour or return to labour alone;

4 the connection, if any, between the 'withering away of the state' and the development of competitive markets.

In this chapter we focus on the third of these points to illustrate some little discussed aspects of the reform's 'Chinese characteristics' as they have emerged in the 1980s. Chinese officialdom claims that the 'new responsibility system' simply means that rural incomes will represent a return to labour. In fact these incomes include rent and profit. Attention is drawn to the persistence of rent-capital and to its vigorous resurgence into a significant submode of production in the overall social formation dominated by socialist ownership forms. The term rent-capital was coined by the German historical geographer Hans Bobek (Bobek 1962) and has also been used in analysis of the Philippines (McLennan 1980; Fegan 1983). One could quibble over the appropriateness of the term. However, the concept is highly relevant to assessing the past 10 years in China and to evaluating the extension of leasing-out, subcontracting and payment of sums of money for the right to set up certain enterprises. The concept of rent-capital is analogous to, but wider than, the payment of interest on capital seen in earlier modes of production. It can be defined as those payments made to obtain an advance of capital or a licence or political permission to undertake business activities. Agreement to supply a minimum value of products in a contract is another, more disguised, form of rent-capital. Under China's post-reform responsibility system rent can be paid to state and cooperative bodies and not only to other individuals or families.

The recent growth of rent-capital accompanying the remarkable upsurge in smaller-scale economic activity in a number of sectors implies a set of human relationships. As a result a much more complex web of social relations exists in China today than pre-1978. In later sections of this chapter we show that these have to be considered in any plan to advance the leading role of socialist social relations of production.

A final problem posed in this introduction is the issue of the time horizon over which the revival of competition, petty-commodity production and rent-capital is to flourish. Rent-capital existed in past modes of production, but it has not generally been a force for profound social change. In the case of the Chinese reform the operation of rent-capital mechanisms will boost incentives and activity in the short term, but it will not of itself transform the productive and social system. The new responsibility system in agriculture may assist in laying the material foundations for a future advance towards socialism, but cannot lead to deep social transformations. How long is the production responsibility system expected to function in the restricted role of productivity booster? In plans for the future operations of the public sector, do the Chinese leaders and theorists support the idea that has appeared in Yugoslavia (Horvart 1964) that the aim should be a kind of market communism? What sectors or classes are expected to group around the push for socialist transformation, assuming that the Four Modernizations are actually achieved? What steps will be taken to monitor and modify the new coalitions of interests that will surely emerge under petty-commodity production if it operates for an extended period of time? Can the mere existence of social ownership of the 'commanding heights of the economy' suffice to shore up the socialist advance against the insistent appeal of 'free enterprise'? Indeed, can we assume that there is in place a socialist reference point for setting goals in the perspective plan, something that would clearly differentiate a socialist economy from a mere 'mixed' economy (Kalecki 1976: 28–30; Xue 1981: 170–7; Hamilton 1987: 16). This may seem a superfluous query, but I do not consider it to be so in view of the fact that many Chinese economists and planners have actually lost confidence in the viability of a publicly owned economy and are greatly intrigued by what has been achieved in Singapore and Taiwan over the last two decades. A clear outline needs to be drawn up delineating which policies will be able to transform most of the presently rejuvenated petty-commodity producers and participants in rent-capital into economic agents willing to function in socially useful ways in a socialist context.

## The economic reform and its role in accelerating economic growth

In the past 10 years China has made great headway in developing its productive forces. In terms of annual growth rate of gross national product (GNP) it has joined the ranks of the world's most dynamically developing countries. This achievement has been noted in publications in Yugoslavia, Hungary and other socialist countries, including the USSR (Matyaev 1988: 17). In the view of those Soviet economists who favour economic reform for the USSR itself, an appreciable role in Chinese growth was played by measures adopted under the economic reform which they describe, quoting Zhao Ziyang, as having 'breathed new life into socialism'.

How much weight should we give to these sentiments? Are these the self-serving views of a technocratic–academic group who have much to gain materially and psychologically if all socialist countries adopted the economic systems and analytical structures found in Hungary (Heinrich 1986: ch. 4), Vietnam (Beresford 1988: ch. 11) and China (Ma 1985; Blecher 1986: ch. 6)? Or do their conclusions flow from the fact that Chinese growth under the reform may, indeed have been fostered by a realistic economic policy which took into account objective bottlenecks in constructing perspective plans (something long advocated by experienced and perspicacious socialist planners like Michal Kalecki) as well as incorporating the distinguishing 'Chinese characteristics' in a search for new growth factors that could be tapped and mobilized for economic growth?

The unleashing of new material incentives, deregulation in many sectors, a smoother functioning of market forces and a deepening of markets for capital funds and labour have all improved China's economic performance. However, there is not an unambiguous link between the reforms of the last decade and accelerated growth. Other factors also played a significant role. In 1965 I argued that the potential of reform to improve the rate of economic growth should not be exaggerated (McFarlane 1965: 46–65); earlier, Kalecki pointed out that a sound central economic plan which achieved a good structural balance of the economy was at least as significant (Kalecki 1963: 9–22). Bottlenecks and the lagging behind of infrastructure played a major role in the slowdown of the Chinese economy in 1965–78 (Ishikawa 1984). What tipped the balance towards the reform was the disproportionality crisis which, combined with excessive rates of national investment, had led to stagnation in real product per man-hour.

One reason why oversimplified correlations cannot be drawn between particular economic policies and rates of growth is that the gestation lags in construction mean that the investments made in earlier periods bear fruit in later periods. A current 'reform' period might be the recipient of the fruits of past labour expended in a non-reform period. Another reason for treating simple correlations with care is that there are two other variables at work which intersect at many points with the reform proper. These are the post-1950 operation of various investment cycles as well as a sort of 'political trade cycle'. At least two, and probably three, kinds of investment cycle have occurred in China since 1950. These are (a) construction or building cycles of the kind called 'Kuznets cycles' in the West, (b) waves of investment activity flowing from spurts in import of foreign technology at various times (Ishikawa 1983) and (c) cycles rooted in the 'shortage economy' and excessive accumulation rates and now conceded to be a significant feature of the East European landscape (McFarlane 1984a, b).

There is disagreement on the causes of such cycles in the Chinese case and on how such cycles might interact with each other. However, increasing research oh the topic (Shimakura 1982; Ishikawa 1983; Maruyama 1983) shows that incorporation of the effects of investment lags and growing gestation periods in project completions prevents simple correlations being made between either the investment rate or the appearance of reform policies and increases in output. For example, China's agricultural policies in the last decade would not have had the results obtained without the infrastructure completed in the labour mobilization drives since the mid-1950s.

Planners are more aware than they used to be of the difference between current investment expenditure and the availability of new capacity. The impact of the policy shifts embodied in China's reform upon output growth can only be established by separating investment data into a number of categories, of which the most important are (a) the value of fixed investment completed and becoming operational in the period under discussion, (b) the value of partly completed projects at the end of the period less their value at the beginning of the period and (c) additions to working capital needed to support the higher flow of output. This is not the place to pursue these matters further[2] but their importance is often overlooked in analyses of Chinese growth since 1978.

There is one cycle which is neither political nor technical. This has arisen as a cycle of centralism – decentralization – turmoil – recentralization (Shimakura 1982; McFarlane 1984b: 190–6), and is a policy cycle that is strongly related to periodic fluctuations in the rate of capital accumulation. In China's case these have been extreme (Ishikawa 1983; McFarlane 1984c). The high accumulation rates forced by government decisions lead to structural imbalances, problems of intersectoral coordination and absorptive capacity, and pressure on consumption. The economy becomes rigid under the impact of vertically enforced administrative directives. In the ensuing outbreak of discontent from consumers, traders and managers a new decentralized system is introduced with transfer downward of many powers of planning and management. The experience in Eastern Europe is that the next phase of the cycle is either a period of confusion or of good results. In the former case a return to centralism is encouraged, whereas in the latter case the result is overconfidence by the Party leading to the return of high-growth goals and excessive capital accumulation rates. The political cycle then begins again. The question now is whether China can avoid the scenario that has been played out in Yugoslavia, Poland and Hungary and maintain a longer-term commitment to the three conditions needed to escape from the 'treadmill' of the cycle: a plan in which the competitive powers of market forces can operate properly, consistency in planning goals and central macroeconomic policy, and development of a unified national market. The wider scope given in China for economic agents to participate in decentralized decision-making and the broader impact of the new prosperity give hope that the exacerbation of the shortage economy and of the ugly 'second economy' of black marketeering which disfigured East European socialism might be less pervasive. There seems more consciousness among China's policy-makers of the need, for political as well as humanitarian reasons, to defend the real incomes of urban workers.

Disruption of the Chinese economy associated with excessive rates of national accumulation and high capital-to-output ratios was not helped by certain decisions taken in 1976–80. In the scramble to import the most modern technology the capital-to-output ratio shot up and there was little consideration of the possibility that the era of extensive development, with reliance largely on the use of more manpower, still had some time to run in which there were dividends to the economy from a lower capital-to-output ratio. Instead, a precipitous leap was made into a technology-driven growth strategy. The temptation to do this again must be strong, but there are great advantages of not doing so and pursuing instead moderate growth rates using more labour-intensive methods alongside modern technology.

How then can we sum up the contribution of the reform to China's improved economic performance? Clearly there has been a considerable medium-term boost to output. This has been due to improved material incentives and greater competition resulting from the reform. Moreover, the reduction in shortages and the achievement of a more balanced structure of investment are making an important contribution towards improving the economic atmosphere. However, the experience of Hungary (Heinrich 1986: ch. 4), Poland (Kalecki 1963: 9–22) and Yugoslavia (McFarlane 1988: ch. 15) suggest that reform will not provide a sustained boost to economic performance unless accompanied by a firm commitment to the following:

1　restricting the gross investment rate to a maximum of 25 per cent;
2　controlling the construction cycle and reducing the average gestation length for investment projects and the period for which resources are locked up in unfinished construction projects;
3　supplying sufficient consumer goods to the peasantry to help maintain their incentives once the exhilarating effect of having cash has been exhausted;
4　carefully handling the process of absorbing foreign technology, which has not always been done in the past.[3]

The combination of a well-conceived investment plan and the integration of increasing numbers of new economic agents into the national market will deepen the social division of labour and promote a sounder, balanced long-term development path than have the cyclical fluctuations of the past.

# The reform: some consequences of the drive towards market socialism

A change as momentous as the Chinese economic developments of the last few years will create many new contradictions in the course of solving old ones such as stifled incentives, a rigid planning system, and ignorance of the working of markets and the role of commodity production.

Yugoslavia has gone furthest down this road, admittedly under very different cultural and political conditions. In that country successful economic reform required improved coordination, in the shape of some kind of indicative plan, overcoming autarky within provinces through the development of a national market and consistency in economic policy (Pjanic 1986; McFarlane 1988: chs 9–12, 15). Recognition of the fundamental role of commodity production and competition was a necessary though not sufficient condition for achieving a successful reform. The Yugoslavs failed because their policies lacked consistency, because they prematurely abandoned all planning and because they did not establish a socialist reference point alongside the goals that the new mechanisms were supposed to achieve. Moreover, they underestimated the power of the revived petty-commodity producers and their allies in local government to pursue small-group interests at the expense of society as a whole.

Today both China and Yugoslavia know that there is no viable practical alternative to a policy of extending commodity production. It takes time to analyse the new contradictions. However, the postponement of a drastic reform of relative prices shows that China's political economists are well able to analyse such problems once they have heard the voice of mass opinion.

We now illustrate these points by discussing four issues thrown up by 10 years of the reforms: (a) the revival of rent-capital mechanisms; (b) the problem of interdependence of markets; (c) the link between the revival of a competitive economy and political democracy; and (d) the effect of the reforms upon social relationships.

## Rent-capital and its revival

Concern about the rapid spread of family-based farming as well as rural private enterprise in trade, construction and industry has been more prevalent among foreigners (e.g. Keating 1984) than in official statements. However, this concern has been largely expressed in terms of the disruption to family-planning schemes and an alleged decline in rural education. However, in examining the social-existence form of labour power (Takahashi 1952, it is useful to recall the observation of Wiles (1961) that the return of decision-making power to economic units can vary widely in character in a socialist system. In the case of the Chinese reforms family incomes are no longer limited to a reward for labour but contain significant non-wage elements.

One source of these is rent-capital. It has been argued by anthropologists and historians that the social relationships embodied in the operations of rent-capital (defined in the Introduction) predate productive capitalism whose major feature is, of course, the dominance of the wage–labour relation. The reference to 'capital' in the term arises because the essence of a rent-capital system is the production of commodities for monetary sale and the extension of this operation. The 'capital' is not applied directly in production. Rather, it is loaned to petty producers and vendors for the purchase of materials or for the borrowers to re-sell goods and materials that they purchase. Rent-capital gives the lender – which can be state or collective bodies – a claim on the product or the right to levy rent which is paid for out of the eventual sale of produce. In earlier societies rent-capital characterized relationships between large and small merchants as well as such things as rentals for permission to use certain sites or transport services or even kilns. In a socialist system like that of China some of the loan and capital advances come from state bodies, and in the new responsibility system the minimum deliveries required in contracts are an analogous form of payment.

In old China part of the peasant's product was extracted to meet rent and debt claims. The collectives established in the mid-1950s did away with this, but the new agricultural taxes and other levies paid to the state for reinvestment in collective consumption, social welfare and national investment must have appeared to peasants as a change of form rather than essence. With the dismemberment of the communes the contract system is a new form of the same thing, bringing forward new economic agents who are willing to pay rent for the right to use land, machines and buildings. Significantly, evidence from the Philippines suggests that rent-capital is by no means confined to agricultural production but can be extended to cover all payment made to rent-capitalists or to people with local power to issue licences and concessions (Fegan 1983). The revival of these forms in China today constitutes not only an important source of improved productivity but a new shape on the landscape of social relations, albeit still in a subordinate position in the socialist mode of production of the mid-1980s.

# Interlocking markets

Events in one sphere of China's reforms have brought about changes in adjacent and related areas of economic life.

In agriculture there has been a spectacular increase in the percentage of output marketed. Cash incomes have increased alongside increased monetization of the rural economy. Wealthier peasants demanded and obtained more labour from outside the household and, despite the disapproval of some officials, a labour market has developed in agriculture. As competition extended its impact in other sectors, labour and capital flowed in to those that were more profitable.

Another example is the pressure that built up to establish capital markets. The growth of savings has been a noticeable result of the success of entrepreneurial families. At the end of 1987 the figure was some 307.5 billion yuan compared with 223.7 billion yuan a year earlier (State Statistical Bureau 1987). Another estimate is that people were holding a further 120 billion yuan in cash. As a result, enormous pressure exists to establish capital markets – both longer-term markets to channel funds to those who want to buy their own homes and a shorter-term market to allow people to enrich themselves by purchase of stocks and shares.

At this stage the development of a short-term money market has taken place mainly in Shanghai (Dai 1988) where some of the 300 million yuan hitherto idle in the hands of Shanghai residents is being mobilized as the local stock exchange operates vigorously to attract them. There is also scope to attract the private holdings of self-employed and family entrepreneurs, the earnings of rent-capital and the reserves of state-run firms. Buying and selling of securities on a daily basis is becoming common (Dai 1988), although shares are not so widely traded as it is still difficult to obtain them and their owners are unwilling to release them. A step-by-step approach is being adopted to proposals to let more enterprises issue stock, although it is considered in circles close to the Shanghai Trust and Investment Company that such share issues as those of the Feile Sonic

Engineering Company and the Shanghai Electronic Vacuum Device Company were successful. There has also been some criticism in relation to rural areas that a form of 'feudal' shareholding has appeared in some areas in which people acquire rights to 'silent shares' – ownership rights and dividends in a rural enterprise by virtue of their social relationships rather than through their investments or work. These criticisms and 'underdevelopment of theory' have been cited as reasons for the fact that up until 1987 the Chinese Communist Party (CCP) did not support the free buying and selling of stocks, and the paraphernalia of stock exchanges and their ramifications.

Among such ramifications is precisely the strong surge of sentiment among the financially successful which favours extension of both longer-term markets to underpin a private housing boom and shorter-term capital markets for making financial gain as such. Success in the final-product markets combined with the returns to be obtained on rent-capital have led to the situation today where very little stands between the desire of economic agents for full-blown capital markets and a government-signalled go-ahead for such a new factor market.

As the reform has unfolded, the interconnections between different mechanisms set up by it have become increasingly pronounced: it has not proved possible to separate the growth of a cash economy from the growth of more competitive and freer labour markets; the development of freer labour markets has been accompanied by greatly increased savings and has caused Li Yuanqi of the People's Bank of China, as well as other financial experts, to call for the development of a long-term capital market; excess demand in labour and capital markets has resulted from the entry into the maximand of firms of new non-profit (in the textbook sense) elements such as the level of rent and interest that can be extracted by the mere possession of loanable funds (of which more discussion later). Some of these interrelationships can be linked to the issue of multimarket stability that is so important in neoclassical economics in its general equilibrium form (see for example Henderson and Quandt 1958: 146–53) which states that, if all the competitive conditions hold, the excess demand for each good is a function of the prices of all goods: a disturbance in one market will throw other markets out of equilibrium, and the stability of a single market depends upon the adjustments following the induced disturbances in other markets.

It would be tempting to conclude that if the reformers can make the necessary adjustments to 'market imperfections' by state intervention (e.g. with certain taxes and subsidies) using indirect economic levers, they might achieve both multimarket stability and an optimization in the allocation of labour, land and capital. In that case, all the properties of Barone's beautiful model of the collectivist economy could be fulfilled (Barone 1908). However, the stumbling block would still be the need to determine the social distribution in advance. Movements in supply and demand are given their initial impulse from the distribution of purchasing power which leads on to the allocation of labour and savings. Thus even in the competitive world of a general equilibrium economist like Barone there is still a vital role for the state and the socialist project. Indeed, without a socialist perspective, the 'new competition', if left unhindered, would undoubtedly bring about the intensification of social strife in China about which economists (Dong 1987: 20) and politicians (Zhao 1988) have warned.

Another role for the state in a more competitive system, and one which forms a key element in the socialist project, is the need to guide savings, interest on loanable funds and net investment. Barone himself has advocated this role for the state, partly to assist in achieving multimarket stability and optimal resource allocation, and partly because money and capital markets are notoriously volatile (as we have seen) and so the state needs to bring savings into line with investment. Nor can the welfare of the future generation be left dependent on the attitude of the current populance to savings and investment in view of its faulty 'telescopic faculties' (to use Dobb's term (Dobb 1960)). In order to take account of the needs of future generations a socialist government worth its salt must generally deduct a greater part of the national income to finance investment than would be deducted by competitive markets.

However, it might turn out that the interrelationships between markets represent more than the model of the general equilibrium economist. If, in fact, they represent the very stuff of change, then the civil society will be wagging the state's tail and it will be increasingly hard to see what role the sphere of the state is to play in a culture that has always been dominated by centralism. In particular, there is now no great sage to decide when to move towards a new phase of socioeconomic development and therefore uncertainty seems likely to increase. In the meantime, with some help from consumerism and from the unleashing of competition, many social layers are enjoying China's period of middle-aged stability.

## Competition and political democracy

That competition between economic agents is important for socialist economies has been rightly recognized by socialist economists (Dickinson 1933, 1939; Nolan and Paine 1986: 58; Fforde and Paine 1987: 60–1) and is a key assumption underlying the Chinese economic reforms. Unfortunately, the concept of 'competition' used has sometimes been of the variety found in neoclassical economics rather than in reality. In modern microeconomics 'competition' is linked to problems of equilibrium and optimal allocation of given resources. The whole approach is static and assumes that the pricing system has only one function – to clear markets by guiding economic agents who are set on maximizing psychologically based utilities on the demand side or profits if the agents are producers. Unfortunately many Chinese economists have adopted this approach rather than the dynamic analyses of Adam Smith or Marx, which are more relevant to analysis of how to get a lively process of capital accumulation under way. Adopting this approach would have avoided inconclusive and time-consuming debates about plan versus market or about the appropriate balance between plan and market.

In his *Theory of Moral Sentiments* Adam Smith argued that the desire for consensus was an important drive in society. He added that capitalism tended to produce a tawdry interest in 'baubles and trinkets'. Later the major work of Smith introduced the vital role of the 'propensity to truck and barter' in many human beings. *The Wealth of Nations* is largely concerned with how this propensity propels people into the marketplace to compete there in order to make profit. It also spurs the desire to accumulate profits and capital, and to apply them in extending the scope of the division of labour within factories and/or in bringing scattered enterprises together. Here competition, linked to the propensity to truck and barter and seen as deepening the social division of labour, has lessons for the socialist economy. The contract system encourages the gathering-in of previously scattered economic agents, villages and regions. Judging from the Yugoslav experience, this is the real role for 'market forces'. Failure to recognize this has led to a fragmentation of the Yugoslav national market with the debilitating effects on productivity and morale in Serbia and Bosnia that have become so evident in recent years (Pjanic 1986; McFarlane 1988: chs 12, 15). Moreover, Yugoslavia has suffered a politically dangerous autarky in its constituent republics that contains dangers familiar from the Cultural Revolution and the horrors of the Pol Pot regime in Kampuchea.

Competition can promote a lively process of capital accumulation in the private sector which can be tapped to feed usefully into the socialist sector. The objections raised to this policy (Gao 1984; Kraus 1984: 675; Louven 1987: 63) are misplaced in the conditions of the reforms so far. It should be possible to obtain public support for the use of windfall taxes in a way that allows capital accumulation from the non-socialist sector to stimulate overall growth. Have we not all learned by now from the cases of Yugoslavia (McFarlane 1988: chs 9–11) and Vietnam (Beresford 1988: chs 9–11) the futility of trying to block this development? Does not the handling of the grain speculators of Shanghai in 1951 (Xue 1981: 20–1), for example, show that a resolute government can protect socialist interests without requisitioning the assets of private traders or capitalists?

Socialist accumulation can also be directly assisted by competition. Capital can flow to the more effective industries. Closure of firms that have been milking the public purse and straining local government budgets will help rather than hinder socialist values for, instead of pandering to small-group interests or some cosy local arrangement that has produced a 'political' factory, it releases funds for increased collective consumption or for setting up new and effective socialist enterprises. Such competition is influenced by incentives, even by the propensity to truck and barter, without being driven by the unrestrained working of 'animal spirits' or the 'dog eat dog' competition that Marx saw as fundamental to the capitalist system and which accounts for his description of the drive underlying capitalist competition as 'Accumulate, accumulate! That is Moses and the Prophets'.

Competition can unlock the blockages which constitute a 'shortage economy'. It is the lack of competition in the Stalinist system that led to loss of social control over accumulation (Shimakura 1982; McFarlane 1984b: 177–88; Nuti 1986: 83–4). The domination over a highly centralized plan of Party goals which were too ambitious led to an anti-consumption pro-accumulation bias. It caused a shortage economy, disruption of the supply system, the appearance of investment cycles and eventual retrenchments as the political cycle finally went into its more pro-reform and pro-consumption phase to cool down the construction rate. A network of legally autonomous competing firms would have made this process less likely by giving the centre more accurate information and stronger advice that it needed to modify its 'government decision function'. While this. would not of itself have ensured observance of the golden rule that no more than 25 per cent of national income would be accumulated annually on average, the chance and motivation to sustain higher consumption that always accompanies the appearance of more competitive forces would have acted as powerful restraints on excesses in accumulation and better protected the interests of consumers.

Can workers' interests also be protected in a competitive framework? This is a question put on the agenda by the constant attacks on 'eating from a common pot' (tenure of job and assured social security) as well as the consistent call for management to have power to hire and fire. The problem of whether free labour markets, a comparatively new development in China, will play a role or whether collective bargaining by corporate-style labour unions will become the dominant form of labour relations has been debated surprisingly little in China itself. The paucity of discussion is rooted in the lack of labour union rights to bargain collectively with managers over work conditions and with China's planners over key elements of the plan. There is a dilemma here. No mechanisms yet exist in China for democratizating the planning process, and the occasional interventions in the People's Committees hardly amount to such a democratization. Yet, in various respects, the older system did not represent a better protection of employed workers. For example, the centralized system essentially pumped out economic surplus by applying high work norms and by various managerial devices to meet centrally imposed targets by productivity drives, of which many were harmful to workers. Workers faced a control structure composed of local administrators, Party appointments under what in the USSR is called 'nomenklatura' and friends of the local power structure. Is it any wonder that many workers have sought to escape by working for themselves or in small-scale enterprises run by relatives and acquaintances?

In his report to the Central Committee of the CCP of 21 March 1988,

Zhao Ziyang noted that for the reform to work well democracy was essential. This is a most important statement coming from such a quarter after almost a decade of the experiences thrown up by the reform. Also significant was the comment of the General Secretary that 'a great number of social contradictions can be solved through economic reforms, but during the reforms new forms of social conflict between different interest groups will inevitably arise'. If Yugoslavia is any guide in this respect, the major problem will be to make sure that in promoting competitive economic activities an attack is also launched on local political structures (which are by no means always democratic) (McFarlane 1988: chs 13, 15). Zhao called for 'honest and clean' government and criticized abuse of power by some state and Party officials 'seeking to extort money, practising graft and embezzlement'. Power exercised in this way is the antithesis of democracy. A more unified national market together with the imposition of the discipline of economic competition upon 'political' factories would, in contrast, contribute to greater democracy.

In so far as reform can dismantle local mafias and replace them with cooperatives and family-based enterprises relying on the market to obtain material rewards, it reduces the incentive for workers to circumvent technical standards and specifications, and for managers to conceal the true capacity and needs of their firms in order to fulfil planners' demands. Such a competitive system which is a more decentralized system would not be inimical to socialist ideals and the 'moral aspect' of industrial life. As Liberman pointed out in his pioneering plea for economic reform in the USSR (Liberman 1962; Gordijew and McFarlane 1964), removal of the overcentralized structure with its conflicting norms imposed on the managements of socialist enterprises would lead to less dishonesty and higher jorale. It would combine material and moral incentives in a way that was lacking in the high-norm factory and in a centralized planning system which possessed a multiplicity of plan indicators and generated an atmosphere of hysterical shortage.

How is it possible to avoid the imposition upon workers of harsh or unrealistic work norms? Two practical alternatives exist. The first (which is preferred by this author) is that freely formed trade unions should take part in the planning process from the beginning and should negotiate collectively on each major item of the national economic plan. The second is the deregulated system. This is not ideal, given the existence of powerful alliances of managers and local political machines of the sort unearthed in the 'market socialism' of Yugoslavia which demonstrated that there is no automatic tendency to promote democracy if workers and consumers operate in horizontal structures rather than in the old vertical bureaucratic systems.

The relationship between a market system and democracy is complex. For example, Yugoslavia went through periods of extreme decentralization of the economy while maintaining a rather centralized and undemocratic political regime. However, in China in the 1980s a powerful move towards a competitive economy seems the best way to loosen up the atmopshere and prepare the ground for an extension of the citizens' freedom to speak out on state policy. There is no unambiguously superior path. However, I would take my stand with the leading Yugoslav economist Zoran Pjanic who has said:

Some economists have talked about the *fetishism of commodities* as a danger to socialism, of the alienation of man, reification etc. Those things may be there but what these people never come up with is any empirical work or estimate of how to avoid the political repression which follows the rejection of socialist commodity production. It is not necessary to speak further about Stalin, Pol Pot or Mao Zedong. Their record is an empirical fact. If commodity production is not an ideal mechanism, it is the only sensible way open for a road of socialist democracy. (Pjanic 1986: 152)

China's economic reform has increased the freedom of some groups in the population. There has been a remarkable increase in consumption by both the rural and urban population, while the tremendous development in education and technology has opened up access to information and to the world outside China for millions of citizens (Zhou 1985: 31). Much of this has flowed from the provision of decision-making power to enterprises (Zhou 1985: 35), while simultaneously strengthening the role of the legal system in both political and economic life. By reducing the atomization of individuals and their alienation from the state, much has been done to prepare the ground for greater democracy. In its combination of more consumption, providing people with more access to information from the media concerning the affairs of state and increased protection from random or arbitrary assault by state and Party bodies, the package of policies associated with the reform has greatly increased the sphere of influence of civil society against that of the state. Most Chinese prefer this situation and it has strengthened democracy.

However, to avoid bias in evaluating the relationship between increased socialist commodity production, petty-commodity production and rent-capital transactions on the one hand and the extension of democracy on the other, the following qualifications are in order.

1  The centralized model of socialist economic planning in China, as elsewhere, also increased autonomy and freedom of choice among some groups of the population, in particular disadvantaged groups, largely by expanding their economic opportunities. Examples of such beneficent and pro-democracy policies are several types of subsidies, regulations affecting working conditions, the environment and opportunities for women, and income transfers to low-income groups, public consumption and infrastructure.

2  Not all can participate in the recent economic boom unleashed in China. There has been a fragmentation of the labour market, in part as

a deliberate strategy of the reform to correct 'rather serious egalitarianism in the previous unified wage system in China' (Zhou 1985: 39), but also as an outgrowth of the revival of rent-capital. The effects of this include not only higher levels of output and trade but also the reappearance of classical forms of exploitation for outworkers and those at the bottom of the pyramid in systems of subcontracting. Features here include dislocation, fragmentation and casualization, and pockets of job shrinkage and negative employment growth in 'rationalized' sectors.

For some citizens the economic reform sun has risen, but for others it has set.

Such a situation cannot be allowed to persist over the long term in a socialist society. It is necessary to consolidate the benefits that competition has brought, while adjusting not only for the economist's 'market failures' but also for such things as massive unemployment, welfare relief and protective measures against abuses in the labour process. If the Chinese authorities want competition to drive incentives and productivity, they also need to allow room for small-scale cooperatives, possibly state funded, working to meet market and state orders. They need some sort of NEP, for the growth of the small-scale cooperatives in the industrial sphere will be accompanied by an extension of the right to employ a small number of wage-labourers in small family-based enterprises. Combined with regrowth of the rent-capital sector, the system would resemble that of the early years of the NEP in the USSR in the 1920s. In that system, a maximum of 50 wage-labourers was permitted in small-scale industrial firms; this was later raised in a number of places to 100 and in one case to 650.

What role would the responsibility system have in such a Chinese NEP? The present situation of increasing production of subsistence goods and surpluses on family-based farms needs peasant incentives if it is to be maintained. The alternative to the responsibility system would be force, for the peasants would resist heavy pressure to rejoin collectives or to be weaned from their leased land. Force, however, is ruled out, not least because a more competitive system has already strengthened the legal system and democratic practices. Granted that the leasing of land to peasants must stay and the richer peasants be allowed to employ a few wage-labourers, more support is needed for what is left of the collectives and communes. In incentive-socialism, the cost of the more rapid development of productive forces will be that 20 per cent will not succeed in enriching themselves. These people need the medical care, welfare relief and support for the elderly which successful family farms are able to supply to their own members. As the system develops it may also be necessary to form a union for the agricultural proletariat. This step would help the Party in checking abuses and to inform it of what the agricultural labourers would like to see in national economic plans. It is difficult to predict the future in a country still in the process of bold experiment. However, once the level of rural production has been expanded to the limits attainable from tapping an extensive labour market in the countryside, inequality might perhaps be controlled to some extent by limiting the formation of what by then could be developing into a true *kulak* class.

## Social relations

In this section we examine the coexistence of various sets of social relations within the socialist mode of production in the light of the new responsibility system, the rapid growth of private small-scale industry in rural areas and the unfolding of urban reform.

China is now characterized by the following:

1　a declining collective/cooperative sector as more and more people feel they can do better by paying a rent (or signing a contract to deliver some minimum value of product) and keeping any surplus earned as their own disposable income;
2　a growth of traditional rent-capital relationships of the kind that are widespread in Asia involving borrowing and subcontracting for non-land expenditures (Bobek 1962; Wolf 1966; Fegan 1983);
3　a strong growth of 'kickbacks' needed to modify deliberate bureaucratic delays while officials shop around for better deals, as well as other milder forms of corruption in many dealings with foreign trade partners – especially those that are smaller and based in Hong Kong and Singapore;
4　rapid development of cottage industry via subcontracting, a process always available and mobilized in the past to meet short-term increases in export orders but now expanding rapidly;
5　partial relinking of Chinese business with the powerful established Chinese capitalists of Southeast Asia who have their own family and 'city of origin' networks (notably from Guangdong and Fujian provinces) and who have in recent years increased their activity (Wu and Chien 1981).

In these new circumstances it is probable that one result of further deregulation associated with any major acceleration of the reforms would be a growing trend to seek a subcontract or to pay rent to the next higher level of economic agent (or political office). This would amount to a revival of rent-capital structures and of analogous economic relations. In the Export Processing Zones (EPZs) and open cities where foreign investors have a presence a new sort of political dealing has already emerged in which power to levy and receive rents is conferred on those favoured by local political machines. While efficiency gains could accure from lubrication of the wheels of commerce, these improvements might easily be outweighed by the growth of 'non-rational' criteria in the allocation of building permits, import licences etc. to those who are well connected. These trends are very likely to be present if the experiences of India, Pakistan and the Philippines are any guide.

The appearance of a new set of social relations has implications of an immediate economic kind, but also throws up political–ideological ones. The growth of putting-out and cottage industries may well slow down the rate of technical progress in some sectors as the labour process in small-scale putting-out is often such that there is no incentive to change production techniques. Attempting to produce, say, more complex textiles which involve extra costs in switching over to new techniques might lead to a fall in the producers' net income. It was precisely the need to socialize these costs that led to the formation of cooperatives. The fact that some cooperatives were not well run does not alter this basic point. The traditional Marxian expectation that social relations of production will be transformed by technical change will not be easily fulfilled in areas where rent-capital has established itself. The extreme longevity of this form of social relations in much of Asia suggests that this is a correct observation. This view is reinforced by the fact that under rent-capital systems there is less direct application of capital to production itself. As with money-capital the connection between those with funds or permits to rent out or with subcontracts to offer are more remote from the labour process than the direct investors and the producers. A stampede towards subcontracting in service and small-scale family-controlled industries might well mean that there will be no 'change in a progressive direction' associated with technical development for a most important submode of production surviving within the overall socialist mode of production.

The issue of such a coexistence has been discussed by theoreticians such as Althusser and planners such as Oscar Lange who recognized the practical importance of this problem for the operation of the Polish economy during the Warsaw debates on economic reform of 1956–7. In China it was Dong Fureng (1987) who drew attention to it. Dong has extended our analysis of the implications of diversification of ownership forms. In particular he has insisted on a point made in 1952 by the leading Soviet agronomist Venzher (who was then criticized by Stalin) that the operation of state ownership alone does not bring about the best methods of achieving economic development and meeting the material needs of the population. Among the benefits of the coexistence of a multiplicity of ownership forms is an exchange of ideas and technology between the private and state sectors. In addition, the private economy, driven by competition, can usually produce better economic returns. The main problem here (as mentioned earlier) has been the tendency of the reform to allow such market forces to widen the gaps in income distribution and spatial differences in material standards between regions over recent years.

Achieving benefits for socialism as a whole will continue to be a major reason for the encouragement of diverse ownership patterns. However, management of the new social relations that will arise from a new balance in the strengths of private, collective and state sectors will not be easy. The current stage reached in the reform provides experience in the evolution of a socialist system that may well enshrine some diversity of ownership forms as a more or less permanent feature. Whether this happens or not could depend on how social conflict breaks out and how it is handled, i.e. on the practice of class struggle under the new conditions.

# Conclusions

In this chapter we have suggested that in the course of the economic reform the Chinese government would do well to remember the importance of an effective democratically decided central plan in setting the necessary basic proportions of the economy. The success of this type of model, combined with Chinese characteristics, in establishing heavy industry and rural infrastructure has been attested to by Chinese economists as well as Ishikawa and others well versed in the developments achieved so far.

However, this proposition is not in conflict with the main objective of the reform which is to find new and more effective mechanisms that will enhance the material basis of the economy and thereby provide a springboard to further socialist advance. Rather, there is a political cycle which forces change in outmoded or failing economic mechanisms. This is linked to periods of developing mass dissatisfaction with the material standard of life. The issue was shown to be related to the system's political economy, particularly, the tensions leading to 'socialist investment cycles', the economics of shortage and excessive rates of accumulation at the macroeconomic level. However, competition was also shown to be a helpful factor and a source for improving the situation.

Revolt against an unfair 'government decision function' by dissatisfied workers and frustrated consumers or the correction sought by the reform of the worst excesses of the investment cycle are examples of the need for the economic mechanism to be informed by a socialist project. Indeed, incompatibility between socialist political-economic goals and key aspects of the reform produces both social tensions and decelerated growth. Other examples given in this chapter were as follows.

1   Delays unacceptable to foreign traders caused by an excessive motivation towards profit have produced unexpected changes to projects and contracts already signed. Some concept analogous to the now unpopular 'serve the people' is needed to stop come Chinese commercial enterprises from entering upon the slippery slope of what in the West is called the 'unacceptable face of capitalism'.

2   Corruption in many economic areas has come into the open as a result of the operation of the reforms. Where economic officials work in partnership with local political machines, a gang mentality and a gang system which have nothing to do with socialist economy (although long practised in Bangkok, Manila and Hong Kong) emerge. This is certainly

not the fault of the reforms *per se*. Rather, it is the freedom of deregulation associated with the reform mechanisms that builds on the nepotism of the earlier system of centralism and shortage economy that can produce a gang system, unless confronted systematically with the detailed socialist project by the leading and most aware sociopolitical organizations of Chinese society.

3   A lack of attention to the standard of life of urban workers during the transition to a new set of relative prices can put a heavy burden on these workers and greatly increase social tension. An increase in inflation, even if its origin is partly in the suppressed inflation of the older planning system, is also dangerous for the political legitimacy of the reform-based system. This kind of problem has shaken the political systems of Poland and Yugoslavia because the governments concerned misjudged and mismanaged working-class reactions to the fall-out from reforms of the price system and taxation.

4   Failure to monitor and control the new social forces at work in the mechanisms of the market-socialist economy could also threaten the legitimacy of the reforms in party circles still firmly committed to the socialist project. Attention has been drawn to the revival in China of a rent-capital system amongst the burgeoning subcontracting mechanisms. This is contributing not only to private capital accumulation but also to some social conflict. While the older collectivist system needed a new and more competitive framework in which to operate, it is also the case that the new economic agents need to be constrained by state-assisted small cooperatives. Some of the newly created material interests are the greatest challenge to Chinese socialism in the future, since the older capitalist and large-landlord classes have already been removed from the stage of history.

# Notes

1   An exception is Dong (1987).
2   An attempt to do this in the context of Indian development planning can be found in Reddaway (1962).
3   One remembers the crazy rush to import turnkey projects from abroad in the early months of Hua Guofeng's ascendancy and the inevitable cancellations of foreign loans that became necessary in the period 1979–81.

# Bibliography

Adler, S. (1957) *The Chinese Economy*. London: Routledge.
Barone, E. (1908) The ministry of production in a collectivist state. Reprinted in F. A. Hayek (ed.), *Collectivist Economic Planning*, pp. 245ff. London: Routledge, 1935.
Beresford, M. (1988) *Vietnam: Politics, Economics and Society*. London: Frances Pinter.

Blecher, M. (1986) *China: Politics, Economics and Society*. London: Frances Pinter.

Bobek, H. (1962) Socio-economic development from a geographical point of view. In P. Wagner and M. Mikesell (eds), *Readings in Cultural Geography*. Chicago, IL: University of Chicago Press.

Burns, J. P. and Rosen, S. (1986) *Policy Conflicts in Post-Mao China*. New York: Eastgate.

Dai Gang (1988) Stocks and shares a hit in Shanghai. *Beijing Review*, 7–13 March.

Deng Xiaoping (1987) *Build Socialism with Chinese Characteristics*. Oxford: Pergamon.

Dickinson, H. D. (1933) Price formation in a socialist community. *Economic Journal*, 43, June, 237–50.

—— (1939) *Economics of Socialism*. London: Oxford University Press.

Djilas, M. (1969) *The Unperfect Society*. London: Irwin.

Dobb, M. (1960) *An Essay on Economic Growth and Planning*. London: Routledge.

Domar, E. D. (1957) *Essays on the Theory of Economic Growth*. New York: Oxford University Press.

Dong Fureng (1987) Socialist countries diversify ownership. *Beijing Review*, 5 October.

Fegan, B. (1983) The establishment fund, population increase and changing class structure in Central Luzon. *Philippines Sociological Review*.

Fforde, A. and Paine, S. (1987) *The Limits of National Liberation*. London: Croom Helm.

FitzGerald, C. P. (ed.) (1968) *Quotations From President Liu Shao-Ch'i*. Melbourne, Paul Flesch.

Gao Hongxiang (1984) Can those from 10,000-yuan households be extolled as new socialist persons? Reprinted in J. P. Burns and S. Rosen (eds), *Policy Conflicts in Post-Mao China*, pp. 333–4. New York: Eastgate, 1986.

Gordijew, I. and McFarlane, B. (1964) Profitability and the Soviet firm. *Economic Record*, 40, December, 554–68.

Hamilton, C. (1987) Price formation and class relations in the development process. *Journal of Contemporary Asia*, 17 (1), 2–18.

Hayek, F. A. (ed.) (1935) *Collectivist Economic Planning*. London: Routledge.

Heinrich, H.-G. (1986) *Hungary: Politics, Economics and Society*. London: Frances Pinter.

Henderson, J. M. and Quandt, R. E. (1958) *Microeconomic Theory*. Tokyo: Kogalaisha; New York: McGraw-Hill.

Hilton, R. (ed.) (1976) *The Transition from Feudalism to Capitalism*. London: New Left Books.

Horvart, B. (1964) *Towards a Theory of Planned Economy*. Belgrade: Yugoslav Institute of Economic Research.

Ishikawa, S. (1983) China's economic growth since 1949. *China Quarterly*, June, no. 94, 242–81.

—— (1984) China's economic system reform. In N. Maxwell and B. McFarlane (eds), *China's Changed Road to Development*. Oxford: Pergamon.

Kalecki, M. (1956) Problems of perspective planning. *Nowe Drogi*, nos 11–12.

—— (1963) An outline of a method of constructing a perspective plan. In *Essays on Planning and Economic Development*. Warsaw: Centre of Research on Economic Development.

—— (1969) *Introduction to Theory of Growth in a Socialist Economy*. Oxford: Basil Blackwell.
—— (1972) *Selected Essays on the Economic Growth of the Socialist and Mixed Economy*. Cambridge: Cambridge University Press.
—— (1976) *Essays on Developing Economies*. Hassocks, Sussex: Harvester.
Keating (1984) In N. Maxwell and B. McFarlane (eds), *China's Changed Road to Development*. Oxford: Pergamon.
Kovalevski, N. (1928) Methodology of the Plan of the Reconstruction of the National Economy of the USSR. *Planovoe Khoziastvo*, no. 4. Reprinted in E. D. Domar, *Essays on the Theory of Economic Growth*, pp. 223ff. New York: Oxford Univeristy Press, 1957. Also reprinted in N. Spulber (ed.), *Formation of a Soviet Strategy for Economic Growth*, pp. 490ff. Bloomington, IN: Indiana University Publications, 1964.
Kraus, R. (1984) Bureaucratic privilege as an issue in Chinese politics. In N. Maxwell and B. McFarlane (eds), *China's Changed Road to Development*. Oxford: Pergamon.
Lewis, P. (ed.) (1984) *Eastern Europe*. London: Croom Helm.
Liberman, E. G. (1962) The plan, profits and bonuses. *Pravda*, 9 September. Reprinted in A. Nove and D. M. Nuti (eds), *Socialist Economics*. Harmondsworth: Penguin Books 1972.
Louven, E. (1987) Chinese economics, 1976–86. *Copenhagen Papers* 1 (1).
Ma Ding (1985) Ten major changes in China's study of economics. *Beijing Review*, no. 49.
McFarlane, B. (1965) Communist economic planning over the last decade. In J. Miller and T. H. Rigby (eds), *The Disintegrating Monolith: Pluralist Trends in the Communist World*. Canberra: ANU Press.
—— (1984a) Economic planning: past trends and new prospects. *Contributions to Political Economy*, 3, March, 1–14.
—— (1984b) Political crisis and east European economic reforms. In P. Lewis (ed.), *Eastern Europe*. London: Croom Helm.
—— (1984c) In N. Maxwell and B. McFarlane (eds), *China's Changed Road to Development*, ch. 4. Oxford: Pergamon.
—— (1988) *Yugoslavia; Politics, Economics and Society*. London: Frances Pinter.
Mackerras, C. P. (1984) Chinese Marxism since 1978. In N. Maxwell and B. McFarlane (eds), *China's Changed Road to Development*. Oxford: Pergamon.
McLennan, M. (1980) The Central Luzon Plain. Manila: Alomars.
Maruyama, N. (1983) The investment cycle in China. *China Newsletter*, no. 45.
Matyaev, V. (1988) 13th Congress of the CP of China: lessons of the past and guidelines for the future. *International Affairs*, Moscow, no. 2.
Maxwell, N. and McFarlane, B. (eds) (1984) *China's Changed Road to Development*. Oxford: Pergamon.
Miller, J. and Rigby, T. H. (eds) (1965) *The Disintegrating Monolith: Pluralist Trends in the Communist World*. Canberra: ANU Press.
Nolan, P. and Paine, S. (eds) (1986) *Rethinking Socialist Economics*. Cambridge: Polity.
Pjanic, Z. (1986) *Anatomija Kriza*. Belgrade: Ekonomska Politika.
Reddaway, W. B. (1962) *The Development of the Indian Economy*. London: Allen and Unwin.
Robertson, R. T. (1984) The cultural revolution in Maoist and Dengist strategies of development. *Journal of Contemporary Asia*, 14 (3), 325–42.

Shimakura, T. (1982) Cycles in the Chinese economy and their politico-economic implications. *Developing Economies*, 20 (4), 374–89.

Spulber, N. (ed.) (1961) *Study of the Soviet Economy*. Bloomington, IN: Indiana University Publications.

—— (ed.) (1964) *Formation of a Soviet Strategy for Economic Growth*. Bloomington, IN: Indiana University Publications.

State Statistical Bureau of the People's Republic of China (1987) Changes in ownership structure. *Beijing Review*, no. 40.

State Statistical Bureau of the People's Republic of China (1988) *Statistics for 1987 Socio-Economic Development*, 23 February.

Strumilin, S. G. (1928). Reprinted in *1963 Collected Papers*, vol. 2, *Na Planovom Fronte*. Moscow: Academy of Sciences of the USSR.

Takahashi, K. (1952) A contribution to the discussion. Reprinted in R. Hilton (ed.), *The Transition from Feudalism to Capitalism*. London: New Left Books.

Wagner, P. and Mikesell, M. (eds) (1962) *Readings in Cultural Geography*. Chicago, IL: Chicago University Press.

Wiles, P. (1961) Communist economics and our economics textbooks. In N. Spulber (ed.), *Study of the Soviet Economy*. Bloomington, IN: Indiana University Publications.

Wolf, E. (1966) *Peasants*. New York: Prentice-Hall.

Wu Yuan-Li and Chien Hai (1981) *Economic Development in South East Asia: The Chinese*. London: Hodder and Stoughton.

Xue Muqiao (1981) *China's Socialist Economy*. Beijing, Foreign Languages Press.

Zhao Ziyang (1988) Speech to the Central Committee of the CCP, 21 March 1988.

Zhou Ying (1985) China's economic development and reforms. *UN-ESCAP, Economic Bulletin for Asia and the Pacific*, 26, December, no. 2.

# 5

# Dynamic Equilibrium in Socialist Economic Reform

## Li Yining

## The social tolerance of economic reform

Equilibrium is an analytical method for examining the movement of the socialist economy and the reform of the economic system. It is not the aim of reform, which is to develop the productive forces in order to realize certain economic and social goals.

Equilibrium is a dynamic concept reflecting the need for a long-term criterion with which to assess the whole process of economic development. In the constant movement of the economy with so many variables at work simultaneously only relative and not absolute equilibrium is possible. Both the formulation of reform measures and the achievement of our economic goals are affected by how we perceive the relationship between different economic variables such as overall supply and demand, budgetary income and expenditure, and international revenue and expenditure. These relationships need to be analysed in terms of dynamic relative equilibrium. This is not the same as disequilibrium. There may be dynamic relative equilibrium within a given boundary and disequilibrium outside it. However, the question of where the boundary is located has not yet been solved in the reform of the economic structure and needs to be studied. Relative dynamic equilibrium is an area surrounding a point of equilibrium which is defined by the limit of what will not adversely affect the normal operation of the economy or hinder the achievement of development goals. Factors which might obstruct the normal operation of the economy can be defined either from an economic or a social point of view.

Economic factors are mainly important ratios – for instance, ratios of consumption to accumulation, or of certain products to others, or between departments and regions – which must be approximately appropriate so that the socialist economy can continue to operate normally. Disequilibrium occurs when these ratios are incorrect. Analysis of the social factors which impair the normal operation of the economy is more complicated.

Economic reform has to be considered from the standpoint of social as well as economic feasibility. Although there may be no problem with economic ratios, social problems can affect the economy. The degree of social tolerance must be taken into account in considering the reforms. If it is low, social stability and the economy will be affected. The degree of social tolerance is variable, is related to psychological factors and has a critical limit. It is influenced by three factors. The first is the level of popular confidence in the government and its policies. The second is economic expectations, which includes the attitude to price increases, market supply, employment, levels of real income, consumption etc. If people are pessimistic about these things, social tolerance is weakened, and vice versa. The third factor is psychological preparedness for economic change. If changes are sudden and unexpected, social tolerance is low, and vice versa. If the population has already experienced similar changes, social tolerance is slightly higher. When we study the limits of disequilibrium in the process of economic reform, we must analyse the degree of social tolerance, i.e. the social feasibility of reform. Socialist and capitalist countries are different in this respect. In capitalist countries social tolerance can be tested by such methods as mid-term elections and public opinion polls. Information feedback also allows government to gauge the degree of social tolerance to some extent and, of course, the experience of government departments plays an important role. The degree of tolerance varies from one country to another and from one period to another. However, in China we do not really understand the degree of social tolerance as yet.

It is very difficult to assess the social tolerance of peacetime price fluctuations in China. During the last 30 years we have enjoyed virtually unchanged prices, and people have come to believe that price stability demonstrates the superiority of socialism. This is quite wrong. In the socialist economy, commodity prices must be regulated and irrationalities corrected. This is appreciated by those who have a certain understanding of the significance of reform, but not by most people who still think that it is best if prices remain unchanged. Price reform must proceed step by step, since there is probably little social tolerance of faster change. At present we need growth with stability; this is consistent with the situation in China and is socially feasible. Reform in the realm of finance, credit, welfare and employment, as well as prices, all require us to identify the boundary beyond which disequilibrium sets in and to analyse the degree of social tolerance.

The task of theoretical economic research is to reduce the distance between theory and reality, and to uncover actual socioeconomic problems. Only in this way can economics become a genuinely useful science. Of course this does not mean that conceptual research has no place in economics. In analysing some specific topics rather than broad questions traditional optimization theory can be used to formulate questions and answer them. The higher is the level of the topic, however, the more generalized it is, and it is less likely that optimization theory can produce clear positive results. Moreover, in these topics economics finds it difficult to identify the existence or location of an optimal point. No wonder that some economists maintain that the purpose of studying economics is to breed scepticism about the views of economists! In analysing general questions we need to proceed from practical principles rather than abstract theory. We need to examine the social feasibility of economic reform and the degree of social acceptibility, and not construct a programme based purely on abstract models.

## Recognizing the reality of 'demand exceeding supply'

As noted above, equilibrium is the centre of an area outside which is disequilibrium and within which is relative dynamic equilibrium or, from a quantitative point of view, basic equilibrium. With respect to supply and demand, either supply may slightly exceed demand or demand may slightly exceed supply. Both are analytically imperfect, and are concerned with totals and not structure. We shall start by examining totals.

Some people consider that in China supply should slightly exceed demand. They argue that a buyer's market will encourage enterprises to raise product quality. Moreover, they argue that prices will be stabilized, and that this will benefit the whole economy. There are problems with this view. First, 'demand slightly exceeds supply' is the reality which we have to face during the reform process in which enterprise autonomy necessarily increases. This includes autonomy of expanded reproduction, allowing enterprises to raise investment, use their own profits to fund development, obtain bank credit and so on. The scale of investment can be reduced only to a certain point; it is hard to force it down further. Moreover, we set out from a relatively low level of consumption, and, alongside growth of production, growth of the consumption fund can only be controlled up to a certain point. An important compound of total income is that of peasants, the great majority of the population, who obtain income in relation to the amount of products they supply. It is difficult to depress this, since peasant income is used either for expanded reproduction or consumption, and if both were limited their increased income would be of little use. This would reduce their enthusiasm for production and cause their level of marketing to fall. Another source of income is that of enterprise staff and workers, and this is linked with the efficiency of the enterprise. If production and economic returns increase, their income should increase correspondingly. We can decide that their income (including bonuses) should not increase more than labour productivity or should be limited to a certain percentage of that increase, but if we force it down economic efficiency will suffer. When these factors are considered over the long term, a slight excess of demand over supply is perhaps suited to the reality of our economic position. The opposite is subjective wishful thinking.

We have seen that when considered from an overall viewpoint there are problems with the belief that when supply slightly exceeds demand the quality of goods will improve and prices will be stabilized. However, further problems arise when the issue of structure is taken into account. If the structure of certain products cannot satisfy demand, the question of quality still will not be solved. Only if there is overall excess production can this be achieved, but this is unrealistic. In addition, there is no guarantee of price stability, because price increases can be caused not only by excess demand but also by structural factors. Our aim is economic growth. By the year 2000 the total value of agricultural and industrial production should double twice; by about 2050 China will be one of the moderately developed countries. A slight excess of supply over demand can stimulate economic growth, but wide historical experience has shown that, even when supply is only 4 per cent ahead of demand, already problems arise. In the long run, China's average annual growth rate should be held at around 7–8 per cent. Our situation is different from that of the West, where private capital bears the loss involved in the deterioration of goods stockpiled as a result of excess production. When supply exceeds demand in socialist countries, where enterprises are mainly publicly owned, goods are stockpiled in public sector industrial and commercial departments or in the warehouses of the enterprises concerned. Either way the final loss is borne by the public sector. Therefore an excess of supply over demand is neither realistic nor necessarily beneficial.

Therefore we have to face the reality of slight excess demand and should learn to proceed with economic construction under these conditions. This will enable the economy to operate normally and allow us to achieve our growth targets. For example, with a slight excess demand we have to consider the scale of financial strength in the short term as well as the question of long-term dynamic equilibrium of government revenue and expenditure over a whole period of sustained growth (not just a year), allowing for a deficit in some years and a surplus in others. Dynamic equilibrium of income and expenditure involves their analysis in a given period of deficit in order to determine whether a temporary increase (or decrease) in income is likely to help achieve sustained growth or a large-scale increase of income in the future. A temporary deficit, if conducive to an appreciable increase in income in the future (and therefore conducive to realizing a financial surplus), is permissible within certain limits. This is what we mean by dynamic equilibrium. If we examine long-term government income and expenditure in the light of such dynamic equilibrium, we shall be able to understand budget deficits and how to remedy them.

# Dualism in the Chinese economy

A 'dual' economy is one which contains advanced and backward elements, modern and old elements and differences in income. Such an economy, including that of China, can be divided into two constituent parts, differentiated according to the degree of development, the technical level, average earnings and so on, in short into a developed and an underdeveloped sector. There are three main characteristics of a closed dual economy. First, the two sectors are completely divorced from each other. Apart from the exchange of commodities between them, there are few, if any, other links. The developed sector sells finished goods to the underdeveloped sector and receives agricultural products from it. Secondly, each sector has its own form of economic activity: one is a commodity economy, whereas in the other commoditization is weak and there are strong elements of a self-sufficient natural economy. Thirdly, the direction of development is different. The advanced sector develops mainly using its own strength, but to some extent also develops at the expense of the weaker sector, whose decline, collapse and disintegration benefit it. In an open dual economic system, however, there is economic exchange between the two sectors. Apart from commodity exchange, the developed sector provides funds, technology and labour, and engages in joint production and management. There is progressive commoditization of the underdeveloped sector, with attenuation of its natural economic self-sufficiency. It develops both by its own efforts and with the help of the advanced sector.

In the process of reform we have to consider how to transform the closed irrational dual system into an open beneficial system. This applies not only to the country as a whole but to every region separately. In the Beijing region, for instance, the relatively developed municipality, the suburbs and the district towns can be contrasted with the towns and the countryside of the 'hinterland'. There are several related questions which need to be analysed. The advantages of different regions and the appropriate scale and orientation of investment need to be determined by investigating the availability of labour and natural resources, the geographical conditions, existing industrial plant and so on. We need to find a way of opening up channels of economic linkage, of opening closed doors. In order to encourage cooperation between the sectors arrangements need to be made so that it is advantageous for the advanced sector to invest in the less developed sector. The dual system is characterized by a vicious circle of low wages and low production; lower incomes mean less accumulation and less possibility of technical improvement; low labour productivity means low wages. We have to find a way of breaking through this vicious circle in the backward regions. Wise investment is essential, but it is slow to take effect. Another solution is to rely on the state, but the financial power of the state is limited and cannot fundamentally solve the problem. For the state to give 'blood transfusions' is no solution: the powers of self-generation must be restored. To rely for a long time on relief funds from the state is no way to enrich underdeveloped regions. A better method is the reorganization of factors of production, with the more developed regions supplying technology and funds and the less developed regions providing natural resources and manpower. Compensatory trade, joint exploitation of natural resources and other methods can be used to assist the backward regions.

Developed regions may become less developed in the future and vice versa, but economic dualism will continue for a long time. This raises the question of how we should envisage the economic future of the various regions, and future economic and technological cooperation. Some cities are in the process of establishing, or already have established, trade centres. Are these economic entities? If they become so, what is the difference between them and existing wholesale enterprises? If they are not economic entities or are principally of a service nature, mainly responsible for commercial coordination and information exchange, what should the relationship be between them and existing wholesale enterprises? The purpose of these trade centres is to facilitate the free flow of trade. If they are merely used as a replacement for existing wholesale enterprises, this will not benefit the free flow of trade which, in contrast, may become impeded and blocked.

Another question relates to the significance of economic areas and their relationship with administrative areas. Are economic areas formed naturally? Does the size of an economic area (or city) continually change as it develops? Our view is that economic regions of variable size form naturally during economic development based on specialization and coordination. It makes no sense to mark out the borders of an economic region artificially, because, if this is done, how can links be maintained between cities in an economic area which belong to different administrative areas? What should be the relations between intraprovincial and intracity joint enterprises? Cities should open up markets and invigorate the circulation of commodities and funds and the exchange of qualified personnel. They should encourage others, including economic units and individuals in the countryside, to do business in towns and cities and develop the skills that they possess. That is, cities should develop horizontal linkages; the more there are, the more the urban economy will flourish and the greater will be the attraction of the towns. As to the method of developing such linkages, we advocate shareholding, an excellent form which should be actively tested and implemented step by step.

# Equilibrium and efficiency

Equilibrium and efficiency is the most difficult problem in economic reform. It is relevant not only to China but to all developed and developing countries in one way or another.

What is the rational distribution of income? There are many problems with distribution according to labour, such as the difficulty of defining 'work' in applying the formula 'equal pay for equal work'. If under socialism everyone receives a labour income and all receive wages, what then is the rational level of wage income? How should the minimum wage be determined? Should this be in accordance with the level of labour productivity? What is the rational differential between maximum and minimum wages? Some work is several times more complex than simple labour, but wage income from it cannot be several times higher. It is argued that ability to undertake complex labour is the result of training provided by society, in return for which a higher contribution should be expected. However, this does not help us arrive at a rational level of differentiation.

With regard to non-wage income, how should we determine the level of income for specialized peasants and contract farmers? There are four components of this kind of income. First, there is 'income corresponding to wages', i.e. the wage that a peasant with particular technical and physical qualifications would receive if he were working in a state-owned factory rather than at home. Second, there is 'income corresponding to interest' or 'income corresponding to renting the means of production'. This is reasonable, since peasant families in the contract responsibility system have to buy their own tools. If this money was put into the bank instead it would yield a certain annual interest. In addition, if a private individual in a family engaged in industry or commerce owns a house which is not used for business, as is the case for specialized peasants and contract farmers, but is rented out, he/she obtains rent income. Thirdly, there is income corresponding to entrepreneurial remuneration. Contractors are entrepreneurs and should have a corresponding income. Fourthly, there is compensation for risk. Individual entrepreneurs run risks which must be taken into account, although the rational level is more difficult to determine than for the other three categories. There is a distinct difference between the wages of staff and workers in state-owned industries and the income of labour contractors, specialized families and individual workers, in that there is no lower limit to the income of the latter categories. Unavoidable problems or simply bad management may result in their having no income at all, or even a deficit. The resources they need for production may be directly reduced or they may experience a reduction in the funds that they need for their purchase. In short, they have to bear risks involving both their income and their purchases, and 'risk money' should be included in the reasonable income of labour enterprises. The amount should be limited – but to how much? One possible approach would be to assume that an insurance company existed specifically for labour-related business conducted by contracting or by specialized families or by working individuals, to which they made regular payments in order to guarantee them a minimum income and to insure that value, after normal depreciation, of the funds set aside for the purchase of essential materials.

The cost of this notional 'insurance' could be included in the reasonable income of these individuals. In theory this is possible, but there are still practical difficulties in estimating the level of such 'insurance costs'.

Income not derived from labour may also be justifiable. For instance, the acquisition of assets is permitted to workers and staff who own shares, and they should be able to receive income from them. Again, the precise amount would be difficult to determine. Another kind of income is revenue from the employment of labour by individuals. In order to contract under the responsibility system for the exploitation of a forest, for instance, it is sometimes necessary to employ labour if the contractor's labour power is insufficient. If the contractor himself/herself is only one of those working, then he/she inevitably appropriates part of the income that the others generate, or the project would not make economic sense. How should we regard this income? Exploiting forests through the responsibility system means that within the space of a few years barren hills can be covered with trees again, which is economically useful. However, it is still difficult to decide on the size of a reasonable limit to income earned in this way.

The state should regulate individual income differentials in the interests of social stability. However, if regulation is not kept within limits, economic efficiency will suffer. For instance, if taxes on the individual are excessive no one will undertake such necessary activities as contracting to replant forests. During economic reform, the question of personal income, including the issue of the lower limit at which contractors become liable for income tax, also needs careful study. The relationship between equality and efficiency is a question of economic ethics rather than pure economics. Most people consider equality to mean income equalization and believe this to be incompatible with efficiency, which is increased if there are income differentials. Efficiency requires that there should be graduated income differentials. However, the issue cannot be left there.

Our view is that social equality does not mean egalitarianism. Rather, it means abolishing exploitation. This stimulates people's enthusiasm and promotes efficiency. Equality in this sense is perfectly compatible with efficiency. Indeed, real efficiency can only exist with the abolition of exploitation and the consequent liberation of the productive forces. Many people judge the degree of social equality by comparing their income and employment conditions with those of others. However, this concept of equality is not genuine equality, and this is a problem at the moment. If a relatively large number of people do, indeed, have this concept of equality and it is reflected in dissatisfaction with differences in income, wages, employment, welfare and so on, social instability may result, not necessarily from social inequality but from an incorrect understanding of equality by a section of the population. They feel that they are 'not equal'. There are three possible solutions to this problem. First, the real meaning of equality should be publicized. Second, the state should take steps to control income, even when it is reasonable. Historical factors should be taken into account and excessive differentiation avoided. Third, the state should take measures to increase some people's employability and income opportunities. Moreover, it should correct some very unreasonable wage and welfare provisions. Such a set of measures would promote social stability and economic efficiency.

Western economists have their own way of looking at the relationship between equality and efficiency, and while it is by no means entirely wrong, it is rather one-sided. We need to examine the relationship between economic efficiency and social stability. If society is stable, economic efficiency increases, and vice versa, but social instability is not necessarily caused by social inequality. Furthermore, we have seen that economic efficiency does not necessarily come from unequal income distribution. Reasonable income differentials can promote economic efficiency, while unreasonable ones will damage it. Although it is reasonable that there should be differentials, if they are too great, social tolerance is affected and economic efficiency is not necessarily increased. Material interest is not the only incentive in production, and it is an oversimplification to believe that all we need do to increase efficiency is to create income differentials.

# Protection policy

Protection should not be protection for the backward. We should determine the level and duration of protection according to prevailing conditions in the sector, enterprise or product concerned. We must create conditions which will allow certain enterprises and products to reach international standards rapidly. Some forms of protection practised now are intended to create the conditions for the removal of such protection in the future. Fierce international competition forces us to raise the level of technology, improve management, reduce costs and increase profits. Only enterprises and products which satisfy the demands of international markets have real vitality, and the more there are of them the better our economic performance will be.

The sectors, enterprises and products which require protection change over time. Some need protection one day but not the next. To prolong protection is not desirable. Sectors, enterprises and products which need protection in any specific period are those which show promise in the early stages of their development. Even in these cases the purpose of protection is still only to facilitate their growth and not to maintain them permanently in a hothouse. We need a long-term protection policy, but no sector, enterprise or product should be protected indefinitely, as this impedes economic progress. In order to open up to the outside, China's foreign trade system should become more decentralized. China must escape from the system of rigid centralized state control and move towards a suitable combination of centralization and decentralization.

We should analyse the reasons for our foreign trade deficit. Apart from problems attributable to low technical standards, fluctuations in international prices and the changing structure of imports and exports, the main reasons are associated with the economic system as a whole. In the old centralized system political and management responsibility were not separated; responsibility, rights and interests were unconnected. Enterprises were dependent on the state, and lacked initiative and creativity. The powers of state and region were not clearly demarcated; regional initiative was undermined, leading to central subsidies for the regions and involving a heavy financial burden for the state. This irrational system led to a lack of vitality in foreign trade organizations, resulting in a low level of administrative efficiency. They did not bother with economic accounting, neglected research into external markets and failed to control the prices of imported goods properly. Bad administration led to a very slow financial turnover, rising interest costs, overstocking and increased losses on internal sales. These problems can only be solved by reform of the economic system. If protection is properly understood, the foreign trade system, after genuine reform, can be suitably adapted to China's needs.

# 6

# China's New Development Path: Towards Capitalist Markets, Market Socialism or Bureaucratic Market Muddle?

## Peter Nolan

## Introduction

System reform is on the agenda across the whole socialist bloc. It promises to reshape international relations and to influence a vast number of people's conception of a desirable form of socioeconomic system. Many Western defenders of the free-market system are delighted at the admissions of system failure in the 'socialist' countries. In fact, Stalinism is almost the only form which 'actually existing socialism' has taken where a whole country has been declared socialist, and it is this which free marketeers wish to see as the only alternative to unrestrained capitalism. Many Western socialists accept this analysis, arguing that Deng Xiaoping and Gorbachev are 'restoring capitalism'. Outside these extreme reactions, a large number of ordinary people in the advanced capitalist economies feel that the reforms in the socialist countries signal defeat for the socialist ideal.

These developments provoke deep reflection on the meaning of 'capitalism' and 'socialism', and their relevance to developing countries such as China. 'Capitalism' is easier to define in an agreed way than 'socialism'. The principal elements of capitalism are a system in which most goods and services are commodities traded in markets, in which labour power itself is

I am extremely grateful to the following people for their detailed comments on a long early draft of this paper: Chris Bramall, Michael Landesmann, Liu Minquan, Bruce McFarlane, Ashwani Saith and Zhang Xunhai. I have also benefited from discussion with Carl Riskin, Bob Rowthorn, John Sender, Ajit Singh and Ravi Srivastava. None of these agrees fully with the views expressed in it.

a commodity, in which resource allocation is controlled by the pursuit of profit, which in turn is shaped by market-determined prices, and in which the means of production are privately owned. In its pure form, capitalism's direction of movement is determined by the logic of competition in the marketplace, the 'invisible hand', rather than by conscious social control. It is unequal. Society is divided into a mass class of propertyless workers and a small minority class of capitalists in whose hands the ownership and control of capital is concentrated. However, in its pure form, capitalism existed at the most for only a short period in one country, namely nineteenth-century Britain. Thereafter, the governments of virtually all 'capitalist' countries intervened in markets, and these countries experienced a certain amount of redistribution of ownership and control over capital away from a tiny 'capitalist' class as well as enormous increases in political rights for the mass of the population. These economies cannot be called 'capitalist' without qualification. Socialist elements developed within them, and in this author's view the advanced 'capitalist' economies are more socialist than the self-styled 'socialist' countries.

It is much more difficult to find an agreed definition of 'socialism' than of 'capitalism'. The simplest approach is that of Stalinism. It identifies the chief shortcomings of capitalism as the anarchy of free markets together with class inequality based on unequal ownership of the means of production; it conceives of socialism as the obverse of this, substituting the administrative plan for competitive markets and 'abolishing' class inequality by nationalization of the means of production. This vision of socialism remains influential even within the advanced capitalist countries.

If 'socialism' is not comprehensible to ordinary people it will not be supported. Its broad aim should be to improve the quality of life of the whole population of a particular country and, indeed, of all members of the human race. Socialism's distinguishing characteristics are commitment to the equal worth of all human beings (from which follows a concern with inequality and citizens' rights) and a belief that collective action is often necessary to improve the quality of life (from which follows a concern with citizens' duties). Neither Stalinism nor free-market capitalism can be enduring political-economic philosophies because both will be, or already have come to be, seen by the mass of the population in different countries to be inadequate in providing them with a better quality of life. Some form of market socialism is the only viable long-term basis for meeting most people's aspirations. In different countries, and at different stages of development, some elements of the quality of life are more important than others.

What does this mean for understanding socialism in developing countries? Socialist development is a long-term incremental process, not a single act of seizure of power. Much of it does not occur through action by political rulers, but rather comes from forces emerging independently among the mass of the population. The full flowering of socialism cannot be constructed by rulers for the people. The advanced economies have already developed the productive forces far beyond the poor countries, with corresponding advances in culture, education and leisure which lay the foundation of democratic life. In contrast, in developing countries the principal objective is transparently simple and one with respect to which people of widely different political persuasions can agree, i.e. improving mass living standards as rapidly as possible. Without this, the most straightforward human needs cannot be met. For poor people all considerations pale before those of improved diet, clothing, housing, education, health and increased availability of consumer durables. The most desirable policy for a poor country is that which advances mass living standards most rapidly, providing the basis in the long run for individual self-fulfilment and democratic life. This generally requires much collective action to interfere with the free market to stimulate growth and to redistribute to groups which lose out in the marketplace.

In this chapter it is argued that capitalist forces of competition and profit-seeking are necessary for successful growth of the productive forces in a developing country and for producing many of the prerequisites of a free democratic society. In the next section it is suggested that China needs these forces and that this is more or less explicitly acknowledged by China's present leaders. However, after years of isolation from the outside world, after the disappointments of Stalinism, and under the influence of an oversimplistic interpretation of the causes of growth in neighbouring East Asian countries and of the relevance of their experience to China, some Chinese economists have an excessively positive view of the virtues of the market. In the third section it is argued that China's policy-makers need to be aware of the great variety of ways in which markets fail with respect to both growth and creating a just distribution of the benefits of growth. In the fourth section it is suggested that Stalinism has served China badly. It is in its death throes as a credible political-economic philosophy in China as it is in almost all the other 'socialist' countries. Stalinism emerged as the antithesis of the system which Marx criticized in *Das Kapital*. Having experienced the shortcomings of Stalinism, it would be a great error for the 'socialist' countries to return to a naive trust in the 'invisible hand'. It is argued in the fifth section that the state has an enormous range of tasks to undertake in a country such as China. China does not need the economics of Milton Friedman, but rather a relevant form of market socialism. An optimistic view would suggest that this is broadly the model towards which China is evolving. However, it would be foolish to underestimate the difficulties of a transition out of Stalinism, especially in an extremely poor country like China. I am convinced that China will not return to such a system, but it is difficult to predict whether it will end up closer to capitalist markets, market socialism or even plain market muddle, since this depends on complex political processes rather than the choice of a model from a menu.

Traditional arguments about socialism and capitalism have been conducted principally with respect to the issues of economic growth, political liberties and distribution of power, goods and services. However, two issues stand above all these, namely international military conflict and the environment. If they are not handled well, there will not be much of a world left to argue about. Examination of these would take this chapter into an unacceptable length and beyond the framework of this book. However, their importance overshadows all other considerations, and both capitalism and Stalinism have serious problems in these respects.

# The benefits of capitalism

## Capitalist dynamism

Capitalism's emergence from feudalism in Europe was characterized by a progressive removal of restraints on competition, by a growing tendency for capital and labour to migrate to activities with higher returns, and by increasing enterprise independence to determine resource allocation, with penalties for failure and rewards for success. This process was associated with widening markets, deepening division of labour, and a growing system of property rights which helped to bring private and social costs and benefits closer together by ensuring that risk-takers and innovators reaped the main part of the reward for their enterprise. Without a well-defined and enforceable system of property rights, third parties can receive some of the benefits from economic transactions. Consequently, socially desirable investments and innovations may not be undertaken because private costs exceed private benefits.

Some of the sternest critics of capitalism's inequalities, notably Marx, recognized the stimulus it provided to economic growth. The late medieval expansion of accumulation, technical progress and market widening were possible because of the emerging capitalist setting. In addition to praising the dynamism of capitalism over feudalism, its critics emphasized its unstable character and an apparent tendency towards concentration of asset ownership alongside the growth of a propertyless class. Unsurprisingly, faced with the growth of monopoly capitalism and the collapse of capitalist production in the early 1930s as opposed to the USSR's dynamism, the generation of socialists whose formative years were between the wars stressed an apparent tendency to stagnation in advanced monopoly capitalism compared with its earlier dynamism. Moreover, capitalist neocolonialism was considered to be incompatible with economic progress in the Third World.

Things turned out differently. Despite continued capitalist instability, with enormous periodic waste from unemployment, socialist economists had massively underestimated capitalism's long-term dynamism. The advanced capitalist economies are, indeed, oligopolistic. However, the fierceness of the global struggle for markets ensures that Schumpeterian rivalry exists among huge firms, powerfully spurring on cost reduction and technical progress. Moreover, instead of stagnation, since the 1950s the Third World has seen a massive, albeit uneven, growth of the productive forces in areas in which capitalism has taken root. The success of the newly industrializing countries (NICs) powerfully challenged traditional socialist interpretations of the relative merits of capitalism and socialism as vehicles for economic progress.

Capitalism is not alien to China. From at least the Song dynasty (AD 960–1275) farmers and petty industrialists producing for the market formed increasingly important 'capitalist sprouts' within the existing mode of production, propelling forward the productive forces. Under extremely adverse political conditions, Chinese capitalism made rapid progress in eastern seaboard cities (especially in and around Shanghai) in the early twentieth century. In the early 1950s, and at any later point when controls were relaxed, petty capitalist forces sprang to life. After almost three decades of administrative planning in China the post-1978 period saw a powerful increase in the impact of the capitalist forces of inter-enterprise competition, independent enterprise decision-making and migration of capital and labour in search of profits, especially in small-scale non-state enterprises and in agriculture, though even here capitalist forces still operated in a far from unconstrained fashion. Overall, the economy performed exceptionally well in this period, with rapid growth of output in the sectors most affected by capitalist forces. The most important results were a sustained growth in the living standards of the Chinese people and a remarkably rapid decline in the number of poor. Naturally, such an exceptionally rapid growth of living standards could not be maintained over the long term, because in part it represented a taking in of the previous 'slack' in resource utilization. However, the period was one of outstanding economic success.

## Capitalist freedoms

Capitalism contrasts strikingly with other political-economic formations in the scope that it provides for individual freedom. Capitalism's essence is freedom of choice in the marketplace, and it is unsurprising that individual freedom is the moral basis of capitalism. This concept was useful to merchants and industrialists struggling to emerge from feudal oppression. However, it also became important for ordinary people. The right to make choices without interference from other individuals and groups or from the state is deeply embedded in the psychology of the citizens of the advanced capitalist countries.

As characteristic as the demand for individual freedom has been the emergence under capitalism of demands for political rights, as individuals' sense of self-worth and rights to choose develop with the emerging market economy. The relationship between capitalist development and political democracy is complex. The early phases of capitalist development have rarely been associated with extensive political freedoms and rights.

However, successful capitalist development has generally, after a certain point, witnessed mass demands for democracy. Successful capitalist development brings an increased sense of individual self-worth, reinforced by a growing sense of membership of an interdependent national community, and by increasing levels of education and, eventually, leisure time in which the mass of the population is able to participate in democratic activities extending beyond the important right to choose periodically local or national rulers. Moreover, there is an international 'demonstration effect' of political concepts spilling over from the advanced to the less developed economies.

In the areas of China affected by modern capitalism pre-1949 there was a ferment of new ideas among, in particular, urban workers and intellectuals, bringing new concepts of freedom and demands for democratic rights. How far can the reintroduction of capitalist forces post-Mao be expected to affect popular consciousness in China? In the 1980s the Chinese leadership made tentative steps to establish a concept of individual freedoms with rights to appeal to an independent judiciary, although the base from which this process set out was extremely low. This was attributable in no small degree to the Cultural Revolution, when the rights and freedoms of so many individuals were trampled upon. The most striking examples of increased individual freedoms were in the cultural sphere, where a real New Economic Policy (NEP) atmosphere prevailed in the 1980s. This new cultural freedom, although still within state-controlled limits, contributed enormously to the improved quality of life.

Will the new areas of freedom and independence accompanying the increased role of market forces be compatible with the continuation of a system of Communist Party control, in which ordinary people have no rights to determine their rulers? The recent history of South Korea and Taiwan might suggest a negative answer, but this is too simplistic. Average incomes and levels of urbanization in these countries are much above those in China. Moreover, 'capitalist' elements still penetrate only part of China's political economy. While important changes in mass consciousness are under way in China, most people still live in relatively isolated rural communities and are mainly concerned with raising personal incomes beyond their still desperately low level. During the USSR's own transition from War Communism's highly centralized economic system to the NEP, relaxation of economic control existed alongside the elimination of the political rights of opposition parties, imposition of centralized control within the Party and a ruthless campaign against left-wing opposition both inside and outside the Party. Moreover, Hong Kong is a striking example of the fact that it is possible to combine an almost complete absence of citizens' democratic political rights with a high degree of individual economic freedom and rapid growth of living standards. However, there is in China an important minority, mainly urban and intellectual, whose concepts are rapidly becoming internationalized, whose concern for political liberties is strong and who will strongly influence China's future political evolution. The impact of China's growing market forces upon the political set-up can be compared with that of the same force upon the power of feudal rule in late medieval Europe. However, the pace and pattern of change are hard to predict.

Some people have suggested that economic reform of the Stalinist system is impossible without fundamental political reform. The veracity of this depends on time and place. By late 1988 the attempts to reform the Soviet economy had made little headway. Gorbachev's special Party Congress of 1988 was an acknowledgement that fundamental political changes were necessary before serious economic reform could begin. However, in China considerable economic reform occurred with little political change. China's more rapid progress was due firstly to the fact that it is easier to reform 'socialist' agriculture and small-scale enterprise than large-scale industry. In the former activities the producers are given direct access or access within a small group to the income from the means of production. Moreover, the long-term suppression of small-scale non-farm enterprises in the Stalinist system opens up immediate opportunities for a rapid expansion of employment. In contrast, reform of large-scale industry carries far more risks for both workers and managers, who fear unemployment and/or income loss. Indeed, some analysts believe that if working practices are changed, up to a third of the workforce in China's large-scale state enterprises could be shed with no decline in output. Moreover, agricultural and small non-farm enterprises are much more flexible than large state enterprises. Under the Stalinist system, large imbalances between supply and demand develop, so that the introduction of market forces is likely to cause large shifts in production structure. It is much easier for agriculture and small enterprises than for large industrial concerns to shift to new activities (in the former case capital is closer to putty and in the latter case it is closer to clay). The relative importance of agriculture and small-scale enterprises is much greater in China, and the potential for expansion of small-scale enterprises was much greater at the start of China's reform than in the USSR because of the much larger relative importance of surplus labour in China. Once tentatively begun in the late 1970s, China's rural reforms snowballed, releasing tremendous pressure from peasants at each stage to push the reforms further. Unsurprisingly, this was not the case with large-scale enterprises.

A second reason for the fast pace of economic reform in China prior to political reform was China's relatively short experience with the Stalinist administered economy. The USSR has operated an administered economy for almost twice as long as China. Moreover, markets were further advanced in pre-1949 China than in pre-1917 Russia, albeit that they mostly connected petty-commodity producers to the market. Bringing the habits of market activity to life was not hard in China. Large numbers of peasants, industrialists and traders had direct personal memories of how markets work and needed to be taught little. A third factor distinguishing China from the USSR is the rapid growth which has taken place around it, often in Chinese-dominated societies or in societies in which the Chinese play a strong economic role – Hong Kong, Taiwan, South Korea, Singapore, Malaysia and Thailand. China's leadership is acutely aware of lost time and lost opportunity. By the mid-1930s the lower Yangtze Valley and other areas in coastal Southeast China had already made considerable strides towards modernization, building on earlier 'capitalist sprouts'. While the East Asian NICs grew explosively after the 1950s, comparable parts of China, cut off from international and domestic markets, and with tight controls over the small-scale labour-intensive manufacturing sector which fuelled much of the early growth in the East Asian NICs, grew much less rapidly. The dimensions of the lost opportunity were brought home vividly once reform began in the 1980s. Industrial output, especially in the small-scale labour-intensive sector, grew explosively in favourably situated parts of East and Southeast China, quite reasonably prompting the Chinese leadership to look upon these areas as 'growth poles'.

## Problems of capitalism

### Capitalism and growth

Economists know little more about why output per person grows more rapidly in one country or epoch than in another than that it is because of the provision of more and better capital, and/or better use of capital. Analysis of growth requires both macroeconomics and microeconomics, but combining these levels of analysis is difficult, especially when the vast range of both economic and non-economic factors is included. However, some general points can be made on the subject. While the emergence of capitalist forces of competition and market expansion are, indeed, essential to understanding why growth accelerated in the modern world, unfettered capitalist free markets are not usually the way in which rapid growth rates are achieved. Unconstrained capitalism normally fails with respect to economic growth at both the macrolevel and the microlevel.

Even with considerable national and international intervention in markets, growth in the advanced capitalist countries has been erratic, with episodes of extremely slow and sometimes even negative growth. Many economists in Stalinist countries, used to decades of direct administrative planning, underestimate the difficulties of regulation through macroeconomic levers to produce sustained growth. It is both difficult technically and involves complex non-technical problems. Once labour markets move away from comprehensive state administration and workers begin to bargain for pay, sociopolitical factors affect the macroeconomy. Moreover, the greater the degree of integration into the international economy, the less independence in macromanagement an economy tends to have.

At the microlevel also there are fundamental problems with pure competitive capitalism. Many forms of microeconomic market failure are recognized in standard Western textbooks. These include competition failure, where barriers to entry exist because of increasing returns to scale (the extreme case is a natural monopoly); public goods, where there is zero marginal cost to additional supply and/or it is impossible to exclude others from using the good; externalities, where the actions of an individual or firm impose costs upon or provide benefits to others for which they are not respectively charged or paid; incomplete markets, where a good or service is not provided even though the cost of doing so is less than people are prepared to pay; and finally goods and services which are not provided because too little information is available. Many examples of static market failure also have growth implications, but in a dynamic setting it is difficult to reach firm conclusions. Markets can fail in different ways at the microlevel with respect to growth, size, culture, level of development, location, conjuncture relative to world economic cycles and many other factors affecting both the nature and degree of market failure and the capacity of a given society to resolve it. Successful growth normally depends on devising institutions to overcome market failure, and countries differ enormously in their capacity to construct such institutions, either through voluntary cooperation within and between groups, or through state action to impose the common interest on economic agents.

The reappearance of open inflation in China in the 1980s provides an example of the difficulty of moving away from Stalinist administrative planning towards indirect methods. Inflation in the prices of some important items is inevitable as the economy moves towards a more market-determined system of pricing. Prices of food, transport, housing and energy were all kept artificially low pre-1978, and economic reform was bound to produce pressure for some of these to rise. However, profit rates on some types of products (especially consumer durables) were extremely high prior to reform and a greater role for market forces could lead to a fall in their price. Moreover, a greater role for market forces produces increased pressure to lower costs of production and accelerate technical progress. It is not inevitable that general inflation should result from economic reform. Large state enterprises responded to increases in the prices of formerly underpriced material inputs not by cutting costs but, in classic oligopolistic fashion, by raising prices for those parts of their output outside direct state control. China had, to some degree, entered the spiral of Western-type cost–push inflation. However, the rate of inflation is closely connected to the relationship between the growth of the money supply and the growth of real output. Enormous sociopolitical influences bear upon the money supply and, to a considerable degree, China's inflation represented a capitulation to those influences. The annual rate of growth of money supply (M1) in China roughly doubled from around 9 per cent in the period 1952–78 to 19 per cent in 1979–86 compared with a reported annual growth rate of real GDP of around 10 per cent in 1980–6. The problem was temporarily exacerbated in 1988 by people's fears about future inflation leading them to reduce their savings and panic buy.

Reforms in the price of basic consumer goods, notably food, in the 1980s were followed closely, in order to maintain political stability, by huge unplanned increases in subsidies to urban workers. Moreover, a relatively large proportion of state enterprises made losses, but the state was not prepared to face up to the political cost of bankruptcy and unemployment. Consequently, huge amounts of state funds at different levels were disbursed to cover these enterprises' losses, further fuelling the growth of money supply. Another political element in inflation was the major decentralization in investment allocation in the 1980s. At the enterprise level there was much unplanned diversion of funds towards consumption, and in the absence of full market criteria for state enterprises, local authorities and especially banks, over which local authorities had considerable influence, there occurred an explosion of unplanned investment with little consideration of the social costs or benefits of projects. China in the late 1980s appeared to be one large construction site. These projects sucked in scarce resources and contributed to inflation of wholesale prices in the semi-reformed dual price market for material supplies, as well as feeding the growth of consumers' purchasing power via payments to the huge number of construction site workers. China's inflation of the 1980s could not be attributed simplistically to 'capitalist elements'. Rather, its main cause lay in the politics of reform, working particularly through the money supply which made possible the rise in the general price level. Most East Asian capitalist countries have low inflation rates and low rates of growth of the money supply, while most of the capitalist countries in South America have high inflation rates and high rates of growth of the money supply. Reforming Stalinist economies like China and Hungary also tend to have quite high inflation rates. The reason for these differences is not capitalism *per se*, but rather the political-economic struggles which capitalist forces unleash and which can be resolved in a variety of ways, some more inflationary than others.

Post-1978, many problems emerged to remind the Chinese leadership that, while excessive state administrative control brings microeconomic problems for growth, so too do free markets. One virtue of the people's communes was their capacity to ensure that key cooperative activities were performed. After China's rural reforms of the early 1980s, it proved difficult in poorer areas to mobilize resources for collective health, education and irrigation. Richer areas could finance these directly from the collective non-farm economy, but in poor areas the funds now had to come from individual levies. Although much of the collective expenditure appeared to be useful for the whole village, and had positive externalities for the whole economy (e.g. by helping to bring down birth rates), it proved difficult in many poor areas to obtain the requisite contributions to collective resources. In poor areas the social returns for the local community to more than minimal education may be low because of the simple range of tasks available, so that, left to themselves, it is unsurprising that peasants in those areas opted for lower levels of education than pre-1978. Also, in many areas the marginal returns to irrigation were low after three decades of labour mobilization to expand the irrigated area. Further improvement in poor semi-arid areas often required major irrigation schemes beyond the reach of local cooperation, so that mobilizing labour for village projects might gain prestige for local cadres in the eyes of higher authorities at a high economic cost for villagers. In each of these cases, neither free markets nor even state-led cooperation can solve the problem. Action by regional or national authorities is necessary.

A second example of the dangers of unconstrained markets was the explosive growth of small-scale enterprises in the 1980s. While much of this was beneficial, rapidly absorbing rural surplus labour, much waste occurred. In part this was due to the still unreformed nature of much of large-scale industry, which resulted, for example, in the expansion of small-scale industries into activities in which a reformed large-scale industry would be more efficient. However, in part, the difficulties also reflected classic problems of uncoordinated competitive markets. Short-run returns in many small-scale activities were sufficiently high to bid labour and materials away from activities which would yield higher long-term social returns for the whole economy. To have had such phenomenal all-round growth of small-scale enterprises at a time of acute shortage in energy, appalling deficiencies in the transport system and shortcomings in the educational system, suggests fundamental failure in microeconomic coordination.

Less serious are the microeconomic mistakes which simply reflect the process of becoming re-acquainted with markets. For decades Chinese industry had operated in a seller's market. In the 1980s many producers, especially of light industrial products, rushed too rapidly into expanding production in high profit lines. Within a short time many markets became saturated, especially those for low-quality products, and huge stockpiles of unwanted goods built up.

## Capitalism and inequality

The concepts of individual freedom and rights associated with capitalism are extremely important. Most people in the capitalist countries value them highly, and they contribute substantially to their quality of life. They should form a core part of socialist values but too often have failed to do so, tending to be set aside in favour of the pursuit of an alleged 'common good'. These freedoms and rights apply equally to all citizens, but under capitalism equal rights produce unequal outcomes, which are transmitted between generations. At the heart of capitalism is a competitive economic struggle, from which all citizens may gain in the long term as the whole system moves upwards. However, unequal distribution of the gains from competition means that equal rights and freedoms are of different value to different social groups. Freedom to purchase an education or to migrate have a different meaning for an unemployed worker than for a rich company director. Freedom of speech will mean different things for an international media tycoon than for an ordinary citizen. Equality before the law has little meaning for a poor person confronted with the risk and payments required to go to law. Freedom to organize politically becomes a right of inequality if one social group has more resources to organize and influence opinion than another. Freedom can only have the same meaning for all citizens if the state intervenes with the market and redistributes resources.

Reintroduction of the elements of a capitalist economy in China in the 1980s was accompanied by the development of wide inequalities compared with those of pre-1976 which deeply worried many socialists outside China. Under Mao remuneration had been kept within narrow boundaries and the key slogan was 'serve the people'. The appearance in the 1980s of the slogan 'take the lead in getting rich' shocked people after years of Maoist egalitarianism. The impact of the new policies on inequalities was strongest in the countryside. A rapid widening of the range of income within a given village occurred and a small number of relatively very rich ('10,000 yuan') rural households quickly emerged, relying on superior skills and better balances between labour power and dependents, and often using better connections in a rural economy which was still not fully marketized. Moreover, in many parts of China concentration of land use began to emerge, encouraged by government policy favouring cultivation by 'farming experts'. Income from renting farmland, hiring labour and usury all reappeared. Intravillage political power began to be affected by the economic inequalities which re-emerged in the villages.

In the 1980s a minority of well-endowed regions (e.g. Southern Jiangsu and the Pearl River Delta in Guangdong province) raised their incomes by relatively large amounts. Under Mao they had been held back both through controls on resource allocation and the level of income allowed to the local population. When these constraints weakened, output and income grew rapidly. The main beneficiaries were eastern seaboard areas close to large cities. By the late 1980s some of these had average incomes many times higher than those in poorly endowed areas. The gap in income between the richest households in these areas and the average income in backward areas was enormous. For example, by the mid-1980s, the richest households in the Wenzhou district of Zhejiang province, which specialized in button manufacture and trade mainly in private enterprises, had annual incomes of over 150,000 yuan, while in poor areas there were still many villages with annual household incomes as low as 150 yuan – a range of rural incomes of 1,000:1! These differentials were large even by the standards of advanced capitalist countries. Many critics asked what could be 'socialist' about a country with such wide inequalities?

# The problems of Stalinism

## Lack of dynamism of Stalinism

The Stalinist economic model pre-dates Stalin's rise to power. The mainstream of European socialism in the late nineteenth and early twentieth century constructed its vision of a socialist economy using Marx's fragmentary writings on post-capitalist society and his critique of capitalism as a negative model. For such late-nineteenth-century socialist economists as Kautsky, the socialist economy meant eliminating the anarchic, crisis-ridden and wasteful character of capitalism by public ownership, direct administration and elimination of the profit motive. Under socialism the whole economy would be administered as a single enterprise. The Stalinist model found clear expression in Bukharin and Preobrazhensky's *ABC of Communism*, published in the USSR in 1920, and was put into effect during War Communism between 1918 and 1921 in the USSR, supported by most of the Bolshevik leadership. In essence, the post-1929 Stalinist economy was War Communism reintroduced. The international appeal of comprehensive planning was increased greatly by high unemployment between the wars and post-war frustration at widespread Third World poverty. A state-directed 'big push' for rapid growth provided the attraction of an apparently simple solution to the problem of economic backwardness.

For a long time it was possible to attribute the economic problems of the Stalinist model to special factors, such as hostility from the Western capitalist economies or growing complexity of the economy. However, it became increasingly clear that fundamental systemic problems existed which applied to the model at all stages of economic development. It is no longer tenable to argue that an economy in which the state attempts to administer the details of economic activity is likely to be satisfactory in relation to technical progress and growth of living standards or in minimizing waste, let alone with respect to its impact upon the environment. Among the many problems which have been identified in a system which tries to substitute entirely administrative targets for market coordination are the following. There are insurmountable problems for planners in trying to obtain accurate information and equally large problems in trying to process the information into a complete operational plan. In such a non-market system, if the plan is to come anywhere near balancing inputs and outputs, the key enterprise target must be some synthetic indicator of output. Other goals (e.g. product mix, quality, cost reduction, technical progress) tend to be downgraded in the interests of achieving this objective. The major driving force for capitalist enterprises to reduce costs and innovate, which stems from the incentive of profit and the fear of bankruptcy, is absent. Economic decisions are frequently taken by technically incompetent political cadres. The dynamic effects stemming from the direct connection of enterprises with world markets are missing. Labour motivation for urban workers is dampened by shortages of wage goods, labour hoarding, irregular work patterns due to shortages of inputs and absence of the threat of unemployment. Rural labour motivation is severely impaired by managerial diseconomies of scale in collective forms.

The economic results of such a system are well known. What appeared to an earlier generation of socialist economists to be the major advantage of such a system, namely the ability to 'mobilize resources' on a grand scale, can now be seen to be a reflection of system failure. The system has a pervasive drive to overinvest, and, indeed, the Stalinist economies have all been characterized by very high rates of investment for their level of development.

In relatively closed economies such inefficiency in investment use is necessarily reflected in the high proportion of output allocated to capital goods production. This sector itself is a high consumer of capital goods, leading to a vicious circle of capital goods expansion. Rapid expansion of the capital goods sector began as a conscious system goal, but priority for this sector over the long term reflects system failure: Kruschev's 'steel blinkers' proved easier to put on than to remove. Moreover, such problems are not offset by technical dynamism once the first great infusion of foreign technology has been made in the early periods of planning. On the contrary, a key problem is the system's inability to generate indigenous technical progress. The net result is high rates of investment and overall growth of gross value of output, but poor performance of final consumption growth.

The highly centralized Stalinist model which operated in China from the mid-1950s to the early 1980s blended well with China's centralist political traditions. There were important differences between the approaches of Stalin and Mao to political economy, but in the fundamentals of economic organization and attitudes towards market forces the two remained close. Even during the Great Leap Forward (1958–9) and at the height of the Cultural Revolution (1966–8), China's economy remained firmly Stalinist in its key features (e.g. commitment to administrative planning, absence of markets for capital or labour, collective farms, bias towards the large scale and relative isolation from the international economy).

The highly centralized one-party system provided the opportunity for a single individual to have a major influence on economic development, with extremely detrimental consequences. This system allowed Mao to stifle economic debate for a long period. At the end of the First Five Year Plan (1953–7) a powerful critique of the monolithic administrative planning system, was emerging, but its ideas were suppressed, reappearing briefly in the early 1960s. Consequently, for over 20 years economics in China was narrowly dogmatic and methods of economic management were virtually unchanged. The Stalinist political system enabled this to happen. The Stalinist economic system persisted because of a political form which allowed a high degree of central control which could crush the expression of ideas different from those of one person or a small group of people at the top.

China's overall long-term growth rate was impressive. Like other Stalinist economies China rapidly attained self-sufficiency in a wide range of products. However, growth was unbalanced with the growth rate of heavy industry much above that of light industry, which was, in turn, much above that of agriculture. Because of Mao's initial opposition to population control and later diversion of attention away from work to control population growth during the Cultural Revolution, population continued to increase rapidly up until the 1970s. Despite enormous growth in total product, there was little scope for growth of the most important indicator, living standards. Output per person of a narrow range of poor-quality industrial consumer goods grew quite fast, but from a negligible base, so that at the end of the Maoist period stocks of these goods per family were still extremely low. Housing availability per person deteriorated over the long term. Consumption per person of the main agricultural products hardly altered, leaving no reported long-term change at all in the average daily calorie intake. In the early 1980s it became clear that the Maoist period had bequeathed a legacy of dire material poverty for perhaps one-third of the Chinese population. Not only had progress of average material consumption at best been slow, but the variety of cultural life had been greatly restricted. As in all the Stalinist systems only a narrow range of cultural products was permitted, which strongly affected the quality of people's lives.

Not only does the Stalinist political-economic system produce long-term problems, but it is also able to make serious short-term errors. Nothing illustrates this better than the Chinese Great Leap Forward (1958–9). Against tremendous opposition from economists and most of China's leaders, Mao was able to use his position of supreme political power to launch an extraordinarily utopian movement. With his confidence boosted by false reports from grass roots cadres of the achievements under new social relationships, Mao intended China to leap directly into the realm of 'communism'. He considered it possible to build new forms of social consciousness which would pre-empt the need for bourgeois management and payment systems in town and countryside alike. Never before or since (even in the Cultural Revolution) has such a challenge been made to the capitalist system. Many foreign commentators, including those in the USSR, considered the whole project to be madness. Combined with detailed, and frequently questionable, economic directives (e.g. mass construction of irrigation works, reduced acreage sown to grain and a national campaign to build 'backyard' iron and steel works) went a belief that it was possible in a mass campaign to change social consciousness away from individualism towards collectivism and patriotism, and that this would liberate people's creative energies in a way that would produce rapid economic progress. The implicit criticism of capitalism's constraints on the creativity of the masses was correct, but the results were disasterous.

There was initially a great deal of popular enthusiasm amidst a national holiday atmosphere, with the mass excitement which accompanies an extraordinary event. However, such an atmosphere is hard to sustain when difficulties are encountered. New agricultural institutions (the gigantic 'rural people's communes') multiplied the problems experienced on collective farms. Scarce peak-period farm labour was transferred to activities with low or negative returns. Egalitarian payment systems caused serious urban and rural motivation problems. Invaluable technical expertise was lost as those with scarce skills were transferred for much of the time to mundane tasks. In the heady politicized campaign atmosphere planning collapsed and greater, more irrational, degrees of local self-sufficiency emerged as enterprises and localities desperately sought to produce for themselves products whose supply could not be relied upon through the planning system.

The economic collapse was catastrophic. The full extent of the agricultural decline was initially hidden by widespread misreporting. Its implications for the consumption levels of large numbers of people were much greater than need have been the case owing to the tight control exercised by the Party over information. Local officials sometimes tried to seal off their areas to prevent the news of mass starvation from leaking out. In more open political systems information of severe localized food shortages would have become national news. Instead, in parts of China large numbers of people died of malnutrition – mainly those in the most vulnerable age groups (i.e. the very old and the very young). The concepts of 'excess deaths' and 'deaths through famine' are extremely problematic, and there will never be a clear answer to the numbers of those whose deaths are attributable to the famine of 1959–61. What is certain is that famine did indeed occur on a scale that dwarfs any other famine of the twentieth century. Its origins lie in the closed centralized system of Stalinist political economy. It is not a coincidence that India has not experienced a major famine since 1947, despite regular widespread malnutrition.

## Inequality and restrictions on liberty under Stalinism

Whatever the political system, substitution of the market-determined allocation of goods and services with bureaucratic allocation introduces dangers of inequalities and restrictions on individual liberties. It establishes a generalized inequality between those who allocate and those who are the recipients of the decisions of bureaucratic allocators. This danger applies even to uncorrupt honest administrators. There are great possibilities for corrupt behaviour in such situations in terms of bureaucrats selling items illegally on black markets, economically stronger people and regions bribing officials, and bonds of dependence being created between ordinary people and bureaucrats such that present-giving to and favour-doing for bureaucrats becomes a regular part of daily life. Constant mass vigilance and a high level of public participation is necessary to ensure that the independence of bureaucrats is minimized. This is difficult to achieve even in advanced capitalist countries with high levels of education, plenty of leisure time and strong democratic traditions. The Stalinist system is the obverse of this.

The main features of the Stalinist political system were established during War Communism in the USSR (1917–21) in the face of a desperate civil war and serious opposition from within the domestic socialist movement. Hammered out in wartime, the Party rules of the Stalinist states bear more resemblance to those of an army than to a Western political party. In a memorable phrase, one leading Soviet economist recently described the system as 'barracks socialism'. The structure over which Stalin seized control in the USSR in the late 1920s already had a system of rules which made possible the concentration of power in the hands of one person. Commentators on both Chinese and Soviet post-revolutionary politics have argued that the centralist elements can be explained largely by each country's specific history, without reference to Stalinism. While not disputing the importance of historical influences, the Stalinist system of political economy, in whatever setting it is applied, provides a favourable environment for centralist elements inherited from the country's history to be put into effect, as well as creating new forms of political centralization.

China's post-revolutionary practice was affected powerfully by pre-revolutionary experience. China has unusual historically bequeathed problems in establishing democratic political rights and individual liberties. No other part of the world of comparable size has such a long tradition of centralized rule by a powerful state. A second factor influencing post-1949 politics was the evolution of the Chinese Communist Party (CCP) pre-1949. Not only was it affected powerfully by the Soviet Stalinist approach towards the Party, but the CCP was involved in a military campaign over more than two decades. Tight inner-Party discipline and limitations on the liberties of non-Party citizens of the Communist Base Areas developed ineluctably during the course of the protracted military struggle. Compared with other Stalinist societies, the 'mass line', which was developed in the Base Areas, did indeed constitute a uniquely close relationship between the Party and the masses, but this was essentially a difference in work style rather than a difference in approach towards political rights. The military–bureaucratic approach towards both inner-Party discipline and the Party's relationship to society developed and was continued after the Chinese revolution of 1949. Stalinist Party organization permits control by one person or a group of people who are able to suppress inner-Party opposition to their views and to shape the very membership of the Communist Party in a way that helps support them. Despite strong inner-Party opposition to collectivization, the Great Leap Forward and the Cultural Revolution, Mao was able to use his power as the head of a highly centralized system to push through unpopular policies.

The Party tightly controlled socioeconomic life throughout the Maoist period. A Party which evolved out of military struggle justified restrictions on liberty in the interests of further struggles: against landlords and capitalists in the 1950s, against massive external opposition, and against those within China who opposed egalitarian socioeconomic policies after 1957. Huge restrictions on personal liberty were put into effect by a tiny group of people during the Cultural Revolution, in the teeth of strong high-level political opposition, in the interests of an egalitarian socioeconomic ethic. Perhaps only North Korea has cut off its citizens so completely from international contacts or imposed such restrictions on cultural output as China's leaders did during the Cultural Revolution. Few modern societies have had such restrictions on freedom of movement as China did then. Even freedom to reproduce was tightly controlled in the latter stages of the Cultural Revolution through the detailed birth plan sent down to production units. Moreover, the mass mobilization led by a small minority with great power, and the absence of an independent judiciary to appeal to, permitted the persecution of groups and individuals in the name of support for the leadership (i.e. Mao) against the 'enemies of the revolution'. Such dangers exist under any situation of mobilization against real or imagined enemies, but were developed to a high degree in the Cultural Revolution. Economic freedom was, of course, confined only to small areas of 'free-market' activity, although even these tiny 'capitalist sprouts' were monitored tightly by state personnel. It is true that large numbers of Party members (perhaps even the great majority) were idealistic and tried to serve their communities well. However, their conception of how their communities would be best served came not from democratic decisions by the community, but rather from their superiors and ultimately from the political leadership. Such fundamental issues as winter-time mobilization of vast amounts of rural labour, the method of income distribution and of factory management were decided within a centrally determined framework, given concrete form in editorials in the *People's Daily*, the *People's Liberation Army Daily* and the *Red Flag*, all controlled by the central Party apparatus.

Under Mao, and especially during the Cultural Revolution, China paradoxically had a system attempting to reduce socioeconomic inequality, but doing so with mass restriction of individual liberties, with little acknowledgement of mass democratic political rights, exercising a highly centralized and concentrated form of political power by a tiny number of central leaders over the mass of the population, allowing the regular exercise of power by local Party members over the mass of the population and opening the door to widespread abuse of that power. These problems, which reached their peak in the Cultural Revolution, cannot be attributed to the shortcomings of certain individuals. The Cultural Revolution simply exhibited in extreme form defects inherent in the Stalinist system combined with features inherited from Chinese history. Individuals matter greatly in history. Had Mao died in 1956 or 1966 rather than in 1976

China's history would have been very different. However, the potential for the creation of political inequality and restrictions on liberty is embedded deeply in the Stalinist political system, whose basic features were established as early as 1921. Both the current Soviet and the current Chinese leadership believe that the Stalinist political system can be reformed from above without altering the leading role of the CCP. This is an optimistic view for which history provides little support.

# The need for state intervention

## State intervention and growth

Conventional wisdom in development economics has shifted against the state. A series of criticisms of state intervention in mixed economies buttressed by system reform in the 'socialist' countries has produced a major shift in thinking. Such a strong swing against state intervention and in favour of free markets is highly problematic. However, it must be acknowledged that socialist economists have tended to be too simplistic in their approach to these problems, assuming that a common model of state intervention can solve problems of market failure. In practice, the necessary level and desirable form of state intervention varies enormously. The experience of a wide range of successfully industrializing countries, from France, Germany and Japan in the nineteenth century through to Singapore, Taiwan and South Korea since the 1950s, demonstrates that a key element in rapid growth is devising appropriate ways in which the state can supplement for market failure so as to bring the decisions of profit-seeking enterprises in line with those that are desirable for the overall economy. Only in exceptional cases, such as Hong Kong, have countries relied on the free market during industrialization. Indeed, even in the case of Hong Kong, with unusual supply-side advantages, the state has done much more to supplement for market failure than is commonly supposed (its role in housing and education, for example, has been vital). The idea that the Asian NICs relied on the free market to attain their striking success is a myth. The key to their success lies in the nature of the state. With the exception of Hong Kong, each of the Asian NICs was extremely vulnerable at the start of their take-off, threatened by larger neighbouring countries. Growth was vital if Singapore, Taiwan and South Korea were even to survive as independent countries. In each case the state was able to take decisions beneficial to economic growth without compromising these actions by placating special interest groups. The package of state actions taken in each case was different, and included intervention in labour markets, land reform, state ownership of key industries, protection, subsidies and rewards to exporters, provision of credit, public housing, education, transport facilities, power supplies and agricultural extension services, construction of strategic plans, direct instructions to different enterprises and state finance for research and development. Not all these interventions were successful. Of course, the extraordinary growth of these economies was helped by the boom in world trade and the inward-looking strategies of their potential competitors, especially China and India. However, much of their success is attributable to the way in which these 'developmental states' constructed a strategy which used the dynamism of market forces but identified the many different ways in which free markets would fail to produce acceptable growth. There is a wide variety of relationships between states and sectional interests. It must be recognized that in some cases, although market failure is considerable and economic performance could be greatly improved by effective state action, the state is so corrupted by the influence of sectional interests and/or by the pursuit of power and privilege for bureaucrats rather than the pursuit of growth, that state intervention could produce worse results for growth than those obtaining with market failure and an absence of state intervention. While there is no reason to accept the extreme pro-free-market view that state failure is always worse than market failure, one should not ignore the fact that some states are more successful than others in overcoming market failure, and that in the last instance there is, indeed, the possibility of state failure's being worse than market failure.

Despite considerable economic reform in the late 1980s the Chinese state still had great influence over economic activity, with a much more comprehensive array of controls than, for example, in any of the East Asian NICs. China was moving away from Stalinist economic management, and the role of market forces had increased enormously. The leadership was attempting to strike a new balance between plan and market, relying heavily on indirect methods, mainly macroeconomic levers, to guide the economy. However, the model towards which the system was moving was unclear. The final balance between plan and market was still uncertain, as was the pace and manner in which reform should proceed.

It was argued above that an important characteristic of the East Asian NICs is the relative autonomy of the state which leaves it free to pursue developmental goals with less need to placate sectional interests than in other countries. The present Chinese state in some respects possesses this characteristic. Firstly, unlike the Indian state for example, the Chinese state does not have to placate the interests of landlords or powerful oligopolistic groups in private industry, or indeed to make deals with any socioeconomic group to seek electoral support. Even industrial labour is unable to exert as much organized political pressure as in most developing countries. Secondly, China has been through a long period of turmoil. This began in late Qing and lasted through to 1949. However, the turmoil did not end there. Unlike, say, the USSR, which has had a long period of political stability since the 1920s, China since the late 1950s has had immense sociopolitical upheavals. The Chinese people feel deeply aware of the development opportunities that have been lost. This attitude is given added force by their strong awareness of China's rich history and of the long period in which it led world historical progress. There would therefore be popular support for a leadership which pursued developmental goals successfully. The traumatic nature of this background is similar in some respects to the political crises which helped provide popular support for the 'developmental elites' in Taiwan, South Korea, Singapore and Hong Kong. However, China still possesses a vast Party (around 47 million members in the late 1980s) and government apparatus. They are closely intertwined, have inherited the country's long habit of bureaucratic rule and have traditions closer to those of India's bureaucracy in recent times than to those of China's East Asian neighbours. Moreover, they benefited in many ways from the semi-reformed state of China's economy in the late 1980s. This apparatus has a strong desire to retain power and privilege. Moreover, the sheer fact of its vast size means that, like India, problems arise from the difficulty of running such a large administrative machine and from the difficulty of attaining unity of purpose when there are conflicting regional interests. To turn China's bureaucracy from an administrative into a developmental state is an enormous task which has hardly begun. It presents a major barrier to continued economic reform. Whenever a problem appears in the course of reform, its instinct is to attempt direct control rather than allow the market to solve the problem. Transformation of the state apparatus is the most crucial and difficult task facing China's leadership for the 1990s. It is extremely difficult to predict the path that China's political economy will take if this is not accomplished.

Despite the need for better functioning markets the economic tasks for the state in China are still enormous, although, of course, the methods and the degree of state activity need to alter dramatically. It is a serious misconception to imagine that macroeconomic levers (e.g. money supply, rate of interest, taxation) alone will suffice to guide the Chinese economy effectively along a high growth path. For example, the market is likely to do a poor job in meeting the Chinese economy's needs for education, health, power supply and transport. Up to a certain point, the social benefits to investment in education and health are likely to be inadequately reflected in the private profits to be made supplying these services. Training and retraining the labour force are vital to economic growth, yet in this area the gap between private and social returns is often wide. State activity is vital. Power supply is notoriously problematic if left entirely to the market. Investments are often enormous and long-term coordination between different forms of energy supply is necessary. The free market might produce inadequate levels of power supply from oligopolistic companies at high prices. Construction of communications networks is also uneven and often beyond the reach of individual businesses. Moreover, many of the benefits to improved communications come in the form of externalities that cannot be captured in the profits of the individual supplier. The precise institutional form in which these needs are met by the state should be carefully investigated and the crude simplicity of Stalinist methods of provision avoided. Indeed, in these areas the state may often usefully operate in tandem with private or cooperative provision. A serious problem from the Chinese economy in the late 1980s in these types of activities was not that the state was doing too much but rather that it was not doing enough. Indeed, in power supply and transport a serious crisis had developed. It makes poor economic sense to have such rapid expansion of light industry while these sectors languish. Although the form of provision may (and should) alter, the state needs to play a considerable role in these activities: the free-market solution will produce slower growth of national output, and macroeconomic levers alone will be inadequate to meet needs.

Mistakes made with respect to agriculture in a developing country are costly. Dismantling the old system of collective labour and income distribution was necessary for the achievement of faster rates of growth of farm output in China, for using farm resources more effectively and for raising national living standards. Agriculture, especially under labour-intensive conditions, is characterized by powerful managerial diseconomies of scale with respect to the direct cultivation of the soil, arising principally from difficulties with labour supervision. However, experience in a wide range of settings from Japan to Denmark has demonstrated the necessity of action above the level of the individual farmer. This can take the form of voluntary cooperation or state action, either direct or through state-organized cooperation. Many activities are frequently beyond the range of the individual farmer, including credit provision, insurance, veterinary facilities, research, quality control, processing, marketing and purchasing large equipment for ploughing, harvesting or spraying. Especially important in large parts of China is the construction and maintenance of drainage and irrigation works. To some degree in China these needs will be met by voluntary cooperation. However, experience in pre-1949 China and in comparable parts of Asia shows how important it is for state action (both central and local) to supplement where voluntary cooperation fails. Many new problems appeared in these respects in China in the 1980s, especially in poor areas where only limited resources were available to the local state apparatus. However, compared with many other parts of Asia, China, despite new problems, still possessed a relatively effective local state structure and there was a strong national policy commitment to supplement for market failure in these vital respects. The historical evidence from pre-1955 Japan, Taiwan and China suggests that full-scale collective farms are not the only way in which these needs can be met.

The state needs to do a great deal to affect the environment in which industry operates: educate, train and retrain its workers; provide direct or indirect support for investment in technical progress; protect selected industries; assist selected industries to compete in world markets; provide assistance for industries which are desirable for the national economy (e.g. due to externalities, lumpiness or long gestation periods) but which the private sector would not set up; support suitable infrastructural construction where the private sector fails to do so. Moreover, the Stalinist system showed the dangers of an economy in which industrial enterprises did not need to compete with each other, and an important function for the state is to ensure that competitive conditions exist.

A key issue is the degree to which direct state ownership is desirable. In China in the late 1980s, virtually all industrial output was produced in 'state' enterprises – even rural 'collective' enterprises were often effectively local state enterprises. Whether or not enterprises are formally owned by the state is less important than the way in which they operate. An enterprise formally 'owned' by the state may be permitted to retain all or none of its profits, to sell freely all or none of its output, to bid freely for and take over other enterprises or to have no such rights. Moreover, the idea that state enterprises cannot in principle operate in a competitive profitable fashion has been belied by many practical examples. None of these is more striking than the turnaround in performance of a succession of British nationalized industries in the 1980s prior to privatization. Much the most important goal for Chinese industry in the 1990s is to devise methods by which the competitive vigour which has already penetrated the small-scale 'collective' industrial sector also enters the large-scale industrial sector. This requires that enterprise management has real independence in the sense possessed in the capitalist countries by those who run (but do not necessarily own) large-scale private capitalist enterprises or the many successful large-scale state enterprises. Operational independence and competition rather than ownership *per se* are the key. However, the issue cannot be dealt with in the abstract. It must be examined with China's situation in mind. China has a long tradition of Party and government intervention in enterprise affairs (e.g. the late Qing system of *guandu shangban* – bureaucratic supervision and merchant operation), so that it is extremely difficult to prise enterprises away from their control. Given this background it is possible that only some form of privatization may break the stranglehold in which large enterprises find themselves. Thus, in China today a substantial amount of privatization of large state enterprises may be necessary, not because it is the only way in principle to provide autonomy, but because it is the only way given China's history. Such action will only be successful in alliance with the substantial array of state actions outlined above.

## State intervention and inequality

Free markets provide an unequal value of freedom to different social groups. Capitalism can, after a certain point, produce some narrowing of inequalities through the workings of the market. However, the main force tending to produce greater equality in the value of freedom is state intervention to tax, redistribute and provide equal access to facilities that enable people to utilize more fully their human potential. A crucial question for any community to decide, especially a poor one, is the degree to which there is a trade-off between growth and equality, and the appropriate balance to be struck in any given circumstance. All communities have to make decisions about the degree to which they are prepared to interfere with individual liberty in order to redistribute and support collective facilities which provide a more equal value of freedom.

Maoist China was characterized by extreme political inequalities and greatly restricted individual freedom. However, intense state action produced an unusually high degree of equality. Maoist policies sprang from a deep socialist conviction that citizens are of equal value and should be given equal opportunities for self-fulfilment. The Maoist critique of 'bourgeois rights', under which equal rights permit unequal outcomes, was simple and coherent. Defenders of free-market values and its inequalities outside China mention Mao only to ridicule him. This is inadequate. For all the fluctuations in policy, for all the trampling on individual rights and for all the undesirable results for the economy, the Maoist years in China can only be properly assessed if we take seriously the sustained efforts to try to ensure that Chinese citizens shared equally in the development process.

Maoist China did not eliminate socioeconomic inequality. Even under Mao there was an awareness that 'absolute egalitarianism' could have disastrous consequences. In the 1970s one was still better off as a man than as a woman, as an urban worker than as a peasant, as a state worker than as a collective worker, as a peasant near a large city than as one in a remote area, or as a peasant with many able-bodied adults in the household than as one with several young children. However, one of the most sustained attempts in modern history was made to reduce inequality and to ensure maximum poverty relief from given resources. This produced certain advances. For example, the disastrous loss of life after the Great Leap Forward has to be set against the fact that prior to 1978 China's food distribution system and provision of basic health care contributed to a more rapid fall in death rates in normal times than was achieved in most developing countries, so that by the mid-1970s the average life expectancy was very high for a country at its level of income. However, the attempt to make substantial reductions in inequality was a factor contributing to the extremely slow growth of average living standards by reducing the effectiveness with which people made use of productive resources. Greater poverty relief could have been achieved through a less severely redistributive strategy which provided greater incentives to the workforce to use resources well and which did not attempt such radical transformations of the division of labour. For example, other parts of the world and, indeed, China itself pre-1955, have done a great deal to meet basic needs without attempting such radical transformations of relations of production as China carried out with its collective farms. Redistribution *per se* can only go so far in alleviating mass poverty. Growth is essential to take mass living standards beyond a certain level and it is this which must be the overriding goal for a country still at China's low level of development. Equality in poverty, albeit somewhat reduced poverty, is not the most desirable condition.

After Mao's death major changes occurred in all these respects. Logic and China's experience before 1949, as well as that in a wide range of developing countries, all suggest that if market forces are left to work freely in China, inequality will increase. Many people outside China think that this is desirable – a welcome and inevitable corollary of China's move down the path towards capitalism. Others consider that this did, indeed, happen in the 1980s but feel that in permitting it China's leaders are betraying socialism. In fact, there appeared to be a substantial measure of agreement among Chinese leaders that, while growth is vital to China's national pride and power, and to the relief of poverty, control of inequality matters greatly. The seriousness with which this was taken separated China from most developing countries and constituted a genuinely 'socialist' element in its development strategy. There was, of course, considerable debate about the appropriate degree of inequality and along which dimensions, about the degree of trade-off with growth goals, and about the methods to be used to influence inequality and relieve poverty.

At the most fundamental levels of human capital formation and culture important changes occurred in the direction of increased inequality. However, mainly through state action at different levels, China still allocated a larger proportion of national resources to health and education than most poor countries and made them available at prices that enabled a high proportion of the population to have access to them. Problems in poor areas partly reflected the fact that, left to themselves, many peasants decided that long years of education were inappropriate to their work needs. Also, to a considerable degree they reflected a new openness in reporting poor conditions rather than an actual deterioration. China's recent record in national and local (including village) state resource mobilization to provide mass access to the basics of human capital formation is still impressive compared with other developing countries. Moreover, the most dramatic cultural change in the 1980s was mass access to international television programmes which had a homogenizing rather than a differentiating impact on culture.

Under free-market conditions inequalities in asset ownership are important in explaining inequalities in income, power and life chances. In China in the late 1980s, only a tiny fraction of industrial assets was owned by individuals, and the private sector produced a small proportion of industrial output. The 'collective' industrial sector embraced a wide variety of different ownership forms and made a major contribution to China's growth in the 1980s, and there was a strong official ideological preference for 'collective' rather than private enterprise, despite the fact that the latter was legal. A wide variety of options was being mooted in relation to industrial share ownership schemes in order to improve the functioning of state-owned enterprises by separating ownership rights from control over enterprise management. Although no single model had emerged as dominant, there appeared to be a strong awareness of the need to devise share-ownership systems that prevent the concentration of share ownership in the hands of a small number of individuals or private institutions such as is the case under Western capitalism.

In agriculture, the key asset is land. China's land redistribution in the 1980s was extremely egalitarian, with locally equal allocations per person being the principal method adopted. This provided an egalitarian basis to the whole rural reform programme. While land operation was becoming more concentrated through forms of rental arrangement, land remained publicly owned. It could not be bought and sold. It seems impossible that there could emerge a minority landlord class, with land ownership concentrated in its hands, which absorbs a large share of the benefit of farm modernization or, indeed, inhibits such modernization.

While major changes in asset ownership had occurred, China's policies in the 1980s separated it from 'capitalist' developing countries. For example, if China is compared with India, where industrial ownership is concentrated in the hands of only a few families and there is still considerable inequality in ownership of farmland, the difference is striking.

A major criterion in assessing the social characteristics of any state is its approach towards regional inequality, which is particularly important in the case of economies the size of China or India. A notorious deficiency of the Indian state has been its lack of a coherent regional policy and, apart from famine relief, the national government has strikingly failed to mobilize resources to assist backward areas. Much understandable concern was expressed outside China at the fact that there were still a large number of people living in poverty in poorly located areas while well-located areas on the east coast, such as Southern Jiangsu province and the Pearl River Delta in Guangdong province, experienced explosive growth of output and income in the 1980s. Unlike most poor countries, in China in the 1980s there was much research and publication about regional inequalities. Under Mao, the fact that huge numbers of peasants lived in abysmal unchanging conditions was simply not referred to in public discussion. Policies in the 1980s were based on an explicit recognition that there are gains for the national economy in allowing some areas with economic advantages to grow more rapidly than others. The 1980s (and, indeed, the 1930s) demonstrated just how fast growth could be in key areas on the eastern seaboard, and it would be foolish to hold them back. Some trickle-down effects benefited poorer areas. However, policy-makers recognized that part of the benefits from growth along the eastern seaboard should be taxed or diverted through the banking system (levels of savings in these areas were high) to assist poverty stricken regions. While more could, undoubtedly, have been done to help disadvantaged areas, the relative level of state assistance for such areas was much greater than in most large 'capitalist' developing countries, such as Brazil or India. While richer areas obtained much larger income growth per person in the 1980s, the combination of rural institutional reforms, a certain amount of trickle-down (e.g. via remittances from migrants) plus state assistance (national and provincial) led to massive reductions in the numbers of

Chinese in poverty. This was not inconsistent with the fact that tens of millions still lived in wretched poverty.

Methods of remuneration altered considerably after 1978 within industry, and inter-enterprise inequality in average incomes was wider than pre-1978 as state enterprises were allowed to retain a portion of their profits with which to remunerate their workers. However, there were many controls still, both on the way in which enterprises allocated retained profits and on the proportion of profits enterprises were allowed to retain. In part, this was because incomplete reform in enterprises' environment, notably the price system, meant that profits reflected many factors besides efficiency. Partly, too, it was because there still existed a strong ethos of what consistuted a just (*gong ping*) differential in average incomes. Within state enterprises, differentials widened, with increased incentives to acquire scarce skills and to work hard. However, differentials were still narrow compared with other developing countries, and there was still a strong sense that differentials beyond a certain level were unjust. Equally, in 'collective' industrial enterprises remuneration was far from being on a free-market basis. For example, rural 'collective' industrial enterprises usually operated under an umbrella body of the local state apparatus, which affected local earnings differentials both directly (e.g. via decisions on wage rates) and indirectly (e.g. via taxation). Again, the concept of a 'just' differential was at the centre of policy.

The new policy of 'take the lead in getting rich' had the most dramatic impact in agriculture. After years of 'serve the people' and 'studying Dazhai' it suddenly became legitimate to seek profits and earn high incomes. The appearance of a group of relatively rich '10,000 yuan' households was taken by many foreign observers as an indication that 'capitalism' had been 'restored' in the Chinese countryside. In fact, this was far from the case. The most striking aspect of the change in rural income distribution was the great increase in the range of regional incomes. It is true that the permitted range of intravillage income differentials widened considerably, but important influences limited their extent. First and foremost was the egalitarian land distribution under the contract system. Second, a wide range of collective services to which poor households had access still operated in most of rural China. Third, the huge expansion of employment in the rural non-farm labour-intensive sector in the 1980s tended to benefit a wide range of villagers in a given area. These same factors helped control income differentials in Taiwan in the 1960s and 1970s. The main source of exceptionally high rural incomes was the private non-farm sector. However, purely private non-farm rural enterprises (as opposed to collective non-farm assets contracted out under various arrangements) still accounted for a small share of the rural non-farm output. Moreover, although tax collection from this sector was far from perfect, the sector was subject to steep progressive taxation.

Large changes in China's income distribution occurred in the 1980s, but although people's positions in the income structure altered and the range of incomes widened, the overall inequality in income distribution was still low compared with other developing countries of similar size and income level. This is not surprising when the range of state influences upon that distribution is taken into consideration. Far from having moved towards free-market principles of income determination, China in the late 1980s was striking in the degree to which state action still limited income inequality. It is possible that permitting greater income inequality (especially at the inter- and intra-industrial enterprise level) than existed in China in the late 1980s could stimulate growth. However, it is essential that such additional income relates to an extra economic contribution and not to exploitation of loopholes in the half-reformed economy. A considerable part of the highest incomes in China in the late 1980s derived from the latter source, reducing the popular confidence in the reforms.

The socialist characteristics of the post-Mao Chinese state were evident not only in its continued concern with 'justice' (*gong ping*) in income distribution, but also with its desire to provide for the basic needs of the poorest people. This was reflected in the relatively high level of state provision of education and health facilities. It was also reflected in many of the difficulties that the state faced in trying to reform the price structure and dismantle the system of direct state allocation of items of consumption. The state was moving only slowly towards bringing the price of housing, personal transport, domestic power and food into closer line with costs (whether they should fully cover costs in all cases is, anyway, highly debatable). Most urban housing was still administratively allocated. A large part of urban grain supply was rationed (as well as some other food items), and price control over food supplies was still important. This partly reflected continued political pressure from the urban population as a whole, but it also reflected the continued concern of the state with guaranteeing 'basic needs'. Although crude, the surest way to do this is to guarantee supplies to the whole population, although this is far from ideal (a targeted programme would be more suitable). In the countryside also, the 'basic needs' philosophy was still reflected in the system of grain supply to poor or disaster-struck areas and in the continuation over much of rural China of collective support for locally poor households.

# Conclusion

It is possible to visualize a feasible form of market socialism for China in the 1990s. It is necessary to continue to move away from Stalinist administrativie planning in order to achieve an acceptable long-term pace of growth of output and living standards. However, the desired economic growth cannot be provided by free markets or simply by market regulation via indirect levers such as interest rates, taxes and subsidies, important as these are in guiding the economy. Indeed, a great deal of direct state action is necessary at China's current stage of development to supplement for the many different ways in which markets do, and are likely to, fail as market forces grow. China has much to learn in these respects from East Asian 'developmental states'. Countries which grow fast are those which have devised sensitive institutional solutions to market failure. This requires something different from the Stalinist approach. Open-mindedness and flexibility are the key. Rigid adherence to certain formulae (whether state, private or cooperative ownership, whether large or small scale) is likely to cause problems, since the degree of market failure with respect to growth is likely to be different in different countries and at different stages of development.

However, improving the quality of life for the whole population of a given country is about more than the attainment of fast and efficient growth of output and average living standards, vital as these are. China's experience under Mao demonstrated the dangers of a static redistributive approach towards poverty resolution and the damage to growth that can result from ultra-egalitarianism. However, because ultra-egalitarianism caused great difficulties does not mean that its obverse is desirable. There is no reason in principle why China cannot improve her already relatively advanced system of provision of the 'basic needs' of human self-realization to all her people in a way that is compatible with the maintenance of incentives.

Some elements of a market socialist system began to be put in place in the 1980s as China moved away from the Stalinist command economy, to which system it seems unlikely that it will return. However, strong elements of the Stalinist economy still remained in the late 1980s. Moreover, no clear model of the new system had been provided to the Chinese people, suggesting considerable uncertainty among the leadership. Politics is essential to the outcome of the reform process. Some argue that without political democracy China's economic reforms will not succeed, nor, they argue, if they did succeed, could China be called a socialist country. Neither of these propositions is correct. It is possible that continued tight political control might be compatible with continued economic reform. Indeed, in China, it may even be a condition of such progress. All socialist goals cannot be achieved simultaneously in a poor country. Attempting to do so may prevent the successful achievement of any of them. The main goal for China in the 1990s is to devise a set of institutions and policies which achieves reasonable growth of output and living standards, and enables all its citizens to move out of poverty, albeit at different rates. The achievement of political democracy is a less important goal for most Chinese people at present, and one which, anyway, is extremely difficult to attain in a mainly peasant low-income country. Moreover, by the late 1980s the economic reform, especially the reform of large-scale state enterprises and agricultural prices, had already involved great social tension, with some social groups gaining more than others, sometimes at the expense of these latter groups, and would result in further tension in the future. Immediate granting of full democratic rights might produce uncontrollable social upheaval, with no benefit to the mass of the population. Moreover, a great advance in democracy might reduce the autonomy of the state, increasing the impact of the groups best able to take advantage of political rights, notably urban workers, bureaucrats and intellectuals, at the expense of less well-placed groups, notably peasants. Under these circumstances, such key reforms as a hard budget constraint on state enterprises, removing subsidies on urban foodstuffs, shifting relative prices in favour of agriculture and controlling growth of the money supply might all be more difficult to accomplish.

The second main political issue in the reforms is the question of whether China's vast Party and bureaucracy can be transformed into a genuinely 'developmental state', intervening only where it is necessary to meet social goals, and being pragmatically prepared to work through the market where that produces the best results and to withdraw if the goal of intervention has been accomplished. This is a huge change from the present situation, in which administrators feel that they have the right to intervene directly in almost any economic activity. This form of political reform is, indeed, essential. With respect to the relationship of the Party and bureaucracy to the economy, China's reform may end up anywhere on a continuum from post-Independence India to Hong Kong under British rule. China has to contend with 2,000 years of bureaucratic rule as well as 40 years of Stalinist administration superimposed upon that. However, there have been periods in China's history, usually early in the life of a new dynasty under the impact of the shock of the collapse of the preceding ones, when the bureaucracy worked uncorruptly and effectively. Moreover, the 'development states' of Taiwan and Singapore came from fundamentally the same Chinese tradition. Will the 1980s come to be seen as the dawn of a new Golden Age for China, analogous to that of the early Qing (1644–1911) emperors Kang Xi and Qian Long, with capable leaders and effective administrators, backed by able advisors, running a form of market socialism which inspires other large Third World countries in the post-Stalinist epoch and lays the foundation for a high-income democratic socialism? Will the 1980s be seen instead as a time of enormous short-term gains from the release of the system from the inefficiencies of Stalinism, but a false down, being merely the prelude to slow long-term growth and market muddle as self-seeking bureaucrats and an authoritarian Party ensure that neither plan nor market works well? Or will the 1980s be viewed as a temporary resting place for the Chinese economy in its transition out of Stalinism to unconstrained capitalism alongside the collapse of both the Party and effective planning? One can only pose the questions and hope that the answer is the first one.

# Part II

## Aspects of the Reforms

# 7

# Prices

## Tian Yuan

Price reform is an important part of China's economic reform, and the changes resulting from it have affected almost all aspects of economic life. No other aspect of the reform has attracted more attention.

## The rationalization of prices is a prerequisite for efficient resource allocation

The optimal allocation of resources in a socialist economy, and the role of prices in this process, have been among the main topics in the historic 'debate on socialism'. The Western scholar Von Mises, who initiated the debate, considered that private ownership of the means of production was essential for rational resource allocation because, he argued, a rational price structure cannot exist in a socialist economy. Two other distinguished Western scholars, Hayek and Robbins, took Von Mises' view a step further: while not denying the theoretical possibility of rational resource allocation under socialism, they doubted that this question could be satisfactorily solved in practice. They argued that equilibrium in a socialist economy requires calculations of such complexity that by the time they were complete the information on which they were based would be out of date. Therefore it is a practical impossibility to achieve rational distribution of resources by means of rational prices.

In answer to this, Lange put forward the theory of 'simulating the market'. He admitted that the key to rational resource allocation is rational prices and searched for a method of achieving this. In his economic model he assumes that a market for consumer goods and labour services exists, but there is no market in productive resources, and so the method of planned government regulation is employed. He considered that in this typical model of a socialist economy equilibrium can be achieved if the state demands that enterprise managers make decisions according to rational prices and observe two rules. First they must select combinations of factors of production which minimize average cost and ensure that the marginal productivity of all factors of production is equal; second they must decide the level of production using the principle that the price of a product is equal to its marginal cost. If these two rules are adhered to, the mechanism for resource allocation in both publicly owned enterprises and enterprises operating in a system of free competition will tend to be the same. The objective condition for equilibrium is a rational price system which equalizes supply and demand. Lange considered this to be very important, since only when the prices of factors of production and products are known in advance can production be arranged so as to employ the least-cost combination of factors of production, and marginal costs to equal the price of the commodity. If these prices are determined arbitrarily, managers cannot select resources properly and are consequently unable to achieve rational resource allocation.

Lange also expounded the theoretical possibility of achieving the rationalization of prices through 'repeated adjustment' (or trial and error). He considered that, in both market and socialist economies, in general only one set of prices can satisfy the objective conditions for equilibrium and balance supply and demand for every commodity. He envisaged the possibility of a socialist economy using trial and error to determine prices, just like a competitive market. The central planning authority starts by randomly selecing a set of prices which enterprises use as a basis for decision-making, according to which the supply and demand for each commodity is determined. If the demand for a particular product does not match supply, the price has to be revised – increased when demand exceeds supply and vice versa. The planning authority thereby determines a new set of prices, which are then implemented and lead to a new set of supply and demand figures. A final set of prices is eventually arrived at through this experimental process. In Lange's view such a system does not require the central planning authority to solve countless equations, but only those relating to the consumer and the factory manager, one seeking to maximize utility from income and the other to achieve the least-cost combination of factors of production and a level of production which allows marginal cost to coincide with price. These equations are the same in capitalist and socialist economies.

Lange's theory was the first to link the problem of prices with rational resource allocation in a socialist economy, and to show that rational prices are necessary both for correct decision-making in enterprises and for a rational industrial structure. Long experience in the socialist economies has shown that irrational prices lead to an inefficient combination of factors of production, to the irrational use and waste of scarce underpriced resources, and simultaneously to long-term overstocking of large quantities of low-priced commodities, also resulting in the waste of resources. If prices are not rationalized, then socialist economies will not achieve rational resource allocation.

For a long period before 1978, prices in China were wholly or partially frozen. The state repudiated price adjustment through market simulation. In a constantly changing economic situation, this allowed the price system to sink gradually into a state of general imbalance, with underpricing of agricultural products, energy and raw materials, and overpricing in the processing industries. This led to a worsening of resource allocation and a large imbalance in the economic structure. In agriculture, underpricing meant that peasants were unable to maintain expanded reproduction. The extremely irrational economic system in the villages led to a critical state of agricultural backwardness; the production of 800 million peasants could not meet the needs of the country, and large quantities of grain had to be imported annually. In industry, underpricing of energy and raw materials increased demand and held back supply, leading to serious shortages. In the service sector, undercharging in transport, housing, education, medical and childcare did not stimulate development, which led to serious and widespread problems in all large cities in service supply, including laundry facilities, hairdressing and restaurants, as well as housing and transport. The irrational price system desperately needed reform, and price reform was a precondition for rationalizing resource allocation post-1979.

## The progress and effects of price reform

Discussion and implementation of price reform began in 1978, and passed through two stages. In the first, from 1978 to 1984, the government used the method of 'simulating the market', i.e. state pricing departments raised the prices of commodities for which demand exceeded supply and vice versa. This led to a trend towards balanced planned prices for some commodities, including particularly large increases in the purchase price of agricultural and sideline products and the selling prices of eight non-staple foodstuffs and products and of cotton cloth; the prices of synthetic cloth, watches, radios and so on were reduced. The second stage began in 1985. Not only was the method of 'simulating the market' used, with the government adjusting the prices of commodities with disequilibrium in supply and demand, but in addition – and this went further than the Lange model – market forces were allowed to intervene in price formation of the means of production. In different ways and to varying degrees the prices of certain means of production were deregulated, creating a new system in which the prices of production within the plan are fixed (low) by the state, while prices for the same product outside the plan are determined, usually at a high level, by market forces.

The main aspects of the progress of price reform, and its effects, can be summarized as follows.

### General trend towards equilibrium in price structure although with major exceptions in some sectors

In Lange's model, rationalization of prices is taken to mean the trend in irrational prices towards equilibrium. This trend can be seen in China's price reform overall. However, because only trial-and-error methods can be used, it is impossible to calculate the equilibrium price of each commodity. No method has yet been worked out to determine the appropriate degree of price rationalization in a given period. The trend towards price equilibrium is shown by the fact that in sectors where prices are low the tax rate on profits from capital funds tends to rise, and vice versa. The divergence of the national average of the tax on profits from capital funds from that of a given sector of the economy (i.e. the weighted average of the divergences, or the coefficient of variation) can be used to approximate the extent of the trend towards equilibrium in the price system. Analysis of the data for 27 sectors (excluding agriculture) gave the following results.

Firstly, in the process of price reform, the influence of a very small number of industries causes the level of disequilibrium in the price system as a whole to increase. However, if we exclude certain industries subject to planning in which there is serious underpricing or in which a deficit is tolerated as a matter of policy, then there is a distinct trend towards equilibrium. In 1978 the overall coefficient of variation between the tax rate on profits from capital funds and the average was 110.98 per cent; in 1985 it was 133.94 per cent. If five major sectors in which a deficit is tolerated (i.e. coal, supply and marketing, foreign trade, grain and the military industry) are excluded, it is clear that there has been some reduction in the level of price distortion. Again, taking the average tax rate on profits as the criterion and excluding the five sectors mentioned, the overall coefficient of variation in 1978 was 92.04 per cent and that in 1983 was 70.82 per cent. Sixteen of the industries had a coefficient of variation of 92.49 per cent in 1978 and 80.75 per cent in 1985. If the coal industry and machine-building industry (except for no. 1 branch) are excluded, then the coefficient of variation fell from 74.91 per cent in 1978 to 65.37 per cent in 1985.

Secondly, the trend in tax rate on profits from capital funds in the majority of sectors is towards equilibrium. There has been some improvement in underpricing in transport, energy supply and raw materials, and in overpricing in the processing industry, but the problem has not been fundamentally solved. In 1978 there was serious underpricing in transport, post and telecommunications, raw materials and energy (mainly coal), but by 1985, after price reform, apart from the underpricing which still existed in the planned sector of the coal industry, prices and the tax rate in the other three sectors were raised, while the tax rate in the processing industries, such as textiles and light industry, tended towards the national average level. However, the fact that prices and the tax rate on profit are too high in processing industries but are too low in energy, raw materials and transport is still a problem. The rank order of profitability for 1985 shows the processing industries such as the automobile industry, petrochemicals, light industry, pharmaceuticals and the engineering industry at the top, while energy and primary product industries, such as coal, electricity, forestry, posts and telecommunications, and non-ferrous metals, remain low.

## The growth of a market economy

China's economic reforms are intended to create a system in which planning regulates the market and the market guides enterprises. The creation of markets is an integral part of economic reform. Achieving this requires the removal of both the restraints imposed by mandatory planning over most products and the planning control over prices, as well as a reduction of direct price administration by the government. Since 1978 there has been important progress in this direction. Whereas in 1978 the prices of 92.4 per cent of agricultural products sold by farmers were fixed by the state, by 1986 this figure had fallen to 37 per cent. Goods whose prices were state guided or market regulated amounted to only 7.6 per cent in 1978, but rose to 63 per cent by 1986 (23 per cent state guided and 40 per cent market regulated). The proportion of principal means of production sold at prices fixed by the state decreased from almost 100 per cent to 64 per cent (23 per cent cent state guided and 13 per cent market regulated). In industrial consumer goods in 1986, 50 per cent of prices were fixed by the state, 23 per cent were state guided and 32 per cent were market regulated. These figures are not entirely accurate, mainly because a certain number of products, after being removed from state pricing control, were then controlled at various levels of local government, and market pricing did not develop. This is a problem in price reform which remains to be solved.

## The trend towards rationalization of the regional distribution of economic benefits

Price irrationality reflects irrationality in the regional distribution of economic benefits, and so price reform is also concerned with this problem. The extreme complexity of regional commodity exchange makes detailed statistical analysis of price movements virtually impossible, but we have used the 1984–5 figures at constant and current prices for all provinces and cities to obtain some kind of representation of the changes in the structure of economic benefits caused by price reform. In industry during 1984–5 the ratio of net revenue from price increases to net output value was higher in Central China than in West China, which in turn was higher than in East China. The reason for this shift in regional economic benefits lies in differences in economic structure and the adjustment of the price structure; because of price increases in energy and raw materials in the eastern region, where manufacturing and processing industries predominate, there was a relative decrease in revenue, while the central and western regions, where energy, raw materials and basic industries predominate, experienced a relative increase in revenue. In agriculture the regional distribution of increased revenue attributable to price rises was extremely uneven. Net income from price increases, after substracting increased material consumption attributable to increased prices, as a proportion of net output value in order of decreasing magnitude shows East China far higher than Central China, and Central China markedly higher than West China. This was mainly due to the fact that price indices for economically developed East China rose faster for the other two.

## Improved resource allocation

The reform has produced some reduction in price distortion and much improvement in resource allocation, which is reflected particularly in the increased investment in primary industries. Thirty thousand new industrial enterprises, including 810 in metallurgy, 642 in non-ferrous metals, 5,086 in chemical industries and 4,144 in construction materials, were set up in China in 1986. Capital construction investment increased by 11.4 per cent in metallurgical industries, by 50.5 per cent in chemical industries and by 64.2 per cent in building materials. In 1986 the volume of investment in raw materials and energy steadily increased from 14.7 to 15.9 per cent of total capital construction investment for the former and from 21.5 to 21.8 per cent for the latter. Investment in replacement and renewal in metallurgy, chemical industries, construction materials, non-ferrous metals and petrochemicals was 41.2 per cent higher than in the previous year. In recent years the main raw materials steel, sulphuric acid and cement increased production by 9.8 per cent per annum, 11 per cent and 10.7 per cent respectively. Generation of electricity increased by 9.4 per cent per annum. This is evidence that, in the macroeconomic sphere, the allocation of resources is becoming more rational.

The analysis of these four aspects of the economy shows that important advances have been made in price reform, which have improved resource allocation and promoted economic reform and development. Nevertheless, some urgent questions still await solution.

## Reasons for stagnation in the price reform movement

Between 1978 and 1984 price reform was mainly concerned with the purchase and selling prices of agricultural and sideline products, and had a considerable influence on improving agricultural resource allocation. In October 1984, after the Central Committee's 'Resolution on the reform of the economic system', the focus of reform shifted from the countryside to the towns, where price reform was very necessary for industrial products which were themselves means of production. However, events did not follow a logical course. In 1985 the centre of attention was still agricultural goods and nothing had been done about the prices of industrial products, other than deregulation of prices in the sector not subject to planning and recognition of the legality of the dual-track price system. In 1986 economic reform in general marked time in preparation for the promotion, the following year, of a comprehensive set of reforms in prices, taxes and finance centred on price reform for means of production. For this purpose the government assembled a large number of researchers, created a large planning group, organized nationwide study and soundings, and drew up a wide-ranging plan for adjusting the prices of means of production. However, since evidence which showed that enterprises lacked the ability to 'digest' or tolerate price rises came from all sides and because of unexpected financial difficulties at the time, price reform of means of production was abandoned completely and replaced by the responsibility system designed to 'invigorate' enterprises.

Why did reform falter at the hurdle of price reform for means of production? The main reason was that the macroeconomic situation was unfavourable. The state was unable to control demand, and this led to the excessive issue of money and to inflation. This increased the difficulty of implementing price reform. Moreover, while plans for economic reform were being studied, deficiencies in the guiding ideas about price reform made its realization more difficult. Too narrow a view was taken of the function of price reform, which was not recognized as the key to rational resource allocation but only as a means of 'forming markets'. Subsequently, the discovery that price adjustment and deregulation had failed to create the desired markets led to a tendency to underestimate the importance of price reform, and particularly of the government's basic method of simulating the market – regulation of the price system. This was the result of an essential misunderstanding of the significance of price reform in a pluralistic economy. In the last analysis, reform of the price system does not serve the intermediate aim of economic reform – the creation of markets – but directly promotes the goal of economic reform as a whole, i.e. improved resource allocation. This requires that prices move rapidly towards a level which equates supply and demand.

The negative, even obstructive, influence which these factors have had on price reform of means of production should not be exaggerated, since even without them price reform could not have been achieved at a stroke and might well have been bogged down. The real obstacle to price reform is not one of subjective understanding, but is inherent in the existing economic system itself; this is clear from the inability of enterprises to accept the tendency for prices of means of production to rise and the financial difficulties which accompany it.

The crucial step in price reform of means of production is to increase the prices of energy, raw materials, electricity, communications and transport. Although no major adjustment of prices was made in 1985, the mere deregulation of prices of productive resources in the relatively small sector outside the plan resulted in a rise of 11.25 per cent in the price index for heavy industrial products. The price of 182 out of 414 major heavy industrial products rose by more than 10 per cent, including 37 products with a price index of over 30 per cent, such as timber (35.28 per cent), firebricks (35.26 per cent), pig-iron (30.67 per cent), ordinary carbon steel and cast steel (42.33 per cent), and high-quality cast steel (34 per cent). Prices of 351 out of 414 products rose, sometimes by as much as 84.8 per cent, including raw materials where the price inflation was 89 per cent. The rise in prices of industrial means of production led to widespread increases in the cost of production. In Jiangsu province the increase was 8.86 per cent in 1985 and 9.63 per cent in 1986, of which 5.3 per cent and 5.33 per cent respectively were due to increased expenditure to meet the higher prices of raw materials, which represented 50 per cent and 55 per cent of the increased cost of production in those two years. According to investigations made by the Jiangsu Provincial Finance Department, of 1973 processing enterprises in the province, increased outlays due to higher prices were 74 per cent in metallurgical raw materials, 17.8 per cent in electricity and 8.2 per cent in dyestuffs.

The rising prices for industrial means of production and the resulting increases in production costs put pressure upon enterprises. The central government called on them to offset the influence of such price rises by increasing efficiency and reducing costs. This hope has not been realized: enterprises faced with rising prices of inputs have usually been unwilling to compromise the interests of their staff and workers by reducing welfare and bonus funds. Instead they have used two means of counteracting the effects of rising input prices. Firstly, they have increased the prices of their own products, thereby transferring the burden to other enterprises. In 1985, for instance, local industry in Jiangsu, by reducing consumption and expenses, absorbed the effects of price increases to the tune of 453 million yuan and earned 511 million yuan from increased production and 1,675 million yuan from transferring the burden in the form of increased prices. Prices of goods leaving factories rose by an average of 6.32 per cent, giving rise to spiralling price inflation. Secondly, they have transferred the effects of inflation to public finance departments. In the present system of financial and enterprise management, enterprises and local government departments form a common interest bloc. Consequently, when enterprises are unable to tolerate the effects of price inflation, they seek help from local government in the form of reduced taxes, interest concessions and even subsidies. The system of dividing revenue between central and local governments also facilitates the transfer of the burden of price inflation to central government through a reduction or change in the ratio of remittances to central finance departments. Passed on in this way, the burden of price inflation affects national finance in a chain reaction: the more price reform unfolds, the greater is the pressure upon enterprises and the more state financial revenue is decreased. Not only does central government suffer a reduction in its revenue as a result of its own price reform measures, it also has to bear the political hazards involved in the reform. In this situation price reform of the means of production cannot make much headway.

The root cause of the faltering in a much-needed reform does not lie in the low capacity of enterprises to tolerate the effects of price inflation, but in the fact that price reform is in direct conflict with the current ownership system. During the development of a commodity economy all countries experience price fluctuations, and even large-scale price inflation is by no means uncommon. For instance, during the world energy crisis in 1973 the price of oil increased tenfold in three years and many enterprises came under severe pressure; their tolerance, as world experience has shown, was due to the use of their owners' assets. The result of the price fluctuations was a whole series of closures, bankruptcies or mergers; these were means of using assets to mitigate the effects of price inflation in a way common in a commodity economy. The precondition for the realization of wide-ranging price adjustment, as well as its results, is the reorganization of the ownership structure.

The demand made during the reform that enterprises in China should internally offset the effects of price inflation reflected the hopes of the government. It meant in practice that enterprises should only sparingly use increased revenue to make up for the effects of considerable price inflation; instead, they should make sacrifices in the interests of society as a whole by reducing collective benefits such as bonuses and development funds. Under the present economic system in China this is very difficult to achieve, because enterprises are unwilling and unable to act in this way. Because of their lack of economic tolerance, well-managed enterprises usually increase prices under conditions of expanding demand in order to reduce pressure on themselves, while badly run enterprises shift the burden on to public finance departments.

Two conclusions emerge from this analysis. Tolerance of price inflation may come from revenue increment or from the stock of assets. The latter is by far the more effective and is much more likely to be able to sustain the pressure of price increases. In Shanghai, for example, the burden of annual price inflation in 1985 and 1986 was only 1,300–1,400 million yuan. After deducting the revenue for increased prices of Shanghai products, it has been estimated that the annual burden of price reform did not exceed 1,000 million yuan, yet Shanghai bitterly complained of an intolerable charge. The crux of the matter is that under the present system of ownership it is not possible to absorb the effects of price inflation through the structure of the stock of assets, so that the whole weight of inflation is borne by revenue increments. This directly threatens the interests of staff and workers in enterprises and inevitably arouses opposition to price reform. If conditions could be created by structural reform whereby the effects could be borne by the stock of assets, then Shanghai, with assets of the order of 100,000 million yuan, could easily have absorbed the effects of price inflation equal to no more than 1 per cent of its capital and price reform would not have become bogged down.

The transformation of economic tolerance is the key to the success of China's price reform. This is not a financial question: it is a matter of radically reforming the present ownership and management system, and the existing mechanisms of public ownership. Such reforms must be carefully studied and planned, and closely related to price reform, so that the reform of the whole economic system can be speeded up.

## A new system of public ownership

The experience of socialist economic systems to date has confirmed Lange's views on the determination of equilibrium prices and the achievement of rational resource allocation by ensuring that enterprises select combinations of factors of production which minimize average cost and equate prices with marginal cost. Experience of price reform in China, and indeed of economic reform in general, has shown that it is necessary for the government to attempt to simulate the market. This tends to encourage price equalization and optimizing behaviour by enterprises, regardless of the government's price operations and management directives. Successful simulation of the market requires a rational economic system.

This cannot be a centralized economic system. Although government manipulation of prices is relatively easy in such a system, even if equilibrium prices are set, the planners have no means of ensuring that enterprises select factors of production which minimize average cost and equate price with marginal cost. Nor can such a system be one in which the state controls property rights, while enterprises have only management and operation rights. The reason why price reform has baulked at the hurdle of means of production, causing virtual inertia in the government's market simulation operations, is that enterprises which only possess operation rights cannot tolerate the burden imposed by price fluctuations. This causes spiralling price inflation and financial difficulties for the state. To avoid this, to find a means whereby enterprises bear the risks of price reform, to alleviate the government's difficulties in price operations and to create a mechanism to constrain enterprises to optimize allocation of factors of production, it is essential to reform the ownership system.

In a socialist economy reform of the ownership system cannot mean substituting private for public ownership. Instead, it must involve changing the operating mechanism of publicly owned assets. To do this we must discover the general laws of efficient asset allocation in a commodity economy by examining capitalist economic operation. In capitalist countries, apart from private ownership of assets, there are three important laws of asset operation. The first is competition in the management of assets, with assets growing or shrinking in a 'survival of the fittest' process. The second is the ease with which assets are converted from one form to another. Material assets (factories, land etc.) can be changed into monetary assets (shares, bonds, money, etc.) and vice versa. The third is the control and supervision of operators by asset owners. These are the fundamental conditions for the efficient use of assets – for ensuring that the combination of factors of production of lowest average cost are selected and that price equals marginal cost. These three laws are the necessary precondition for rational resource allocation in a capitalist economy and in a society where private property exists. If any one of them is absent, efficient resource allocation cannot be achieved.

We need to study how to apply the laws of asset movement in a capitalist economy to a socialist economy in which the system of public ownership is to be maintained. In a socialist economy it is not only necessary to simulate the market, but also to 'simulate capital' and to establish a new kind of ownership system with the following characteristics.

1 Unified public ownership should give way to pluralistic public ownership, including ownership by all levels of government – central, provincial, municipal and county.

2 Many different forms of asset management companies (including investment companies, foundations, insurance companies and so on) should be established. Central, provincial and local governments vested with public ownership rights should have the right to assess the returns from assets, to allocate income and to appoint managers. Apart from this they should leave the right of management entirely to the organization in question, i.e. the rights and duties with respect to indebtedness should belong to the operating organizations themselves. These organizations should operate entirely as enterprises responsible for their own profit and loss, with equal rights under the law and with no administrative subordinacy. Their fundamental task should be to increase the value of their assets, and their basic management operation should be to carry out investment policy decisions (including setting up new enterprises, the purchase of bonds and shares issued by the state or other companies, the purchase and sale of enterprises etc.). They should also bear the risks of investment, participate in major management decisions by dependent enterprises, distribution decisions, the appointment of managers and so on.

3 A competitive asset management market should be established in which such organizations and enterprises compete and in which the principle of survival of the fittest is reflected in the constant adjustment of the asset structure. The assets of some poorly managed companies will gradually shrink, while those of others will grow. The market may function through shareholding (i.e. management of assets through the share system), or by a non-share system (i.e. creating enterprises by direct investment or by the buying and selling of enterprises).

4 Revenue from asset management should be distributed by local governments and assets management organizations according to the public interest and needs.

If China's economic system moved towards a system of 'simulating capital', the main problem of bearing the risks of price reform and other economic measures could be solved. The adjustment of benefits brought by price reform would no longer put pressure on incremental revenue or on the interests of staff and workers in enterprises, but would take the form of adjustment of the asset structure with growth or shrinkage of assets in various companies. The mechanism for economic tolerance of price reform pressure by means of asset holding could function effectively. Obstruction of price reform would be correspondingly reduced and the government's ability to influence prices would be increased. Moreover, in the process of economic development, the competitive asset management system and the many asset management corporations would effectively constrain enterprise managers and ensure that a least-cost combination of factors of production was selected and that prices equalled marginal cost.

The establishment of a new system of public asset management and of property rights is a precondition for a more thorough price reform, and indeed for reform of the economic system in general. The possibility of this kind of reform has already been confirmed with the recent emergence of investment companies with publicly owned capital. However, the reform of the whole system of property rights, making publicly owned assets effectively simulate the movement of capital, is a far more complex question which requires specific study and research.

# 8

# Enterprise Reform

## Jiang Yiwei

The focal point of Chinese economic reform was initially in the country-side. Reform in the urban areas, where the economic system was far more complex and there was much debate about strategy, began in 1979. Some wanted to start with reform of the planning structure, and others with enterprise reform. In two papers published at that time (Jiang 1979, 1980a) I attempted a theoretical explanation of the relationship between enterprise reform and reform of the overall economic system. Enterprises are the cells of the national economy and only if they are revitalized can the rigid musculature be transformed; they are where the social forces of production operate, and are the direct expression of the relations of production and the basis of the whole economy. In line with the Marxist theory of the economic base determining the superstructure, the reform of the economic system must be firmly based in the enterprises and macroeconomic management must start from the premise that they are living cells. These ideas were generally welcomed by those working in enterprises, but they caused much controversy in government economic organizations and amongst theoreticians. Whether reform should begin at the microeconomic or the macroeconomic level was much disputed in the first years of reform. Not until the Third Plenum of the 12th Congress in 1984, when it was clearly stated that the central link of reform of the whole economic system is the revitalization of enterprises, was the debate concluded.

Despite the controversy, for the last nine years urban economic reform has in fact centred on reform of enterprises. The series of measures taken to revitalize enterprises has met with considerable success – enterprises are more autonomous than they were and economic results are better – but reform is still incomplete. Many fundamental questions about socialist institutions are involved, and these need to be resolved in order to create a new model of socialism. This is a complicated task, which will be achieved gradually in the process of reform. In this chapter I discuss some of the main problems which have arisen and present some personal views.

# Defining the nature and status of enterprises

The ultimate purpose of economic reform is liberation of the productive forces through reform of inappropriate relations of production or elements of the superstructure which impede their growth.

The former system was characterized by a high degree of centralization. The whole of the national economy was directed by administrative commands from the state, which also directly managed enterprises. These became appendages of the state organs: their production was controlled by mandatory planning, materials and funds were allocated by the state, products were distributed by the state, and all profits went to the state which was also responsible for losses. Enterprises had no autonomy and needed none. This mode of operation was typical of the whole moribund system, and so from the outset urban reform was concerned to give enterprises more independence.

At the beginning of reform it was far from clear what sort of autonomy enterprises should have and how the rights and responsibilities of the state and enterprises should be defined. The answer depends on the nature and status of enterprises: are they government bodies or independent economic entities? I concluded (Jiang 1979) that, since our socialist economy is a commodity economy, socialist enterprises should be independent commodity producers. There was much discussion at the time as to whether a commodity economy was compatible with socialism, and my views on the nature of enterprises was one of the subjects of debate. Fortunately, the Third Plenum of the 12th Congress of the Party, after considering foreign and Chinese experience, came to the conclusion that China had a planned commodity economy with public ownership as its basis, and that enterprises should be socialist commodity producers which were self-managing, responsible for their own profit and loss, capable of reforming and developing on their own, and legal entities with defined rights and responsibilities. This was a great breakthrough – a development of Marxist theory which provided a theoretical basis for the reform of the whole economic system. It was a new concept of the nature and status of enterprises, which pointed the way for their overall reform.

Redefining enterprises as commodity producers was a basic change in their nature and the starting point for their reform. However, the practical application of this principle involved a whole series of questions, including that of ownership, the mode of operation, the system of labour distribution and the method of leadership, as well as reorganization and linkages. The reconstruction of these systems so that they match the laws of a commodity economy while retaining their socialist nature is the difficult task which enterprise reform has to face.

# Ownership

Urban reform started by increasing enterprises' autonomy of operation. It was not initially concerned with ownership, but as the reform progressed the ownership question became increasingly important.

First, as reform tackled the prejudice in favour of 'large scale and public ownership', individual and collective economies were allowed to grow, and private enterprise using hired labour appeared. A socialist economy with public ownership as its basis leaves room for the existence and expansion of a small measure of private ownership and private operation. How to deal appropriately with this sector has become an important problem. Secondly, forms of ownership in the public sector have changed considerably. In the traditional concept of socialism only two forms of public ownership were recognized: ownership by the whole people, and collective ownership (cooperative enterprises in which working people pool resources and labour). Collective ownership declined owing to the preference for 'large and public', but flourished after reform began. 'Large collective enterprises', in which assets are neither state owned nor raised collectively but are formed by self-accumulation over time, have existed for several years. In the past these 'large collectives' were virtually regarded as owned 'by the whole people' and were directly administered by the state. After reform started they increasingly became independent self-administered enterprises, responsible for their own profit and loss, and grew considerably. This is undoubtedly a form of public ownership, but no one quite knows how exactly its property rights should be defined. In fact this is a form of socialist enterprise ownership. Ownership of enterprises in the public sector is vested in the state, but their actual subordinacy takes different forms: some belong to departments of the central government, and others to local government. Their property rights are very unclear. In the process of reform, when enterprises become more horizontally linked and some encourage staff and workers to become shareholders or else sell shares to the public, the ownership structure is even more complicated. Thirdly, the question of ownership has become more complicated because the policy of opening up to the outside world and attracting foreign capital has led to the appearance of joint Sino–foreign and even purely foreign investment enterprises.

The 13th Congress of the Chinese Communist Party approved the resolution that China is in the primary stage of socialism. In this stage, although public ownership is the basis, the auxiliary role of the private sector is not rejected, which implies the adoption of a system in which different forms of ownership coexist. The question now is: is it necessary to implement reforms in the public ownership system itself in order to correct the long-term state of affairs in which no one is responsible for or cares about public property because property ownership relations are unclear? Two views are held about this question: one is that of the two forms of public ownership, 'ownership by the whole people' is the higher form and that anything that weakens it weakens socialism; others consider that public ownership can take many forms and that, as long as publicly owned assets are dominant, there is no fundamental weakening of socialism. I support the latter view (Jiang 1985).

In the primary stage of socialism it is necessary that public ownership should dominate the economy, but it should take different forms, including not only ownership by the whole people but also collective enterprise ownership (large collectives), cooperative ownership by staff and workers (small collectives) and mixtures of these two forms.

All forms of ownership apart from ownership by the whole people are pluralistic, and the rational handling of property relations demands the adoption of shareholding. If this is done, most shares in enterprises will be publicly owned and an appropriate proportion of private shares will not alter their nature as socialist enterprises. With this mixed private and public ownership, the socialist economy with public ownership as its main component cannot be measured by the number of enterprises but only by the proportion of assets in the country as a whole which are publicly owned. For this reason I strongly advocate a system of shareholding.

# Reform of operation and management

The problem of transforming enterprises (mainly those in the public sector) into autonomous economic entities responsible for their own profit and loss has been explored since the beginning of reform. The Third Plenum of the 11th Congress proposed achieving this by separating the functions of Party, government and enterprise, but the appropriate structures have yet to be established.

The resolution of the Third Plenum of the 12th Congress on the separation of operation rights from ownership opened the way to further autonomy in enterprises. The rationale of the old system was that ownership gave the right of management: therefore enterprises 'owned by the whole people' should naturally be run by the state. Now, applying the principle of separation of powers, enterprises in the public sector are adopting the following forms.

## The contract responsibility system

The contract responsibility system began in 1982. Lin Ling, Deputy Director of the Sichuan Academy of Social Sciences, and I recommended to the State Council the practice of the Capital Iron and Steel Company of handing in contracted profits and contracting of management and operation (Jiang 1982). The system was approved and extended to some large and medium enterprises, and resulted in better economic results. It did not spread further because of the implementation of tax reform, although it now appears that the contracting of operation and management is appropriate to the period of transition between the old and new systems and can effectively realize the latent capacity of enterprises. At present it takes several forms. In general, the department which controls an enterprise hands over its assets to be operated and managed by the contracting party, which may be an individual, a collective or the enterprise itself as a legal entity. A contract laying down the time limits within which the terms of the contract have to be met, including the handing in of profits, is signed. The contracting party is selected by tendering, i.e. by introducing market competition. After the contract is drawn up the government department concerned no longer interferes directly with the operation or management of the enterprise. This is the system most widely practised in large and medium enterprises.

## Leasing

The system of leasing is very effective for small enterprises and shops. After the assets of an enterprise have been checked and evaluated, a rent is fixed for individual or collective responsibility operation. Apart from the obligation to pay rent, the contractor is entirely free to run the enterprise as he sees fit.

## Shareholding

Several forms of shareholding have appeared since the beginning of enterprise reform. Whether this is compatible with socialism is a subject of much controversy. Some people consider that shareholding is a capitalist form of organization not suited to socialist enterprises, but most academics believe that it is the natural consequence of the development of the commodity economy and is suited to both capitalism and socialism. The 13th Congress supported this point of view and stated that the distribution of bonds or shares is a necessary attribute of large-scale socialized production and the commodity economy, and is not unique to capitalism. The Congress also concluded that the shareholding systems which had appeared during reform, including those in which the state held a controlling share or in which departments, local government, enterprises or individuals hold shares, are a socialist form of asset organization and experiments with them can continue.

Enterprises which employ shareholding are now flourishing; most of them take the form of 'limited companies' and issue shares to their own staff and workers but not to the public. However, some are 'limited stock companies' and can issue shares to the public. Experimental stock markets have been established in a few cities. For socialist enterprises to adopt a shareholding system makes for pluralism and identification of ownership, correcting the formerly prevalent situation in enterprises owned by the whole people in which no one cared about the property. It also normalizes the separation of management and ownership. The owners only have shareholders' rights and have no right to interfere with the running of the enterprise. Furthermore, the adoption of shareholding favours the linkage of enterprises and increases economies of scale. It has not yet become the main form of enterprise in China, but with the further development of the socialist commodity economy it is bound to do so, and the contract and leasing systems may well be absorbed by it.

## Reform of the distribution system

There are two questions here. First, how can the socialist principle of distribution according to work be applied to the income of staff and workers; second, in the distribution of benefits between the state and enterprises, how can it be ensured that the latter have the capacity to improve and develop independently.

Distribution of income according to work done is a basic principle of socialism; but for many years, while observing the principle in theory, Chinese enterprises have not practised a policy of 'the less you work the less you eat' but one of 'all eating out of the same pot'. The state regulates wages by a unified system which applies to enterprises across the board, regardless of performance; therefore enterprises 'all eat out of the same pot'. Moreover, within enterprises, apart from the differences in basic salary scales of staff and workers, labour efficiency has no effect on wages, i.e. 'all eat out of the same pot'.

Since reform started the bonus system has been restored, and this has been quite effective in realizing the principle of distribution according to work. However, the state has attempted to control the growth of this system by means of a bonus tax in order to constrain inflation of the consumption fund. In practice many specific problems remain and the 'big pot' has not been entirely eliminated. Fundamental reform of the wage system remains a major problem.

Since 1981 I have advocated that in a socialist economy income cannot be directly distributed to the individual according to work, but only by a 'two-tiered' distribution according to work (Jiang 1980b, c), i.e. distribution to the enterprise as a whole is dependent on its results whereas distribution to each individual within the enterprise itself is dependent on that individual's work. This proposal has given rise to considerable controversy in theoretical circles, but experiences has shown that it is inevitable. Since reform began, many enterprises have calculated the total wage bill according to output or according to the amount of wages in the net value of output; the total wages bill (including bonuses) varies with performance and is distributed to staff and workers within the enterprise according to work done. The Third Plenum of the 12th Congress made two points about reform of the wage system: first, the total wage fund and bonus funds of an enterprise should be related to its performance; second, wage differentials within enterprises should be appropriately increased, with a greater range of grades and full implementation of the principle of more pay for more work. This is, in effect, the principle of a 'two-tiered' distribution according to work. However, fundamental reform of the wages system is still under discussion.

Rationalization of enterprises requires that they be given autonomy. In the early stages of reform the autonomy of enterprises was increased and they were allowed to return a proportion of profits, most of which was put aside for technical improvement; this gave enterprises greater vitality. This was followed by the implementation of 'tax instead of handing over profits' which meant that enterprises could retain all their profits after tax. However, the tax was rather high and the amount retained was usually very limited, and so many enterprises had difficulty in financing their own expansion. Further separation of profit from tax is needed, with tax paid to the state as a matter of duty, while profit is determined by contract, lease or shareholding and suitably distributed between owners and enterprises. As long as state revenue is not diminished, enterprises should be allowed to increase by their own efforts the amount of profits that they retain, and so increase their enthusiasm for production.

## Reform of the labour system

In state-owned enterprises under the old system, staff and workers were employed and allocated to enterprises by the state. They then had 'iron rice bowls' with complete security of employment, and the state or the enterprise decided any subsequent move. They had no choice of trade, nor could enterprises really chose their own staff and workers. This labour system was very detrimental to the motivation of both the enterprise and the workers. This has now been replaced by a contract system, in which newly employed staff and workers enter into contracts with the enterprises. In this way both sides are given a choice, and a labour market has been created which encourages the national mobility of labour. There is a rational side to these reforms and the labour system has improved but many problems remain, especially those relating to the position of staff and workers as the masters of socialist enterprises.

I agree with some kind of contractual labour system, but I do not believe that the whole labour force should be under contract. Nor do I agree that contracts should be between the factory manager and the individual worker, because this is bound to lead to a hiring relationship which will undermine the position of workers as masters of their enterprises, and these will therefore lose their socialist characteristics (Jiang 1984, 1987a). The contract system should be replaced by a 'joint pledge by staff and workers'; if newly employed staff and workers are to enter into contracts, they should be between individuals and the labour collective, which should be the socialist enterprise itself.

# Reform of leadership

For a long time Chinese enterprises were run by a factory director under Party Committee leadership together with a committee of staff and workers. The Party organization became the highest organ of power, creating a situation in which the functions of Party and government were not separated, but power was separated from responsibility. The Party secretary had power but no responsibility; the director had responsibility but no power. The status of the committee of staff and workers was very unclear, and often it existed only in name. This system was entirely unsuited to the objective needs of large-scale socialist production and the commodity economy, and in 1980 research began into the reform of leadership. Regulations concerning the functions of the committee of staff and workers, and the work of directors and grass-roots Party organizations were drawn up. However, the problem of the division of labour between Party and government is still not completely solved.

The Third Plenum of the 12th Congress emphasized the need for a strong unified, efficient production command and administrative system, and pointed out that only the director responsibility system can meet these requirements. The main task of the Party organization in enterprises is to ensure the implementation of Party and state policies, to strengthen the Party's ideological and organizational work, and to undertake political work among staff and workers. In 1986 the Central Committee and the State Council promulgated three further sets of regulations and, while confirming the director responsibility system, clarified the functions of and relations between the Party, the government and the workers. At present these regulations are being implemented in state-owned enterprises throughout the country.

The long-standing problem of lack of separation between Party and government has therefore been solved, and this is, of course, an important development in leadership reform in Chinese enterprises. However, another major problem – the relationship between managers, staff and workers – has not yet been properly solved. In most cases, because it is the manager or director who is responsible or who is the lessee in the responsibility and leasing systems, disagreements between managers and workers have often occurred. This is also something which future reform will have to deal with.

For several years I have advocated the idea of 'staff and workers as the main body' (*zhigong wei zhuti lun*), which should be one of the main characteristics of a socialist enterprise. Staff and workers should be shareholders; apart from a small number of enterprises which will still have to be owned and run by the state, management rights should be handed over to the labour force as a collective, and should be based on democratic decision-making and a highly collective system of manager responsibility. I initially proposed these ideas in 1980, and have developed them over the past few years (Jiang 1980d, 1987b).

## Horizontal linkages

There are almost 500,000 industrial enterprises in China, of which 80,000 are large and medium sized. The majority are small. Even among the large and medium-sized enterprises, most are 'all-round' factories with a low level of specialization, which is a major reason for low efficiency in Chinese industry. Specialization and coordination are hindered by the subordinacy relations inherited from the old system. Every enterprise belongs to a department or to local government, so that they cannot establish coordination with each other, and each goes its own way. Whether large or small, each becomes an 'all-round' factory, there is little batch production and the economies of scale are small.

In 1979, when reform began, questions of reorganizing and combining enterprises were raised. However, as long as the old system had not undergone any fundamental changes, any measures of this type were invariably carried out by directive from the regulating department concerned for its own administrative convenience; enterprises were forced to merge or separate with no consideration for their actual needs. The number of management levels and the number of non-productive staff were usually increased, but not efficiency. Moreover, the increased autonomy which had been granted to enterprises was usually usurped by these new companies.

However, during the process of reform there have been several cases of enterprises voluntarily merging to form joint concerns, and they have been very successful. For instance the Dong Feng Joint Automobile Industrial Company was organized around the Hubei No. 2 Automobile Factory. Enterprises associated with it are found in 29 different provinces, cities and autonomous regions; they operate a division of labour and coordinate production of the Dong Feng range of automobile products, and the company has had considerable success (*Renmin Ribao*, 30 November 1984). Another example is the group based on the Chongqing Jialing Machine Factory, whose Jialing motorcycle has captured 50 per cent of the Chinese market.

In 1986 the State Council promulgated regulations concerning the promotion of horizontal combinations and emphasized that they must be voluntary and based on mutual interest; a time limit was also given for the abolition of administrative companies in which there was no separation between government and enterprise. This gradually put the reorganization and combination of enterprises on the right path.

The combination of enterprises in this way is a means of raising productivity and improving economic returns. The more successful mergers seem to pass through three stages which take them from loose cooperation to actual combination. In the first stage there is coordinated specialization of production, and in the second there is total combination of production (for instance, the Dong Feng Automobile Company practise total combination in production, supply and sales). In these two stages, the enterprises retain their independence and their subordinacy relationships are not altered. As reform has developed, a third higher stage of combination has appeared with the combination of capital as well as production. Most of these enterprises take the form of rather large shareholding companies or groups. A typical group of this kind – the China Jialing Stock Company – has now been formally established in Chongqing, which is a pilot city for reform. This is one of the national groups approved by the State Council, and other groups are preparing to adopt shareholding. We can expect some powerful stock-holding companies to appear in the near future and to become strong pillars of Chinese industry.

# References

Jiang Yiwei (1979) Qiye benweilun chuyi (Opinions on the 'enterprise selfishness philosophy'). *Jingji Guanli*, June, no. 6.
—— (1980a) Qiye benweilun (The philosophy of enterprise selfishness). *Zhongguo Shehui Kexue (Social Sciences in China)*, January, no. 1.
—— (1980b) Guanyu anlao fenpeide jige wenti (Some questions of distribution according to work). *Gongren Ribao*, 21 March.
—— (1980c) Shilun quanmian wuzhi liyi yuanze. *Renmin Ribao*, 14 July.
—— (1980d) Lu shehui zhuyi qiyede lingdao tizhi (On leadership in socialist enterprises). *Hong Qi*, no. 21.
—— (1985) Lun shehuizhuyide guodoxing (On the transitional nature of socialism). In *Shijie Jingji Daobao Chuangkan Wuzhounian Tekan (Fifth Anniversary Special Edition of World Economic Report)*, p. 81.
—— (1982) Cong Shoudu Gangtie Gongsi kan zhiti gaige (The Capital Iron and Steel Company and reform of the economic system). *Jingji Guanli*, July, no. 7.
—— (1984) Shixing zhengsi gong, hetonggong he linshigong xiangjiehede laodong zhidu. *Shijie Jingji Daobao*, 15 October.
—— (1987a) Guanyu laodong zhidude ruogan wentide tantao (On some questions concerning the labour system). *Jingji Guanli*, September, no. 9.
—— (1987b) Jianchi qiyede shehuizhuyi xingzhi, fayang zhigong dangjiazuozhude zhurenwen sixiang (Maintain the socialist character of enterprise and carry forward the spirit of staff and workers as masters of their enterprises). *Gongren Ribao*, 14 May.
*Renmin Ribao* (30 November 1984) Cong Dongfeng Qiche Gongye lianying gongsi kan yi gugan qiye wenzhongxin tuidong qiye ziyou lianhede daolu.

# 9

# The Stock Market in a Socialist Economy

## Ajit Singh

### Introduction

The General Secretary of the Chinese Communist Party, Zhao Ziyang, in his report to the 13th National Congress of the Chinese Party, made the following observations in relation to 'restructuring' the Chinese economy:

The reform we have already carried out includes the development of different types of ownership, public ownership remaining predominant, and even allows the private sector to exist and develop. This reform is determined by the actual condition of the productive forces in the primary state of socialism, and it is the only way to promote their development. Some of the things we have introduced in the process of reform, such as expanded markets for means of production, funds, technology and labour service and the issuance of stocks and bonds, are phenomena which are not peculiar to capitalism but are bound to appear in the wake of large-scale, socialized production and the development of the commodity economy. Socialism can and should make use of them, trying at the same time to minimize their negative effects in practice. (Zhao 1988)

The main purpose of this chapter is to consider the usefulness of the institution of the stock market in the present circumstances of the Chinese economy. Specifically, the following questions are raised by such an investigation:

1  How, if at all, will a stock market help the 'development of productive forces', i.e. economic and industrial development in China?
2  Will a stock market be system compatible, i.e. conform to socialist values, even those of 'socialism with Chinese characteristics'?[1]
3  If a fully fledged stock market is indeed introduced, can its evident 'negative influences' (speculation, stock-market booms and crashes) be minimized?

In recent years, China has established embryonic stock markets in

Shanghai, Beijing and other large cities with limited trading in company shares. Professor Li Yining of Beijing University, a leading exponent of economic reform in China, told the *New York Times* (5 December 1988) that 'By 1995 virtually every state-owned corporation will have issued shares that will be publicly traded on exchanges around the country'. Professor Li believes that the government should retain control of at least 25 per cent of most companies but that the remaining 75 per cent or less of the shares should be freely traded. He is reported as saying, 'There is no turning back. We have no other way to go.' More significantly, in the same despatch, General Secretary Zhao Ziyang, is quoted as telling an audience, 'The shareholding system will be carried out step by step.

Although there is evidence of a slowdown in the pace of reform this year in the face of China's economic difficulties, the questions outlined above will continue to be important. Moreover, the signficiance of these issues extends beyond China since many other socialist countries, e.g. Yugoslavia (Uvalic 1988) and Hungary (Nuti 1988a) are also experimenting with share ownership and stock-market institutions at present.

# The functions of a stock market in a capitalist economy

A natural starting point for a discussion of the desirability of establishing a stock market in a socialist economy is to ask what functions the stock market performs in a capitalist society where such markets have long been in existence. Following Hughes and Singh (1987), we note that in theory the stock exchange has a triple role: first, to pool together society's savings dispersed among individual savers; second, to channel these savings selectively to companies with the best investment prospects; third, to encourage the efficient use of assets embodying past savings. Two interrelated mechanisms are involved: a primary market mechanism whereby new share issues are made by companies wishing to raise funds, and a secondary market mechanism whereby trade in existing shares of companies is carried out. A company whose equities are traded at a relatively low price will find it more expensive or even impossible to raise new funds in the primary market. It may also be subject to the threat of a take-over in which a majority ownership stake in its equity is acquired by another company whose objective is to change policies to improve the stock price. Management teams can thus compete in a market for corporate control, and take-overs on the stock market can then be interpreted as an essential part of the competitive selection process in a capitalist economy.

A central question is how well, in fact, these supposed functions are actually performed by the real world stock markets? There is voluminous literature on these issues, but for the purposes of the analysis in this chapter the essential points can be summarized as follows. As far as the savings function is concerned, it turns out that the stock market makes at best a very limited contribution to social savings. For a number of reasons, managers in large corporations avoid going to the stock market to raise funds by means of issues of stocks and shares (Baumol 1965; Singh 1971; Stiglitz 1985). In a recent paper, Mayer (1988) used flow-of-funds accounts to show that, between 1970 and 1985, new issues in the two leading stock-market economies of the United Kingdom and the United States made a *negative* contribution (i.e. there were net redemptions of shares due to take-overs) to net investment in the non-financial corporate sector. In these two countries the non-financial corporations financed most of their net investment from retentions (in the case of the United Kingdom, more than 100 per cent).

The investment in large corporations in capitalist countries is thus carried out overwhelmingly through retained profits or through borrowing from banks. Moreover, there is evidence that the retained earnings are not as profitably utilized as they might be: the rate of return on ploughed back profits tends to be considerably less than on new issues or debt (Baumol et al. 1971; Whittington 1972).

Crucial to the allocative and the disciplinary function of the stock market is the efficiency of the pricing process. Only if the trading activity on the stock market is such as to yield relative share prices of firms which more or less correspond to their relative expected profitability will the market be at all able to carry out these tasks effectively – rewarding the profitable enterprises by making funds available cheaply to them to expand and punishing the unprofitable companies by making them decline or disappear.[2]

There are many studies purporting to show that stock-market prices are 'efficient' in the sense, for instance, of rapidly incorporating new information (Keane 1983). However, there is not much to suggest that share price movements are systematically related to the current, past or subsequent underlying performance variables of companies or to longer-run equilibrium considerations rather than to those of short-run equilibrium (Little and Rayner 1966; Nerlove 1968; Shiller 1981, 1984; Summers 1986). It is the influence of 'short termism'[3] and of speculators on the stock market that led Keynes to observe:

Speculators may do no harm as bubbles on a steady stream of enterprises. But the position is serious when enterprise becomes the bubble on a whirlpool of speculation. When the capital development of a country becomes a by-product of the activities of a casino, the job is likely to be ill-done. The measure of success attained by Wall Street, regarded as an institution of which social purpose is to direct new investment into the most profitable channels in terms of future yield, cannot be claimed as one of the outstanding triumphs of laissez-faire capitalism. . . . (Keynes 1936)

Although 'efficient' prices in the sense outlined above are a necessary condition for the stock market to perform its essential tasks, they are not sufficient. Sufficiency requires, in addition, that the 'take-over mechanism' be efficient so that all those companies whose profitability under their existing managements was lower than what it could be under any other management were acquired by the latter. For large management-controlled oligopolistic corporations in capitalist economies, for which the natural selection process on the product markets may not work, the take-over mechanism is the only effective market-based disciplinary device.[4] However, modern theorists of the firm and economic organization have argued in recent contributions that, for a number of powerful reasons, even in principle the take-over device may not work effectively even when prices are 'efficient' (e.g. Grossman and Hart 1980; Stiglitz 1985).

More significantly, empirical studies of the actual nature of the take-over selection process on the stock market show that in general it is not the case that only the unprofitable companies are taken over, or that the greater the profitability or the stock-market valuation of a company, the correspondingly lower are its chances of acquisition. Evidence from a wide range of studies for the United Kingdom, the United States and other industrial countries indicate that the take-over selection takes place only to a very limited degree on the basis of profitability; it does so much more in terms of the size of the company. A large relatively unprofitable company has a much greater chance of being immune from take-over than a small but much more profitable company. In fact, in the real-world stock markets, making an acquisition to increase size might itself become a tactic to avoid take-over (Singh 1971; Greer 1986).

If we turn from the question of what kinds of companies are taken over on the stock market and by whom to the question of what happens to resource use following take-over, the empirical evidence is no more reassuring. In addition to their disciplinary role, take-overs also provide an important mechanism in a capitalist economy for the reorganization of the capital resources of the society in response to changing tastes in technology and market conditions. However, a wide range of empirical studies comparing pre- and post-merger profitability indicate that on average the profitability of merging firms does not improve after merger. To the extent that monopoly power of the acquiring company in the product market may increase as a consequence of take-over, this evidence is compatible with reduced efficiency in resource utilization following mergers.[5]

Finally, in relation to the actual behaviour of stock markets and their impact on economic development in the capitalist countries, it is useful to note that until recently the stock market has played a major role only in the US and UK economies. It has historically been much less important in countries like the Federal Republic of Germany, France, Japan or Italy. Until the 1980s, a comparatively small number of companies were listed on the stock markets in these non-Anglo-Saxon industrial economies. Trading was relatively thin as share ownership was not as widely dispersed as in the United States and the United Kingdom. In the Federal Republic of

Germany, for example, the banks have played a much larger role in savings, in the allocation of capital and in the disciplining of firms than the stock market (Cable 1985). It is significant that the overall economic performance of the stock-market-dominant economies of the United States and the United Kingdom over the last 40 years has been much poorer than that of the non-stock-market economies. It is indeed true that during the 1980s financial markets have been liberalized in most advanced countries, including the non-Anglo-Saxon countries. However, the impetus for such liberalization in countries like Japan and the Federal Republic of Germany comes from the current imbalances in the world economy and from US political pressure rather than from the exigencies of economic development (for a fuller analysis see Cosh et al. 1989b). There is reason to believe that the 'forces of production' in the hitherto non-stock-market economies are more likely to be harmed than helped by the globalization and liberalization of financial markets which is now taking place (Cosh et al. 1989b).

## Stock markets and share ownership in socialist economies

In the textbook theories of socialist economics, the allocation of investment has usually been regarded as one area where socialism has a clear advantage over market economies. There are several reasons for this view which are well known in literature.[6] Briefly, first, as Scitovsky (1954) pointed out a long time ago, in the absence of complete futures markets, market prices in a capitalist economy do not provide necessary information for the *ex ante* coordination of investment plans of firms. This serious deficiency of market economics can then only be remedied by the government planning of investment resources. Secondly, the planners can in principle allocate social capital on the basis of social needs rather than private profitability which may not always coincide with such needs. Thirdly, the government can ensure full utilization of resources which the market economy, left to itself, may not necessarily be able to achieve – the usual Keynesian argument. In view of these considerations, even in the Lange–Lerner economy of market socialism and decentralised profit maximization by the managers of individual firms, the control of investment decisions was envisaged to be vested in a government planning agency.

However, as opposed to this idealized picture, the actual experience of 'realized socialism' has been rather different (e.g. Bauer 1978; Kornai 1980; Nuti 1988a). Total investment has often turned out to be 'excessive', contributing to Kornai's 'shortage economy' syndrome in socialist countries. There are well-known investment cycles, and at the microeconomic level there are many examples of inefficient utilization immobility and misallocation of resources. For these and other reasons a number of planned economies in Eastern Europe as well as in China have embarked on an economic reform programme which essentially involves marketization and managerial autonomy. The process of reform has normally been piecemeal and protracted, leading at each step to difficulties whose resolution, in the eyes of the reformers, requires further reform.

Thus in China, following the death of Mao, first the agricultural sector was liberalized by the abandonment of people's communes. Next, the reformers turned to the urban economy and over time a large number of commodities have been taken out of the hands of the central planners for their prices is to be determined 'freely' by market forces (Naughton 1986). At the same time, several steps were taken to provide greater managerial and enterprise autonomy. In 1984 the government published a list of ten principles which were intended to make a significant increase in the ability of managers in state-owned enterprises[7] to make their own production, marketing and pricing decisions (Griffin 1986). Managers were also given *more* discretion to determine the inernal organization of the firm, to choose their management teams and to recruit workers. The state enterprises were also permitted to dispose of or rent unneeded fixed capital assets (provided that the capitalized value of the enterprise remains the same) and to retain 70 per cent of the depreciation funds.

Following the classic dynamics of reform, these changes in turn have led to calls for a review of the questions of ownership and of property rights. Two important arguments are made in this respect. First it is suggested that the present position where in principle a state enterprise is 'owned by the whole people' is too abstract and does not provide the proper incentives for managers and workers to make best use of the enterprises' resources. Secondly it is argued that 'managerial autonomy' can only be properly assured by a change in property rights – by selling shares in state-owned enterprises to specific institutions (e.g. banks, provincial or local governments) or private individuals. Thus, Gu and Liu (1988) observe:

. . . the noteworthy problem is that when the property rights remain ambiguous, the redistribution of benefits is not able to make the enterprise have long-term aims and truly form a self-restricting and self-promoting managerial mechanism. Therefore the reform aimed at radically improving the enterprises managerial mechanism should start with the rationalisation of the relations between property rights and determination of property ownership. This requires that the profits obtained by the enterprise, after delivery to the state of the returns on state assets and taxes, should belong to the enterprise and so should the reinvested amount of the retained profits and returns from them. The enterprise, according to law, has the right to own, use, collect income from and dispose this part of assets.

They go on to claim:

we can thus see that the introduction of the system of shares into state owned enterprises is not simply a subjective choice, but represents an objective demand by China's economic life after the reform and constitutes the basic chain of change in the enterprise mode.

Once shares have been issued, the next step in the line of reasoning of the reformers is to suggest that there should be a market for these shares. This is thought to have two significant advantages:

1 it would make it possible to weed out inefficient management teams by market rather than political processes;
2 the 'missing' capital market will help in the efficient allocation of resources without government interference.[8]

Turning from theoretical considerations to actual practice, the *New York Times* estimates that currently 7,000–10,000 Chinese companies have issued shares. There are stock markets in Shanghai, Beijing, Shenyang and a few other provincial cities. The largest market appears to be Shanghai, where more than 350,000 people own shares issued by over 1,000 companies. However, the shares issued are more in the nature of bonds than equities since they carry a fixed interest and do not provide clear ownership rights. Many of the shares are held by enterprise employees and various government agencies. Trading tends to be rather limited as few people sell shares once they have purchased them. However, it is reported that a group of financial institutions are attempting to establish a national stock exchange modelled in part on the exchanges in New York, Milan and Tokyo.

Nuti (1988b) reports that there has been a bond market in operation in Hungary since 1983. There is both primary issues of bonds and secondary trading for enterprises (non-state guaranteed) as well as households (guranteed). Bond issues have increased overall thirtyfold over a five-year period and purchases by households have increased a hundredfold. It appears to be the case that ordinary shares have also been issued by some state enterprises and are retraded but until now exclusively among the enterprises themselves.

In Algeria, which until recently was run as a traditional centrally planned economy, economic reform has taken a different approach to share ownership and enterprise management. Following the government decree of January 1988, the state-owned enterprises were turned into joint-stock companies with shares owned by the state. Eight independent holding companies (not entirely specialized by sectors), known as *fonds de participation*, were set up to manage these state enterprises. Fund managers, whose performance is supposed to be judged by the financial results of their portfolios, can alter their holdings by trading with each other. The purpose of the system is apparently to simulate the disciplinary and allocative functions of a stock market (Nuti 1988b).

To sum up, the above account suggests that although share ownership and stock markets in China and other socialist countries are at present at a rudimentary stage, in the eyes of many of the reformers their future role in these economies is potentially very important.

# The stock market and economic development in China

In what ways and through what channels will the institution of the stock market promote the 'forces of production' in the Chinese economy? The first crucial point to note here is that by conventional macroeconomic criteria China has an exceptionally successful industrial economy. As table 9.1 indicates China's industrial growth rate during the period 1965–80 was quite respectable by international standards, even though the first 10 years of this period involved all the upheavals of the Cultural Revolution which particularly affected industry. China's industrial economy expanded at a faster rate during these 15 years than that of most developing countries including the highly successful Latin America giants Brazil and Mexico.

China's industrial record in the 1980s has been spectacular: industry has developed at a faster rate in that country than almost anywhere else in the world. Whereas the tempo of industrialization in the Latin American countries such as Brazil and Mexico has succumbed to the debt crisis and the slowdown in world economic growth during this decade, the Asian semi-industrial countries have continued to expand.[9] However, the Chinese industrial growth in the 1980s has been even faster than that of South Korea. Table 9.2 indicates that China's overall economic performance in the 1980s – at least in terms of growth of gross domestic product (GDP) – has also been extremely good. It was just creditable but not

**Table 9.1**   Growth of industrial production and share of industry in gross domestic product in semi-industrialized countries: 1965–1980, 1980–1986

|  | Growth of industrial production (% per annum) | | Share of industry in GDP | |
|---|---|---|---|---|
|  | *1965–80* | *1980–6* | *1965* | *1985* |
| China | 10.0 | 12.5 | 38 | 46 |
| India | 4.0 | 7.1 | 22 | 29 |
| Mexico | 7.6 | −0.1 | 31 | 39 |
| Brazil | 9.9 | 1.6 | 33 | 39 |
| South Korea | 16.5 | 10.2 | 25 | 42 |
| Developing countries | 7.2 | 4.6 | 31 | 36 |
| Middle-income developing countries | 7.2 | 2.1 | 33 | 36 |
| Low-income developing countries | 8.4 | 1.2 | 25 | 30 |
| Industrial countries | 3.2 | 2.5 | 40 | 35 |

*Source*: *World Development Report* 1988

**Table 9.2**   Growth of gross domestic product in semi-industrialized countries: 1965–1980, 1980–1986

|                                        | *1965–80* | *1980–6* |
|----------------------------------------|-----------|----------|
| China                                  | 6.4       | 10.6     |
| India                                  | 3.7       | 4.9      |
| Mexico                                 | 6.5       | 0.4      |
| Brazil                                 | 9.0       | 2.7      |
| South Korea                            | 9.5       | 8.2      |
| Developing countries                   | 6.1       | 3.8      |
| Middle-income developing countries     | 6.6       | 2.3      |
| Low-income developing countries        | 6.5       | 1.8      |
| Industrial countries                   | 3.6       | 2.5      |

*Source*: *World Development Report* 1988

outstanding in the earlier period, mainly because of the relatively much slower growth in agriculture.

Nevertheless there are at present serious macroeconomic imbalances in the Chinese economy and it is believed by the reformers that the development of the stock market will help to correct such disequilibria. The most important of these is reflected in the high rate of inflation which China is currently experiencing. Further, the rate of investment is thought to be too high and its sectoral allocation is regarded as being inappropriate. In addition, the reformers point to a wide range of microeconomic inefficiencies in the economy. We consider below the implications of the establishment of a stock market for each of these areas.

### Inflation, savings, investment and the stock market

Table 9.3 indicates that China has long been a low-inflation country. Until 1980, there was hardly any recorded inflation at all. However, with the progressive decentralization of the economy, inflation began to accelerate in the 1980s and had reached very high levels, by Chinese standards, by 1988. The oficial rate of inflation was 7.8 per cent in 1987 and 20.7 per cent in 1988 (*IMF Survey*, 1 May 1989). In the early months of 1989, inflation was reported as running at an annual rate of over 30 per cent (*Economist*, 25 February 1989) – clearly a cause of immense concern for the Chinese people and the leadership.

It is argued by the reformers that the creation of a proper stock market will help reduce inflation by promoting savings. However, this argument is not convincing for at least three reasons. Firstly, as table 9.4 suggests, China already has one of the highest rates of domestic savings in the world. At 36 per cent of GDP in 1986, it was considerably higher than that of the

**Table 9.3** Rates of inflation in Asia and Latin America: 1963–1984 (average annual rates of growth of consumer price index in percentages)

|  | 1963–73 | 1973–9 | 1979–84 |
|---|---|---|---|
| *Asia* | | | |
| China | 0.5[a] | 0.6[b] | 3.0 |
| India | 8.3 | 6.3 | 10.0 |
| Indonesia | 42.1[c] | 19.7 | 12.5 |
| South Korea | 13.2 | 17.9 | 12.1 |
| Malaysia | 2.1 | 6.2 | 6.0 |
| Pakistan | 5.1 | 14.8 | 9.2 |
| Philippines | 7.9 | 13.3 | 19.8 |
| Sri Lanka | 4.3 | 7.3 | 17.0 |
| Taiwan | 3.5 | 12.0 | 12.9[d] |
| Thailand | 3.2 | 9.7 | 8.3 |
| Median | 4.7 | 12.0 | 10.0 |
| *Latin America* | | | |
| Argentina | n.a. | 181.5 | 222.8 |
| Bolivia | 8.2 | 17.4 | 195.6 |
| Brazil | 31.4 | 38.6 | 121.6 |
| Chile | n.a. | 167.9 | 22.1 |
| Colombia | 11.2 | 23.7 | 22.8 |
| Ecuador | 5.9 | 14.5 | 23.6 |
| Mexico | 4.5 | 19.8 | 53.7 |
| Peru | 9.9 | 38.2 | 82.8 |
| Venezuela | 2.2 | 8.9 | 13.0 |
| Median | 8.2 | 23.7 | 53.7 |

n.a., not available.
[a] 1965–70.
[b] 1970–9.
[c] 1966–73.
[d] 1979–82.
*Source*: *World Bank Data Bank*

various groups of developing countries as well as of the Third World as a whole. It was also greater than that of South Korea. Nevertheless, to the extent that it is suggested that domestic savings in China should increase still further, higher real interest rates on bank deposits and/or, better still, extension of modern banking to rural China are likely to be better ways of achieving this objective than the attractions of an equities market which may be subject to considerable volatility.[10] The banking system or the financial institutions could also introduce some additional more flexible instruments for savings deposits as indeed some banks have already been doing in recent years.

**Table 9.4**   Gross domestic investment and gross domestic savings as a percentage of gross domestic product: semi-industrial countries: 1965 and 1986

|  | Investment (%) | | Domestic savings (%) | |
|---|---|---|---|---|
|  | 1965 | 1986 | 1965 | 1986 |
| China | 25 | 39 | 25 | 36 |
| India | 18 | 23 | 16 | 21 |
| Brazil | 20 | 21 | 22 | 24 |
| Mexico | 22 | 21 | 21 | 27 |
| South Korea | 15 | 29 | 8 | 35 |
| Developing countries | 15 | 29 | 20 | 24 |
| Middle-income developing countries | 21 | 23 | 21 | 24 |
| Low-income developing countries | 17 | 19 | 16 | 17 |
| Industrial countries | 23 | 21 | 23 | 21 |

*Source*: *World Development Report* 1988

The important point is that inflation is a macroeconomic phenomenon caused by too high a level of aggregate demand. This is in part due to a very high level of investment (the gross domestic investment as a proportion of GDP was 10 percentage points greater in China in 1986 than in South Korea (see table 9.4)). This in turn is due to the growing loss of central control over investment decisions made by enterprises since the beginning of the economic reform (Naughton 1986). Other significant causes of inflation include decentralized bonus payments to employees by individual enterprises and the consequent breakdown of what had effectively been a strict incomes policy until the late 1970s (Singh 1979; Griffin 1986). At a deeper level, the inflationary problems arise from the fact that although the overall rate of economic growth in China has been very high, there is no longer any social consensus on the distribution of income and thus there are conflicting claims over the national product. However, the essential point is that the reasons and remedies for inflation lie in the macroeconomic sphere and the institution of the stock market is unlikely to help in this respect; on the contrary, it could make matters worse. The Chinese government has been reluctant to use macroeconomic stabilization measures because of the fear of causing 'stagflation' in the economy. Without such macroeconomic stabilization, a probable stock-market boom in inflationary conditions would make control over prices more rather than less difficult.

## Sectoral allocation of investment

The question of the overall level of investment has been discussed above. As far as the allocation of investment is concerned, there are two broad issues: (a) the allocation of investment between the broad sectors of the economy; (b) its allocation among enterprises within a sector or industry. We shall briefly consider (a) here; (b) will be examined in the next section.

At the end of the 1970s, the Chinese government identified many important structural imbalances in the economy: the share of industry in the GDP was too high and continually increasing, and the share of services was too low; growth of agriculture was sluggish; there was an excessive share of heavy industry in the industrial product (World Bank 1985). Since 1980, many of these imbalances have been greatly reduced to the clear benefit of the standard of living of the Chinese people. There has been a great improvement in both the quantity and the quality of available consumer goods. A number of new products, e.g. colour television sets and video cassette recorders, have been introduced. Urban housing has vastly improved. However, as Riskin (1988) rightly points out, many of these changes have been brought about by the macroeconomic actions of the central planners (rather than through 'reform' as normally understood) through, for example, allocating greater investment resources to the consumer goods industry, housing etc. In the circumstances of China's institutions, it is unlikely that a stock market would have been able to bring about such enormous changes in the *broad* sectoral investment allocation more quickly or more effectively than the country's central planning mechanism.

## Microeconomic efficiency and intrasectoral investment allocation

The reformers believe that Chinese industrial enterprises have a number of serious weaknesses at the microeconomic level.

1   As a consequence of the soft budget constraint in the socialist countries, there is a considerable degree of $X$-inefficiency in Chinese firms.
2   Managers in state-owned enterprises – 'owned by the whole people' – do not have appropriate performance incentives. This contributes significantly to $X$-inefficiency.
3   There is inefficient allocation of intra-industry investment resources since there is under-utilization of capacity in some enterprises whilst there is over-utilization in others. Resources do not flow from enterprises which are using them less efficiently to those who are, or could, utilize them more effectively.
4   There is no clear-cut arm's length mechanism for changing inefficient management teams. At best this is done through political processes,

rather than on the objective basis of the quality of enterprise management.

A central question is whether share ownership and the institution of the stock market are the only or the best way of solving these problems. Several observations are in order with respect to these issues. Consider (a) the question of $X$-inefficiency. First, as noted earlier, notwithstanding all the essentially a priori concerns as well as casual evidence about $X$-inefficiency in Chinese industrial enterprises, it must be stressed that China's overall industrial growth rate has been extremely high, among the highest in the world. Secondly, to the extent that it is argued, quite correctly, that if $X$-inefficiency is reduced, overall industrial growth would be higher still, this goal is likely to be better achieved through competition in the product markets rather than through the disciplinary mechanisms of the capital market. As seen earlier, even in advanced capitalist economies with highly organized capital markets, the stock market is a poor disciplinarian of large management-controlled corporations.

Turning to the question of managerial incentives in state-owned Chinese enterprises – it is important to reflect that share ownership and the stock market are by no means the only ways of inducing optimal managerial performance. The growing literature on privatization of state-owned enterprises in the advanced as well as the developing countries is relevant here. Kay and Matthew (1988) have noted on the basis of their comparison of state-owned and privatized enterprises in the United Kingdom that privatization is neither a necessary nor a sufficient condition for improving enterprise performance. Rather, they suggest that the promotion of product market competition is a greater spur than the transfer of ownership to microeconomic efficiency. Similarly, the experience of the giant Korean state-owned steel company POSCO is instructive. POSCO is by far the most successful steel producer in the world, even more successful than the Japanese steel companies. Aylen (1987) notes that its success is due to its being set clear-cut goals, given managerial autonomy and being subject to market competition. Managerial autonomy is clearly not ruled out by state ownership.

It is also important to bear in mind that profit sharing can be, and indeed is, used as an incentive for workers and managers in state-owned enterprises in many countries, including China, without either share ownership or a stock market. Moreover, if it is felt that employees will have an even greater incentive to perform better if they had in addition an ownership stake in the enterprise, they could be issued shares without there being a stock market in these shares. In fact, this particular incentive can work best only if the workers are obliged to retain their stake in the firm and not to sell it.

Let us now examine the issue of interfirm allocation and mobility of capital. Would it be best facilitated by the stock market or by other mechanisms? The first important point to note in this connection is the normal volatility of stock-market prices. In the wake of the stock-market crash of October 1987 in New York, London and elsewhere, there has been an important debate on the question of whether, as a consequence of liberalization of the world stock markets and introduction of new devices such as program trading in recent years, the markets have become more volatile than before. Although the evidence from the Brady Commission (appointed in the United States to investigate the 1987 crash) and other sources suggest that the volatility has not increased compared say with the 1930s (Cosh et al. 1989b), the fact remains that the share prices on the stock markets are normally highly volatile. It is useful to reflect here on the recent behaviour of some Third World stock markets. Between 1982 and 1985 share prices on the Brazilian stock market rose fivefold in US dollar terms; two years later they had dwindled to 28 per cent of their 1985 value. In 1988 the market had risen again by 40 per cent. In Taiwan, the stock market more than quadrupled from the beginning of 1987 to mid-1988 before crashing; it is still almost 40 per cent of its 1988 all-time high (*Economist*, 29 April 1989).

In the light of such volatility of share prices, interfirm allocation of investment resources through the stock market would not appear to be a very sensible course. Indeed, in a different but related context Williamson (1970) regarded such volatility and other imperfections of the stock market as an important reason why a so-called M-form corporate organization will perform better than a U-form organization. The 'central office' of the M-form organization, acting as a 'surrogate' capital market, can provide a superior mechanism for allocating investment resources to the different subsidiaries relative to the real-world stock markets. The practical implication of this view for China's industrial management is that, instead of establishing actual stock markets, they should attempt to create surrogate markets for intra-industry resource allocation. One method of doing this would be to establish state-owned holding companies and entrust them with the overall management of groups of industrial enterprise – much like a M-form organization. These holding companies should be allowed to compete with each other, and their managerial performance should be judged by their financial results.

With respect to the related question of the change of inefficient managements through the market rather than political processes, the experience of the stock-market economies of the United States and the United Kingdom with the take-over mechanism is far from happy. For many of the reasons discussed above, an increasing number of scholars regard the involuntary take-overs as a costly, inefficient and cumbersome mechanism for forcing a change in corporate management. There are often huge transactions costs (particularly if the take-over bid is defended) and enormous speculation in shares, and at the end of the day it is far from clear whether the management which actually succeeds in a take-over battle is in fact better at long-term industrial management rather than simply being more adept at short-term financial manipulation. These considerations have led to calls, both in the United States and the United Kingdom, for separating the market for shares from that of corporate control.[11] It is suggested that it would be better for management changes to occur through active participation by financial institutions (who now hold the bulk of corporate shares in the Anglo-Saxon countries) in corporate affairs than by the take-over process. It is interesting to note in this regard that in countries like Japan there are hardly any involuntary takeovers on the stock market. In the light of the experience of the advanced countries, it would not seem sensible for a developing country like China to adopt such a costly and uncertain system of enforcing management changes in industrial enterprises.

# Conclusion

The foregoing analysis suggests that as far as the promotion of 'forces of production' is concerned, the institution of the stock market is unlikely to make a positive contribution in the present circumstances of China's economy. In the inflationary conditions which have prevailed in the country in recent years, a stock market could in fact have a negative influence on economic and industrial development by contributing to overall instability. In this chapter it has been suggested that the 'negative features' of the capitalist institutions which General Secretary Zhao referred to in his speech at the 13th Congress (see Introduction) are best overcome in the case of the stock market by not having an actual stock market but rather by simulating its functions via the establishment of new financial institutions. These would in effect be competing holding companies of industrial enterprises. The holding companies would have managerial autonomy and their performance would be judged by financial results. Further, it is argued here that, at the present stage of China's development, to increase microeconomic efficiency the reformers should pay greater attention to the promotion of competition in the product markets.

The question of the system compatibility of the stock market with socialism has not been given specific attention in the above discussion. This is mainly because 'socialism with Chinese characteristics' seems to be rather catholic in its embrace. The 'primary stage of socialism' and the development of 'the commodity economy' appear to be compatible with almost all institutions of a market, i.e. the capitalist economy. In contrast with the Mao era, the main focus of the post-Mao Chinese leadership is clearly not socialism as such but the development of the 'forces of production', or more specifically the 'four modernizations' adumbrated by Deng Xiaoping a decade ago. This is perhaps as it should be, but that in any case is the standpoint adopted in this chapter in relation to the question of the usefulness of the institution of the stock market in the present conditions of the Chinese economy. However, the question of system compatibility of the stock market remains important in a country like Yugoslavia where there has been a serious discussion of the extent to which the workings of the stock market would conflict with socialist values and institutions, particularly with those of labour-managed firms.[12]

## Notes

1   The title of General Secretary's Zhao's report is 'Advance along the road of socialism with Chinese characteristics'.

2   In the normal calculus of a capitalist economy, private profitability is taken to be an indicator of 'efficiency'. There are well-known reasons why private and social valuations and private and social costs may differ even in a perfectly competitive equilibrium market economy.

3   This term refers to the short-term time horizon of many important players on the stock market, e.g. fund managers of financial institutions whose own performance as managers is judged by short-term results (Cosh et al. 1989a).

4   See further Alchian and Kessel (1962), Manne (1965), Meade (1968) and Singh (1971, 1975). Because of the so-called principal – agent problems in the large management-controlled corporations, shareholders dispersed throughout society may not be able to persuade the managers to act in the shareholders' interests rather than in the managers' own self-interest.

5   For systematic evidence on this subject from a number of industrial countries, see Mueller (1980).

6   For one of the earlier analyses of these issues see Dobb (1939).

7   There are over 60,000 state enterprises in China which account for about 75 per cent of aggregate industrial output. Out of the total non-farm workforce of 133.4 million in 1988, state-owned enterprises employed 97.9 million workers, collectives employed 34.9 million and private enterprises employed 0.8 million (*Economist*, 21 January 1989).

8   A number of differential proposals concerning share ownership and trading in shares have been made by Chinese reformers. A notable recent contribution is that of Hua Sheng, Zhang Xuejun and Luo Xiaopeng; their views, first outlined in *Economic Research*, were given an airing in the *People's Daily* in January 1989.

9   For an analysis of the different performance of Asian and Latin American industrial economies in the 1980s, see Singh (1989).

10   On the question of volatility, see below. To the extent that it is argued that the Chinese households are not risk-averse, but prefer risk, the state can indulge such tastes by running lotteries, as indeed many socialist countries already do. A straightforward state-run lottery is better than gambling on the equities market with real enterprises.

11   See Charkham (1989); in the United States a number of individual states have adopted laws to restrict involuntary take-overs.

12   For a recent survey of this discussion, see Uvalic (1988).

## References

Alchian, A. A. and Kessel, R. A. (1962) Competition monopoly and the pursuit of pecuniary gain. In *Aspects of Labour Economics*, pp. 157–83. Princeton, NJ: NBER.

Aylen, J. (1987) Privatisation in developing countries. *Lloyds Bank Review*, January, no. 163, 15–30.

Bauer, T. (1978) Investment cycles in planned economies. *Acta Oeconomica* 24 (3), 3–4.

Baumol, W. J. (1965) *The Stock Market and Economic Efficiency*. New York: Fordham University Press.

Cable, J. (1985) Capital market information and industrial performance: the role of West German banks. *Economic Journal*, 95, March, 118–32.

Charkham, J. (1989) Corporate governments and the market for control of companies. Bank of England Panel Paper 25, March.

Cosh, A. D., Hughes, A., Lee, K. and Singh, A. (1989a) Institutional investment, mergers and market for corporate control. *International Journal of Industrial Organization*, 7, 73–100.

——, —— and Singh, A. (1989b) Openness, innovation, and ownership: the changing structure of financial markets. Discussion Paper WP 74, World Institute of Development Economic Research, Helsinki.

Dobb, M. H. (1939) A note on saving and investment in a socialist economy. *Economic Journal*, 49, December, 713–28.

Greer, D. F. (1986) Acquiring in order to avoid acquisition. *Antitrust Bulletin*, 31, Spring, 155–86.

Griffin, K. G. (1986) Reform of state industrial enterprises in China. Presented at ORSTOM Conference, Paris, 26–27 February 1987.

Gu Peidong and Liu Xirong, 1988. Study on turning state-owned enterprises into stock companies. *Social Sciences in China*, Autumn, 25–45.

Hughes, A. and Singh, A. (1987) Takeovers and the stock market. *Contributions to Political Economy*, 6, March, 73–85.

Joint Economic Committee, US Congress (1986) *China's Economy Looks Towards the Year 2000*, Washington, US Government Printing Office.

Kay, J. and Matthew, B. (1988) The impact of privatisation on the performance of the U.K. public sector. Paper presented at the 15th Annual Conference of the European Association of Research in Industrial Economics, 31 August–2 September.

Keane, S. M. (1983) *Stock Market Efficiency*. Oxford: Philip Allan.

Keynes, J. M. (1936) *General Theory of Employment, Interest and Money*. New York: Harcourt, Brace.

Kornai, J. A. (1980) *The Economics of Shortage*, 2 vols. Amsterdam: North-Holland.

Little, I. M. D. and Rayner, A. G. (1966) *Higgledy Piggledy Growth Again*. Oxford: Basil Blackwell.

Manne, H. G. (1965) Mergers and the market for corporate control. *Journal of Political Economy*, 73, April, 110–20.

Mayer, C. (1988) New issues in corporate finance. *European Economic Review*, 32, June, 1167–89.

Meade, J. S. (1968) Is the 'New Industrial Estate' inevitable?' *Economic Journal*, 78, June, 372–92.

Mueller, D. C. (ed.) (1980) *The Determinants and Effects of Mergers*. Cambridge, MA: O. C. & H.

—— (1984) Stock prices and social dynamics. *Brookings Papers on Economic Activity*, 2, 457–98.

—— (1975) Takeovers, economic natural selection and the theory of the firm. *Economic Journal*, 85, September, 497–515.

Naughton, B. (1986) Finance and planning reforms in industry. In JEC-US.

Nuti, D. M. (1988a) Competitive valuation and efficiency of capital investment in the socialist economy. *European Economic Review*, 32, March, 459–64.

—— (1988b) Remonetisation and capital markets in the reform of centrally planned economies. EUI working paper 88/361.

Riskin, C. (1988) Reform: where is China going? East Asia Institute, Colombia University, June.

Scitovsky, T. (1954) Two concepts of external economies. *Journal of Political Economy*, 62, 143–51.

Shiller, R. J. (1981) Do stock prices move too much to be justified by subsequent changes in dividends? *American Economic Review*, 71, June, 421–36.

—— (1984) Stock prices and social dynamics. *Brookings Papers on Economic Activity*, 2, 457–98.

Singh, A. (1971) *Takeovers: Their Reference to the Stock Market and the Theory of the Firm*. Cambridge: Cambridge University Press.

—— (1975) Takeovers, economic natural selection and the theory of the firm. *Economic Journal*, 85, September, 497–515.

—— (1979) The basic needs approach to development versus the new international economic order: the significance of Third World industrialisation. *World Development*, 7, 585–606.

—— (1989) The state of industry in the Third World in the 1980s: analytical and policy issues. Cambridge, Faculty of Economics.

Stiglitz, J. E. (1985) Credit markets and the control of capital. *Journal of Money, Credit and Banking*, 17 (2), 133–52.

Summers, L. H. (1986) Does the stock market rationally reflect fundamental values? *Journal of Finance*, 41, July, 591–601.

Uvalic, M. (1988) Share holding in Yugoslav theory and practice. EUI Working Paper 88/330, Florence.

Whittington, G. (1972) The profitability of retained earnings. *Review of Economics and Statistics*, 54, 152–60.

Williamson, O. E. (1970) *Corporate Control and Business Behavior*. Englewood Cliffs, NJ: Prentice-Hall.

World Bank (1985) *China: Long-term Development Issues and Options*. Baltimore, MD: Johns Hopkins University Press.

Zhao Ziyang (1988) *Report to the 13th National Congress of the Communist Party of China*. Beijing: Beijing Review Publications.

# 10

# The Rural Economy

## Du Runsheng

Since reform of the rural economic system started at the end of 1978 it has resulted in some remarkable achievements. However, overall productivity in the rural areas is, still very low, and many important problems with respect to the rural economy remain to be solved. Some are inherited from the past, while others are new problems which emerged after the reforms had already made some progress. Continued reform is the only way to overcome these difficulties and to continue rapid economic development in the countryside.

China has a population of over a billion, of whom about 80 per cent live in the rural areas and constitute the largest low-income group, with a per capita income only about half that of the urban population. Expanding agricultural output and raising rural income are inseparable goals in our rural development strategy; they must be solved simultaneously. The ultimate solution to these two problems is linked to the task of transforming China from a traditional agricultural economy into an advanced industrial economy. The two aims promote and condition each other; only when the problems of agricultural production and farm income are considered in the context of the economy as a whole can we understand their inner workings and arrive at correct solutions.

After 1949 China went ahead with programmes of socialist transformation of agriculture, capitalist industry and commerce, and entered the primary stage of socialist development. At that time, there was no mature international experience available which could be drawn on in order to guide China's transformation into a modern industrial country. Moreover, just as economic reconstruction started, China was subjected to an international market blockade. In these unfavourable circumstances China opted for a highly centralized planned economic system and a strategy of giving priority to the development of industry, particularly heavy industry. Capital was generated from agriculture, through monopoly control of urban–rural trade, to provide initial investment for industrialization. This was the only practical choice in the situation at that time. In the first six or seven years of the 1950s, careful attention was given to balancing the relationship between industry and agriculture and between town and countryside, and the national economy grew rapidly and embarked smoothly on the path to modernization. For a long time however, because priority was given to industry, especially to heavy industry and large-scale state-owned enterprises (which were highly capital intensive and mostly concentrated in large cities), labour absorption was limited. By 1978 great progress had been made in the modernization drive. The foundation of a modern industrial system had been laid; the share of industry in the gross value of industrial and agricultural output had climbed from 10 per cent in the early post-liberation years to 74.4 per cent. However, no corresponding changes had taken place in the structure of employment: agricultural labour still accounted for 76.1 per cent of the total labour force, and the rural population was still about 80 per cent of the total. With a growing population, the per capita availability of cultivable land and other agricultural resources declined year by year. Although significant progress had been made in urban industry, the growth of labour productivity in agriculture, and of farm income, was slow; between 1965 and 1977, the average net income of farmers increased by only a little more than one yuan per annum. In the long run, this stagnation could neither create effective demand for industrial goods, nor provide adequate food and raw materials for urban and industrial development. With agricultural products in short supply, population flow to the cities had to be restricted and the development of small towns limited. Basically, only urban producers had access to industrial resources; farmers were restricted to agricultural resources. We had created a dual structure of modern urban industry and traditional agriculture, isolated from each other and mutually exclusive. The people's commune, which was characterized by a highly centralized collective management, contributed to the rigidity of this structure. For over 20 years goods were exchanged between the rural and urban areas according to the unified purchasing price system, which biased the terms of trade against agriculture and the farmer in favour of industry and the urban population. All this slowed down rural development. Compared with other developing countries at the same stage of industrialization, China ranks low in the supply of modern inputs to the countryside and the ratio of agricultural to industrial employment. With respect to the integration of the urban and rural economies in particular, China's industrialization remains incomplete, and this makes it essential to re-examine and revise our economic development strategy. Now that the industrial system has basically taken shape, we should carry out economic reform, break down the barriers between the urban and rural areas, shift rural manpower to the secondary and tertiary industries, and promote urbanization. Industrial development must not only provide agriculture with more and more modern inputs; more important, it must also create more new job opportunities for rural people. As we establish a dynamic symbiotic relationship between industry and agriculture, town and countryside,

China will move smoothly from a low-income to a medium-income country.

China's rural economic reform marked the beginning of a new era. After 1979, a series of reform policies was implemented, the purchase prices of agricultural products were considerably raised and structural deviations in income distribution were rectified. The contract responsibility system was introduced throughout the countryside, with remuneration linked to output from publicly owned land. Farmers were given decision-making power, and efficiently re-allocated their own resources, greatly raising their productivity. From 1979 to 1984, agricultural output value increased at an average annual rate of 9 per cent, per capita grain production grew from 319 to 395 kg and the supply of farm products rose by 24.2 per cent; this eased long-standing agricultural shortages. Opening up the labour market set free the surplus labour which had been tied to the land. Their day-to-day needs having been met, farmers generated a certain amount of accumulation; farm households took over as the main investors in the rural economy, whereas previously the state was virtually the only investor. The sources of investment were also diversified. Industrial development in the rural areas surged forward; numerous job opportunities were created and more and more farmers transferred to the secondary and tertiary sectors. In 1986, the total output value of township enterprises reached 354 billion yuan, accounting for 31.7 per cent of total industrial output value. These enterprises employed 79 million peasants, equal to 61.6 per cent of urban employment in that year.

Rural economic development also created conditions for urban indust-rial development. From 1979 to 1984, about two-thirds of new purchasing power came from peasants. This expansion of domestic demand stimulated the production of manufactured goods, and the nation's total industrial output value during this period increased at an average annual rate of 8.9 per cent. This was the result of synergic interaction between the urban and rural areas. Rapid industrial growth promoted specialization in urban enterprises, which increasingly transferred products to the countryside for processing. Technologies, skilled personnel and funds flowed to the rural areas. Cities and villages jointly operated various undertakings, and the barriers separating the resources in industrial areas from those in the countryside were gradually removed; factor markets began to operate. Experience over the past few years proves that when we talk about efficiency under existing conditions, we need to pay attention not only to the internal efficiency of an enterprise, but also to external efficiency in terms of social employment. This is the only way to ensure the balanced development between urban and rural areas and facilitate the mobilization of China's rich labour resources for modernization.

The grown of rural industry has restarted the urbanization process which had been suspended for about 30 years. The appearance of enterprises in small towns has produced linkage effects, increasing job opportunities in the service sector. Urbanization helps communities to break down their isolation, and encourages enterprises to be independent in their operations and to develop horizontal linkages. In the last five years, 23 million peasants have entered the cities; 3.8 million of them have settled there and are responsible for their own food-grain. More than 8,000 fairs have recently started in small towns in the countryside. Although the peasants involved in these developments comprise only a small proportion of the rural labour force, their activity has put the primary rural labour market into motion. Economically developed coastal regions in the east have now absorbed thousands of labourers, who flow in from other provinces every year to work in township enterprises or engage in crop cultivation. These regions, in turn, send roughly the same number of skilled workers to the underdeveloped central and western regions to assist technological diffusion. The flow of manpower, technology and funds has re-allocated resources, thereby increasing the efficiency of rural resource use.

If, under present conditions, the migration of large numbers of peasants to large and medium-sized cities, long isolated from the countryside, is permitted, conflicts and difficulties will occur and urban reform will be affected. We should now implement a rural industrial policy of encouraging peasants 'to leave their land but not their native place'. Meanwhile, in order to accelerate the process of urbanization and the appropriate concentration of industrial and service sectors, the development of small townships and migration between rural areas should be encouraged. With the deepening of reform it is inevitable that peasants will begin to migrate to large and medium cities. As the reform of enterprise management unfolds, allowing enterprises to assume sole responsibility for their own business profits and losses, it will be necessary to reform the personnel and wage systems and develop the labour market. Relaxing control over the manpower flow between town and countryside and permitting peasants to enter the urban labour market will not only effectively curtail wage inflation, but will also create a more rational gap between the wages of skilled and unskilled labour, and between those of blue-collar and white-collar workers, while raising labour productivity in the economy as a whole.

Because natural agricultural resources are scarce in China, an excessive number of farmers crowded onto insufficient cultivable land would not only keep rural income depressed, but also hinder the improvement of agricultural labour productivity and rational resource use and lead to environmental deterioration. Today, more than 300 million peasants work no more than 100 million hectares of arable land; this fact reminds us that we must make unremitting efforts to shift at least 100 million people out of agriculture by the turn of the century and solve the employment problem for the rural population.

Raising rural incomes by changing the rural employment structure will not solve all the problems of agricultural development. With the increase of rural non-farm employment, the rising opportunity cost of agricultural labour will inevitably decrease the supply of labour to agricultural production and in particular to grain production. The present low price of grain must be raised, and the government is investigating how to implement this. The law of value should be applied to all production in rural areas, but price policy should not be our only means. As industry develops, it is necessary to promote constant technological innovation in agriculture, increase the supply of inputs and change the extensive exploitation of land into an intensive pattern. For these purposes it is also necessary to encourage the consolidation of land.

The restructuring of the rural economic system which started in the late 1970s has done away with the agricultural management and organizational methods of the people's commune system, which was characaterized by highly concentrated production and unified distribution: instead, the household-based contract responsibility system, with remuneration linked to output, has been introduced. This change, by the simple principle of 'more pay for more work done', has increased farmers' enthusiasm and forcefully stimulated production.

However, we must recognize that the same reform is leading us inexorably to the subcontracting of land. At present, each farm household manages on average only about 0.5 hectares; such small-scale operation is obviously incompatible with technological progress, the reduction of costs and the improvement of labour productivity. However, we cannot repeat the process of collectivizing the land and adopt the method of concentrated labour and unified distribution; to do so, with no change in traditional technology or the ratio of land to worker, would inevitably revive the egalitarian practice of 'eating from the same big pot'. The eventual scale of farms in China will depend on how much labour is moved away from the land. In recent years we have noticed that as non-agricultural rural production develops and after about 60 per cent of the labour force has moved out of farming, a demand for machinery arises and the concentration of cropland becomes really practicable. This is because the development of local non-agricultural production provides a new economic basis for grass-roots economic organizations. When the income of peasants who have taken up other jobs is guaranteed, grass-roots cooperative organizations, acting as landowners, can readjust contract cropland, recuperate all or part of the land from farmers who have transferred to other jobs and in this way expand the scale of production. Such conditions now exist in the suburbs of some large cities and in the southeast coastal areas, and we are now conducting systematic experiments there which will provide a scientific basis for formulating policies and laws.

Land remains the primary guarantee of local farmers' incomes in most regions. We cannot rashly change the contractual relationship governing land use. Instead we should develop local non-agricultural production, promote the transfer of land usage rights with compensation and then gradually help farmers to move out of farming. In this process, they can own small plots of land and at the same time engage in other commodity production in order to increase their cash income. Of course, this method has its drawbacks, but it is unavoidable. At the present stage we should concentrate on improving social services in order to realize economies of scale. It is important to develop vigorously various kinds of social service organizations for production supply and marketing, which can carry out those projects which are beyond the capacity of one household. In this way we can popularize advanced technology, reduce production costs, open up outlets for products and improve economic returns in agriculture. The contracting system, based on an egalitarian mode, embodies a kind of welfare principle which is consistent with the farmers' immediate interests. From the long-term point of view, in order to develop social productive forces we need to stress the principle of efficiency, i.e. to change to a management system which yields better economic results and to an optimal operation scale. In fact, this is a contradiction, but we must create suitable conditions for its resolution.

There are more than 195 million peasant households in the rural areas: a huge group of small and diversified operation units. Obviously, it is beyond the government's capacity to face them directly, to control them efficiently and to provide them with all the necessary services. In addition to paying high circulation costs in markets, such small diversified households cause sharp fluctuations in market supply, and are in a weak position to raise their own economic situation through market transactions. Therefore, on the basis of household operation, individual households should form larger organizations.

Through the cooperative and people's commune movements, we have established a very rigorous system in the rural areas which, before the rural economic reforms, included every peasant, almost without exception. Nevertheless, the system had an obvious weakness: it organized traditional agricultural production by industrial methods. Management was subject to inappropriate administrative inference, and incentivies were depressed because people were unable to see the direct connection between efforts and rewards. Therefore the system lost its vitality; moreover, it was an obstacle to the development of a commodity economy. Economic reform in the countryside has abolished that system, and it is neither possible nor desirable that it should be revived as the rural economy develops.

It is not easy to establish a genuine cooperative economic system which will be welcomed by peasants not only because historically China did not have a cooperative tradition, but also because in the past the cooperative movement was implemented in a rash and unsuitable manner. Peasants do not have a proper understanding of what a good cooperative system should be, and so we need to ensure that current rural policies are stable over a long period during which peasants can learn from their own experience. Therefore at this stage there are two basic approaches to the problem of increasing the size of peasants' organizations. First, while stabilizing the household contract responsibility system, we have gradually changed the original community-based collective organization, with the land cooperative as its basis, into household operation, separating politics from business; various productive services are provided to individual households in order to organize them into unified cooperative associations. Secondly, all kinds of economic association are encouraged – cooperative, part-nership or joint-stock company. They may be seasonal or long-term stable associations; they may be associations of one part of the production process or of all of it. Peasants have already voluntarily formed various kinds of new economic associations in the countryside. This reflects an irreversible trend towards the development of a peasant cooperative economy, based on household operation, and also the need for Chinese peasants to educate themselves in the process, particularly on the necessity for a formal organizational system. We intend to develop cooperative organization by means of demonstration, not by administrative interven-tion. Meanwhile, an individual household's diversified operations can also be led towards this goal by means of all kinds of large agricultural technology service organizations, or the organized activities of processing and marketing enterprises.

The establishment of the household contract responsibility system created a new starting point for organizing the peasants. However, it is only a starting point. To meet the objective demands of rural economic development and the hopes of peasants, we shall continue, for as long as is necessary and without sparing any effort, to promote peasant organiza-tions.

Grain has been the people's primary concern in the supply of farm products. China can produce enough to ensure that her people have sufficient to eat. According to a survey conducted by the Chinese Academy of Medical Sciences Nutrition Research Institute, China's daily per capita food intake was 2,485 calories in 1982, 5.7 per cent higher than the average for developing countries and 0.2 per cent more than the indicator recommended by the Society of Physiology for the Chinese. In future, as the population grows, food supply will have to be continually increased. China has great potential for grain production: from 1979 to 1984, the average yield of grain per *mu* (1/15 hectare) increased by 72.5 kg, an average of 12 kg per annum. If, by the year 2000, per capita grain production is an estimated 400 kg and the area sown to grain decreases annually, then in the next 12 years the average yield per *mu* will have to increase annually by almost 6 kg. About two-thirds of the existing cultivated land consists of low-yield fields; in addition, about 100 million *mu* (67,000 hectares) of wasteland could be reclaimed. However, both must be improved, transformed and developed before the requirements for increasing total production can be met. Additional inputs are essential. State investment is necessary, but the greater part of the investment should come from the farmers themselves. The prerequisite is that they should have the necessary motivation. A favourable policy environment should be created; otherwise the potential for increasing production will not be realized. The key to this is correct pricing. A substantial part of the grain now purchased is low priced. When farmers feel that growing grain is not worthwhile, they will turn to production that gives higher returns. The state should implement an appropriate price protection policy for grain production.

As far as grain consumption is concerned, the new situation confronting us is that the demand for enough to eat gives place to a demand for better food; in the future, feed grain and distilling will be the main areas of growth in grain demand, and if the consumption of animal products and liquor is allowed to grow unchecked, the grain needed will hardly be met by a per capita production of 1,000 kg, let alone 400 kg. Such a high level of demand obviously far exceeds China's grain-supply capacity. Therefore it is necessary to exercise guidance over grain consumption. An appropriate price policy is the most effective measure: the price of grain must be reasonably fixed so that producers have an incentive to grow grain while consumption is curbed. The present price system holds down production and stimulates consumption. The retail prices of food for urban consumption contain a large subsidy. Meanwhile, because of the present welfare system, other items for urban consumption are very limited. As a result, when urban income increases, the additional money is spent mostly on non-staple foodstuffs. To change this situation, it is necessary gradually to reform the system for the purchase and marketing of food, as well as the wage and welfare systems. We should work out a reasonable purchase policy and change price subsidies for all town-dwellers into welfare subsidies for those on low incomes. It is essential to balance supply and demand through market price signals. If the system of monopoly purchase and marketing is reinstated merely because of the shortages in grain supply, the only result will be to aggravate the shortages. This has been borne out by years of experience. Therefore reform of the circulation system, which takes the establishment of market adjustment under the control of state plans as an objective, should be carried out resolutely and cautiously.

In summary, our consistent principle with respect to the problem of grain is to rely on the development of domestic production to guarantee supply. However, this does not exclude the limited use of the international market to diversify variety and balance annual surplus and shortage. It is necessary to ensure that people have enough to eat and that those on low incomes have a stable food supply. We should try as far as possible to ensure better food for the people, but this should not be achieved at the expense of all other social and developmental goals.

# 11

# Income Distribution

## Zhao Renwei

Income distribution is an important problem in the reform of China's economic system and in economic development. In this chapter some questions connected with personal income since reform are analysed, but before this is done some of the characteristics of the previous system are examined to clarify the starting-point for reform and future trends.

## Some characteristics of personal income distribution before reform

Reform of the Chinese economic system began in late 1978 and early 1979. Broadly speaking, personal income distribution at that time had the following characteristics.

1   Income was relatively equal. There are various estimates of this, most of which use the Gini coefficient. According to the *World Bank Report* (1981) in 1979 China's national Gini coefficient was 0.33 (0.31) in

**Table 11.1**   Gini coefficients for developing countries

| | | |
|---|---|---|
| India | 1975 | 0.38 |
| Indonesia | 1976 | 0.44 |
| Malaysia | 1973 | 0.50 |
| Rural | | |
| India | 1975 | 0.34 |
| Sri Lanka | 1969 | 0.35 |
| Philippines | 1970 | 0.39 |
| Malaysia | 1970 | 0.50 |
| Urban | | |
| India | 1970 | 0.42 |
| Pakistan | 1970 | 0.36 |
| Indonesia | 1976 | 0.43 |

**Table 11.2** Rural and non-rural levels of consumption

| Year | Level of consumption at current prices (yuan) | | | Index (1952 = 100) at comparable prices | | | Comparison of consumption levels (at current prices) | |
|------|------------------|-------|---------------|------------------|-------|---------------|-------|---------------|
| | Total population | Rural | Non-rural | Total population | Rural | Non-rural | Rural | Non-rural |
| 1952 | 76 | 62 | 148 | 100.0 | 100.0 | 100.0 | 1 | 2.4 |
| 1957 | 102 | 79 | 205 | 122.9 | 117.1 | 126.3 | 1 | 2.6 |
| 1965 | 125 | 100 | 237 | 132.9 | 125.2 | 136.9 | 1 | 2.4 |
| 1978 | 175 | 132 | 383 | 177.2 | 157.6 | 213.2 | 1 | 2.9 |

*Source:* ZTN 1987: 670–1

the rural areas); in 1980 it was 0.16 in urban areas (Liu 1984). However, some workers consider that the estimate for the rural areas was too high. Li Chengrui, former head of the State Statistical Bureau, put the rural figure in 1978 at 0.237 and the urban figure in 1977 at 0.185 (Li 1986). Adelman and Sunding (1987) estimated the rural Gini coefficient for 1978 at 0.222 and the urban coefficient at 0.165. Whatever the estimate, it is clear (table 11.1) that the figure is lower than that in a number of other developing countries (Liu 1984). It is well known that China has one of the lowest levels of income inequality. Before reform, income equalization, especially in the urban areas, was quite marked. This was due, firstly, to the fact that in general individuals had no income from private property apart from interest and cash deposits. Secondly, the belief that social equality is an aim of socialism led to a policy of low wage and salary differentials. Thirdly, there was a certain egalitarian tendency in traditional Chinese culture, typified by the Confucian dictum 'insufficiency is less to be feared than inequality', though to divorce equality from efficiency tends to blur the distinction between common prosperity and general penury.

2   There was relatively large differentiation between urban and rural income and consumption. Table 11.2 shows that the rural consumption level has been lower than the non-rural consumption level over a long period, and that the difference increased over the period 1952–78 from a ratio of 1:2.4 to 1:2.9. The difference between consumption levels in rural and urban areas, apart from historical reasons, was also the result of policy. For instance, before reform, agricultural prices were consistently kept low in order to support accumulation for industrialization. Rural–urban migration was strictly controlled, which contributed to the sharp division between levels of income and consumption.

3   The method of distributing consumer goods emphasized the distribution of actual goods – the supply system – which reduced the role of the market. This took the form of either per capita rationing, in order to provide for basic needs in grain, cloth, cooking oil etc., or free distribution according to a person's position, through which certain consumer goods and services, such as cars, telephones etc. were provided to those who needed them. Moreover, the large-scale subsidy of consumer goods and services was a disguised form of supply system. For example, rent for urban housing was, and still is, only nominal, and the housing stock is basically maintained by subsidies. The supply system limits the individual's freedom of choice, and encourages waste and corruption. In these circumstances, the level of income does not properly reflect the standard of living, nor do income differentials reflect actual income. The extent and long duration of distribution in kind in China is exceptional. It arose mainly from the low level of development and the lack of resources, but an important reason for its survival is that it was regarded as a socialist policy and evidence of the superiority of the socialist system.

4   The long-term wage freeze has created an income distribution pattern unfavourable to young people. Except in certain occupations, an individual's labour contribution is greater when in the prime of life, and income should correspond to this; however, in the 20 years from 1956 to 1976, wages were effectively frozen. Of course, the prices of consumer goods – particularly those which were rationed – were also frozen in this period. Although this 'double freeze' superficially made everyone equal, in fact this was not the case. In 1976, university teachers in their twenties earned as much as those in their thirties and forties, i.e. after a 20-year freeze too many employees were underpaid. Figure 11.1 shows that the distribution of wage income to employees in 1976 is neither the bell-shaped curve A nor the skewed curve B, but is represented by the sharp curve C. The effect of this income distribution on different age groups has been discussed elsewhere (Zhao 1985). The undesirable social and economic consequences of this income distribution structure have not yet been entirely obliterated. The continued low income of middle-aged intellectuals is clearly connected with the former system (see below).

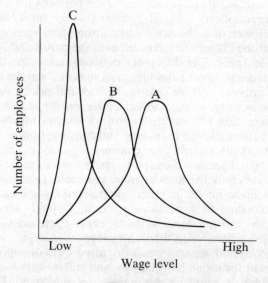

**Figure 11.1**

# Some changes in personal income distribution since reform

Since the beginning of reform there has been a substantial increase in the level of rural and urban income and consumption. For example, according to data obtained by the State Statistical Bureau during the period of the

Sixth Five Year Plan (1981–6), the average income available for living expenses for urban families was 752 yuan in 1985 compared with 439 yuan in 1980, an increase of 313 yuan (71.3 per cent) or an average annual growth rate of 11.4 per cent. If these figures are corrected for price inflation, the annual increase was 6.9 per cent. The equivalent data for rural inhabitants gave the average income for rural families as 397.6 yuan in 1985, which is 206.3 yuan (or over 100 per cent) higher than the 1980 figure of 191.3 yuan, an average annual increase of 15.8 per cent or 13.7 per cent after correction for price inflation (State Statistical Bureau 1986: 84, 88). In 1985 the national average level of per capita consumption stood at 407 yuan, an annual increase of 8.8 per cent over the five-year period (State Statistical Bureau 1986: 151).

The increase in income and consumption levels can also be seen from changes in the structure of consumption. Between 1978 and 1985 the proportion of average annual urban family consumption spent on food (the Engel coefficient) fell from 57.5 to 53.3 per cent, and that of the rural population fell from 67.7 to 57.7 per cent. The proportion spent on grain decreased, while that for meat, dairy products and superior vegetables increased. Expenditure on woollen cloth, silk and woollen goods increased more than on cotton cloth. Electrical goods showed a marked increase: in 1986 there were 93 television sets for every 100 urban families compared with 17 per 100 rural families. Between 1978 and 1986, the average living space per head in towns rose from 4.2 to 8.0 square metres, and in the countryside it rose from 8.1 to 15.3 square metres (ZTN 1987: 693, 700, 710).

Since reform there has been a general increase in income, with that of the lower-income groups increasing proportionately more. The modal income is rising. For instance, 61.6 per cent of rural families had an income of less than 200 yuan in 1980, but this had decreased to only 12.2 per cent in 1985; the number of families with an income of 200–500 yuan increased from 36.8 to 65.5 per cent, the number with an income of 500–1,000 yuan increased from 1.6 to 20 per cent and the number with over 1,000 yuan increased to 2.3 per cent. In other words, during the Sixth Five Year Plan, 49.4 per cent of peasant families escaped from poverty (an income of less than 200 yuan), 28.7 per cent moved into the category of 'those with enough to eat and enough to wear' (200–500 yuan), 18.4 per cent became 'well-to-do' (500–1,000 yuan) and 2.3 per cent became prosperous. In this period the average (modal) peasant income moved from the poor group with an income of less than 200 yuan (61.6 per cent) to the group of those 'with enough to eat and wear' (65.5 per cent) (State Statistical Bureau 1986: 88). A similar development took place among urban families: in 1977, 65.03 per cent of individuals in such families had an income of less than 300 yuan, while 62.7 per cent had moved into the 420–600 yuan income group in 1985 (Li 1984).

The change in urban and rural income and consumption differentials is worth noting. In general, the increase in the rural areas has been faster than in the towns and cities, and so the differential has decreased to some

**Table 11.3**   Income and consumption of urban and rural families

| Annual average per capita (all members of family) | Absolute value at current prices (yuan) | | Average annual rate of increase (based on comparable prices), 1979–84 (%) |
|---|---|---|---|
| | 1978 | 1984 | |
| *Urban families* | | | |
| Per capita income | 316.0 | 607.6 | 8.2 |
| Per capita consumption expenditure | 311.2 | 559.4 | 7.0 |
| *Rural families* | | | |
| Per capita income | 133.6 | 355.3 | 15.0 |
| Per capita consumption expenditure | 116.1 | 273.8 | 13.2 |

*Source*: Li, 1986

extent. This is clearly shown in the period 1978–84. Table 11.3 shows that whereas peasant and urban family income and consumption expenditure levels were both growing quite rapidly between 1978 and 1984, that of peasants was faster and consequently the difference between them decreased. As noted above, in 1978 the ratio between peasant and non-agricultural population consumption was 1:2.9. This decreased to 1:2.5 in 1981 and to 1:2.2 in 1984 (ZTN 1987: 670). This was caused, among other things, by the change in rural economic structure following the rapid increase in agricultural production and the considerable increase in the state purchasing price for agricultural products. However, after 1985, the influence of these factors weakened and the former momentum in production, income and expenditure subsided; thus the ratio of agricultural to non-agricultural consumption was 1:2.3 in 1985 and 1:2.5 in 1986 (ZTN 1987: 670).

Although urban incomes have risen considerably since reform, their distribution has tended to become more equal. According to Li Chengrui, the Gini coefficient of income for urban families was 0.185 in 1977 and fell to 0.168 in 1984. The main reason for this is that their wages are still subject to a unified state wage system, with its low differentials, and in the early stage of reform emphasis was on raising the income of the lower paid groups.

The growing role of the market in economic life had led to an expansion of the monetization and commoditization of income and consumption. In the 20 years before reform, basic consumer goods such as food and clothing, and even other items of daily use, were distributed by ration coupon. Until the 1970s, 73 items were still rationed in China (Jiang 1987). Since reform started, rationing has decreased considerably, and cloth rationing, which lasted for nearly 30 years, came to an end in 1983. Rationing has now been virtually abolished, except in the case of grain, oil and a small number of consumer goods in great demand, although there is seasonal rationing of meat, eggs and so on, depending on local supply. The proportion of commoditized expenditure in total peasant living expenses increased from 39.7 per cent in 1978 to 62.8 per cent in 1986. This includes the cost of accommodation, which is already 98.2 per cent commoditized. The commoditization of urban accommodation is far more difficult, but experiments are already under way.

What worries people most in all this reform and change is whether the policy of allowing a few to enrich themselves will not create polarization, with the rich become richer and the poorer. Indeed, since reform a small number of people have become rich, but the reasons and results are different and policies must be adapted accordingly (see below). In general it is not true to say that polarization has already appeared or is imminent in China. The trend in both peasant and urban families towards a decrease in the number of low paid and an increase in the number of better paid is clearly not polarization, but poor and rich both becoming richer. The Gini coefficient of income distribution for urban families has tended to decline in recent years, and in general the problem is excessive equalization rather than polarization. The Gini coefficient of rural income distribution, in contrast, has risen to some extent, which is proof of increasing income differentiation. The question is whether this has already reached the stage of polarization. According to the State Statistical Bureau the Gini coefficients between 1978 and 1986 were as follows: 1978, 0.2124; 1980, 0.2366; 1981, 0.2388; 1982, 0.2318; 1983, 0.2459; 1984, 0.2577; 1985, 0.2636. Although there has been some increase in the rural figure, it has not been excessive. Some Chinese specialists consider that in China the maintenance of a Gini coefficient of 0.3–0.4 for a relatively long period would be appropriate; less than 0.2 would be excessively egalitarian, while 0.4 would be too great a differential (Huang 1987). Thus the increase in the rural Gini coefficient only indicates that chronic egalitarianism has been corrected to some extent, and from the point of view of encouraging growth the present differentials are not too high but are rather on the low side.

To achieve a correct balance between efficiency and equality, income differentials should show an inverted U-shaped curve (small–large–small). Efficiency and equality should receive different emphasis at different stages of economic development: in a situation of extreme underdevelopment, such as in the difficult post-war period in China, equality should be emphasized in order to guarantee food for all; however, when the economy starts to modernize (the take-off period), efficiency should be emphasized more in order to stimulate economic development. In a developed economy, when the material base is solid and the population has achieved a higher spiritual level, then equality should again be stressed. At present our economy is modernizing in the first stage of socialism and pre-reform egalitarian tendencies are still marked; therefore priority should be given to efficiency, and due attention should be paid to social justice. In other words, a policy of income distribution based on the principle of 'higher efficiency' as a premise for the realization of social justice' (Zhao 1987: 39) is the correct choice.

# The problems to be solved and prospects for the future

China's economic structure is in the process of reform; income distribution is also in a period of considerable change with new problems arising before old ones are solved, creating a situation of great complexity.

## The rapid enrichment of a few people

Egalitarian ideas about income distribution still survive, but the dissolution of the old rigid economic structure has allowed some people to achieve rather high incomes, and this has led to debate. We should distinguish between two different forms of enrichment. Some have become rich through honest work and good management, and they should be encouraged. For instance, it is reasonable that the income of lessees or contractors is higher than that of an average employee, reflecting the rewards for innovation and risk-taking. Naturally, if individual income exceeds a certain limit, it should be legally regulated by income tax. Moreover, some owners of private enterprises make a relatively high income from employing labour. If this income is obtained legally it should be permitted, but it should be limited and regulated according to policy. However, illegal income is sometimes obtained either by taking advantage of opportunities presented by changes in the economic structure, especially with respect to prices and taxes, or by trickery or cheating. This should indeed be forbidden by law. Only by making such distinctions and devising policies accordingly can the problem of polarization and an excessive range of income be avoided.

There are two aspects of this policy: one positive and encouraging, and the other negative, restrictive and even prohibitive. They are complementary; the positive advantages should not be rejected merely because there are negative aspects. Some economists have suggested that in order to encourage production, the enrichment of three categories of people should be encouraged: good managers (in both state and private enterprises), those contributing to the natural and social sciences, and exceptionally hard workers in any walk of life who make outstanding contributions to society (*Guangming Ribao*, 24 December 1987).

## Creating conditions for equal competition and equality of opportunity

Complaints about the rapid enrichment of a few and increasing income differentials are really directed against the inequality of opportunity which lies behind them. The problem of how to provide equal competitive opportunities to individuals, enterprises and industries has not yet been solved in China. For instance, the restrictions on population movement and the movement of qualified personnel are a barrier to equal opportunity, particularly between urban and rural residents. These restrictions have been severely criticized: the World Bank report commented that China's 'structural reform is faced with a fundamental question – the assignment of labour and the restrictions on population movement. This policy undoubtedly has its political and social rationale, and any change must be gradual. But from the point of view of economic efficiency and equality, this policy is difficult to justify' (World Bank 1981). These restrictions have their own history and cannot be abolished overnight, but conditions which will allow their gradual removal must be encouraged. This is a necessary requirement for the further progress of reform.

At present China is suffering from the contradictions and friction arising from the transition from one economic system to another; during the reform process, new inequalities in competition may emerge from the coexistence of different systems of ownership and different industries. For example, in areas where the private economy has developed rapidly, state-owned industry has often found itself disadvantaged with respect to private industry with regard to prices, taxation etc., leading to marked differences in wages in the public and private sectors. Consequently, if employees in state-owned industry cannot find themselves a second job, they sometimes have no choice but to encourage their wives to engage in private economic activity in order to supplement family income. In areas where private industry and commerce has mushroomed, labour income is higher than in agriculture. According to an investigation of the Yishan District of Wenzhou (Zhejiang) Municipality (Economics Research Institute of the Chinese Academy of Social Sciences 1987: 55) the remuneration in agriculture, industry and commerce is in the ratio 1:5:11. The problem of low income from agricultural work and the shrinking of the agricultural sector has been solved to some extent by 'using industry to supplement agriculture', i.e. supplementing low agricultural revenue from the relatively higher incomes from involvement in industry and commerce at the level of *xiang*, village and even family. In the long term, however, it will be necessary to achieve a suitable balance between industrial and agricultural incomes if the shrinkage of agriculture is to be prevented. In order to do this, apart from increasing economies of scale in agriculture, it will be necessary to provide equal competitive conditions with respect to prices and taxation in different sectors.

**Table 11.4** Comparison of the average monthly income from manual and non-manual labour, February 1982

| | Sample size | Monthly income (yuan) | | | | | | | | |
| | | Under 25 | 26–30 | 31–5 | 36–40 | 41–5 | 46–50 | 51–5 | Over 55 |
|---|---|---|---|---|---|---|---|---|---|
| Manual workers | 1,110 | 66.60 | 74.23 | 77.65 | 85.39 | 90.03 | 96.92 | 105.01 | 114.73 |
| Non-manual workers | | | | | | | | | |
| Industry | 261 | 57.10 | 64.25 | 72.30 | 77.48 | 83.10 | 95.09 | 101.55 | 103.30 |
| Services | 851 | 62.99 | 63.06 | 70.95 | 77.34 | 76.18 | 85.84 | 107.51 | 143.22 |

*Source:* He, 1982

## Speeding up the monetization of distribution methods

Monetization of income and consumption has increased since reform, but only slowly. In the distribution of food, clothing and utilities, monetization has grown relatively fast, but because of the low base from which it began, owing to economic fluctuations and other reasons, it has been impossible to eliminate distribution in kind entirely. Although in general it has been decreasing, in some areas it has increased. The commercialization of housing has been slow because of opposition from vested interests, among other reasons. Because rent, water and electricity prices have been frozen, the proportion of total expenditure of urban families on rent has fallen from 1.93 per cent in 1978 to 0.9 per cent in 1986; similarly, expenditure on water and electricity fell from 1.35 per cent in 1978 to 1.11 per cent in 1986 (Li 1986: 9; ZTN 1987: 692). The government has been forced to make substantial increases in its subsidies in order to achieve this. According to Li and Zheng (1987), the subsidy to urban families (e.g. rent, grain subsidy, free medical care and education) is equal to about 80 per cent of their wage income. No figures are available for subsidies on higher levels of consumption. The commercialization of this category, though affecting only a small minority, would be highly sensitive and should eventually be linked to reform of the whole wage system. With the development of reform of the economic and political system this problem will have to be put on the agenda.

## Low income from non-manual labour, particularly middle-aged intellectuals

For a long time the income of non-manual workers in China has been low. Table 11.4 shows the results obtained from a sample of 2,000 individuals in a survey carried out in February 1982. Another survey performed in 1985, in departments employing a relatively large number of scientific, educational, cultural and medical workers, shows that average salaries were about 10 per cent lower than those of employees in industry and construction.

The problem of the income of middle-aged intellectuals is particularly striking. Most of them graduated from universities in the 1950s and 1960s, and they have been the chief victims of the virtual wage freeze over the last 20 years. Although this group has now been given high-level titles and receive commensurate salaries, they are still underpaid. For example, in the Beijing area in 1956 the minimum monthly salary of an assistant professor was 149.5 yuan. After preliminary wage reform in 1985, the minimum salary was 122 yuan, and even when length-of-service allowances were included it was only 135 yuan – lower than in 1956, and substantially lower if price inflation is taken into account. One consequence of this is the high mortality rate of middle-aged intellectuals. The majority of the 82 intellectuals employed by the Chinese Academy of Social Sciences who died in 1986 were middle-aged. In 1987 nine 50-year-old researchers and high-ranking engineers died. The ratio of mortality of old compared with middle-aged intellectuals is 1:3.3. Another consequence is that there has been a change in the attitude of those taking up employment, with some young people abandoning their education to go into business. These problems have already caused concern. Future wage reform, and indeed economic strategy in general, must include appropriate measures to deal with them.

## Controlling the growth of income

Since reform there has been a substantial growth in average income. However, in recent years the growth has become excessively rapid. In 1984, for example, cash payments made by the banks for wages increased by 22.3 per cent, whereas labour productivity increased by only 8.7 per cent and national income by only 12 per cent. In 1986, the national outlay for wages and salaries was 20 per cent higher than in the previous year, a real increase of 12.2 per cent if the effects of price inflation are taken into account. This was 7.4 per cent higher than the increase in national income and 4 per cent higher than the increase in labour productivity (Hu 1987). This rapid increase in incomes has become an important cause of inflation which, in turn, has caused a decrease in real income for some people. The State Statistical Bureau estimates that in 1986 a fifth of the urban population suffered a decrease in real income and that in the first half of 1987 this increased to two-fifths, mainly as a result of price increases (Ji et al. 1988). Bringing income growth into line with the growth of national income and productivity is an important part of macrocontrol of income distribution.

## References

Adelman, I. and Sunding, D. (1987) Economic policy and income distribution in China. *Journal of Comparative Economics*, September, 444–61.

Economics Research Institute of the Chinese Academy of Social Sciences (1987) *Zhongguo Xiangzhen Qiyede Fazhan Yu Jingji Tizhi (The Development and Economic System of Township Enterprises in China)*.

*Guangming Ribao* (24 December 1987) Rang nayibufen ren xian fuyu qilai – fang Xiao Zhuoji (Who should first be allowed to enrich themselves – a visit to Xiao Zhuoji).

He Xiaopei (1982) Guanyu muqian naoli laodong he tili laodong baochoude ruogan diaocha. *Jingji Yanjiu*, August, no. 8.

Hu Aidi (1987) Lishi yu xianshide bijiao – guanyu woguo jumin xiaofei shuiping de duihua. *Jingji Ribao*, 13 October.

Huang Daoxia (1987) Nongcun you meiyou liangji fenhua (Is there differentiation in the countryside?) *Banyuetan*, no. 22.

Ji Naifu, Chen Naijin and Chen Yun (1988) Guanyu wujiade tongxin. *Guangming Ribao*, 13 January.

Jiang Bo (1987) Biaozheng de bian qian. *Jingji Ribao*, 15 October.

Li Chengrui (1986) Guanyu Zhongguo jinjiniande jingji zhengce dui jumin shouru he xiaofei zhuangkuang yingxiang de tongji baogao. *Jingji Yanjiu*, January, no. 1.

Li Tiejung and Zheng Lianming (1987) Shilun shixian xiaokang shuipingde tiaojian he te dian. *Jingji Ribao*, 18 July.

Liu Guoguang (ed.) (1984) *Zhongguo Jingji Fazhan Zhanlue Wenti Yanjiu (The Study of Some Questions Concerning China's Development Strategy)*. Shanghai.

State Statistical Bureau (1986) *Liu Wu'qiujian Guomin Jingji He Shehui Fazhan Gaikuang (The National Economic and Social Development During the Sixth Five Year Plan)*.

World Bank (1981) *China: The Development of a Socialist Economy*. Washington, DC: World Bank.

Zhao Renwei (1985) Laodongzhe geren shouru fenpeide ruogan bianhua qushi (Some trends in the distribution of workers' personal incomes). *Jingji Yanjiu*, March, no. 3.

Zhao Ziyang (1987) Yanzhe you Zhongguo tesede shehuizhuyi daolu qianjinzai Zhongguo gongchandang di shisanci quanguo daibiaodahuishang de baogao (25 October 1987). In *Zhongguo Gongchandang di Shisanci quanguo Daibiao Dahui Wenjian Huibian*. Beijing: Renmin Chubanshe.

ZTN [*Chinese Statistical Yearbook (Zhongguo Tongji Nianjian)*]. Beijing: Zhongguo Tongji Chubanshe, various issues.

# 12

# Technological Policy

## Peter Wiles

The government and people of China are extremely interested in technical progress, but there does not appear to be a settled definite technological policy, nor even a clash between two or more definite policies. In this chapter a policy is suggested: hold back certain areas as 'game preserves' of labour-intensive technology to ensure fuller employment and greater equality. In doing this much of the elementary modern economics of technological choice is discussed, and thus this chapter also serves a didactic purpose.

Human beings and their governments have or, in the latter case, should have some overriding economic goals. Their economies must ensure (a) more consumption, (b) at least some employment for all who are able and willing to work, (c) national income growth to finance the investment and technical progress necessary for (a) and the investment necessary for (b), and (d) avoidance of gross inequality. It suffices for most of this chapter to leave this grossly oversimplified statement as it stands.

Our first step must be to explain (b): why is work good rather than bad? In Western microeconomics work is wholly bad: we sacrifice our leisure in order to extract money from the market by work. We do not wish to do this; we are forced to by the threat of poverty. We would prefer never to work. It is hardly necessary to point out that this is not merely undesirable – many undesirable things are true – but also false, though not invariably false. For instance, it appears to be true of Australian aborigines, whose many languages contain no word for work. Much more importantly for us, it is true of all work done in overtime or in unsocial hours. This is the important point: we all take a 'work is bad' attitude when we are fatigued or find our family life disrupted. There is also, of course, dirty and dangerous work.

Apart from this, work is definitely good for normal people. By work each individual asserts himself as a citizen: he/she achieves a sense of worth. It is his/her contribution to society, and the wage obtained,[1] even a market-determined wage under capitalism, expresses society's recognition. If one has no work and no wage, one has no self-worth and society gives one no recognition. Moreover to do no work is to be bored, to have surplus energy which is easily diverted into crime and eventually to become, through loss of self-confidence and atrophy of skill, unemployable. In my opinion, Karl Marx exaggerated when he said work was an honour, even under full communism. Indeed, no factory worker would have written that! But his is still a far superior attitude to the cynical and untruthful approach of the neoclassical economists that work is exclusively a disutility. He erred only in that the non-pecuniary benefits of work over unemployment are also very considerable under capitalism. It is that system's failure to provide moderately satisfying work for all who are able and willing that we who live under it complain of most. It should also be noted that, as a practical matter, the wage is not there only to enable us to live but is an integral part of the earner's self-worth.

Our central question is as follows. Here is the sum we are willing to set aside, as a nation, for investment and research and development (R&D);[2] how shall we best use it for the short- and long-run welfare of the people? For technological choice in connexion with a new investment can give work to many or to few, at a low or a high wage respectively.[3] It is the main point of this chapter that welfare is not just the remainder of the national income after deducting investment, not private consumption alone, not even private plus public consumption, not indeed any kind of expenditure alone, but also a job and a wage[4] and the ensuing consciousness of citizenship and worth. That wage must be a 'living' or 'fair' wage – adjectives on which people put their own interpretation. We relegate the zero-wage commune, a totally different human system, to the appendix.

Thus work is partly good and partly bad. Figure 12.1 shows the appropriate adjustment to the neoclassical labour supply diagram – if any serious and genuinely worthwhile adjustment can be made. However, since it is not only a cost of production but also a benefit, *it is not necessarily right to economize it*. This great truth – for I can call it no less – has a number of consequences, some very upsetting.

First, it may not be profitable for an enterprise to change technologies and economize labour, since the capital cost of the alternative technology might be so high as to raise total cost per unit output. This is a perfectly simple possibility that troubles nobody. Our problems begin where it is profitable to the enterprise or ministry to economize labour. Assume that the accountancy is correct and that the prices upon which it is based are a rational representation of the relative scarcities of the various inputs and outputs: should we be guided by profit and dismiss labour because the new technology demands it?

Of course, the 'most profitable' is not necessarily the 'most advanced' or newest technology. Let us consider a choice between three technologies: A is the one that we have and know; B is newer than A and the cheapest; C applies the very latest discoveries, but it uses rare materials and/or too much capital. The costs of C per unit output are little less than those of A. However, it must be said in defence of C that the prices of all these other

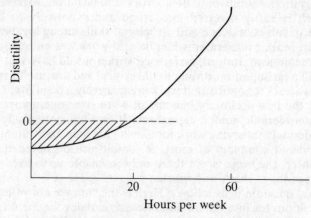

**Figure 12.1**  Curve of marginal disutility. The longer the working week the more displeasure is manifested at the addition of an extra hour, and at 60 hours the curve becomes vertical which means refusal to work more. The shaded area that cuts off at 20 hours is of negative disutility, and attempts to represent in a neoclassical manner the positive feelings that we have towards *some* work. Textbook diagrams place the whole curve above zero, but they do not say why. Needless to say, this two-dimensional diagram is still a substantial misrepresentation of many human attitudes to work.

inputs vary in different countries. Thus it will not be surprising if C is the most profitable in the United States but B is the most profitable in China.

Shall we substitute B for A? Acquiescence in the market has a very high cost of unemployment. Resistance also has a very high cost – loss of output. By refusing B, we forgo the extra outputs it will produce for the same cost. It is not simply the profits of some (capitalist or socialist) enterprise that we sacrifice, it is extra output for the use of the nation as a whole. Therefore when we make these choices there is a trade-off between employment and output. We should be grateful that very often, perhaps almost always, we make other kinds of choices in problems were employment and output point the same way or are irrelevant. When two important principles clash we face much perplexity, and may have to settle for an illogical compromise.[5]

The importance for us here of the apparently irrelevant C is that it catches the imagination, is prestigious and makes us all feel proud. Therefore a hypothetical China – not, we hope, the real China – will import it at vast expense and then set it up without the correct labour, materials and ancillary equipment. Then, in addition to the loss that it would have made anyway because the relative prices of these inputs are unsuitable (see above), a super-loss is made because the labour input lacks the proper training and the material inputs are not of the precise quality required, and so the technology does not even work. This is technological snobbery, which is a disease of poor countries above all, although medium-rich countries like the United Kingdom have also been known to imitate the super-rich unprofitably.[6]

Socialism is particularly prone to this disease, since its enterprises and planners are so much less constrained by profitability. The capitalist public sector is, of course, more socialist than capitalist and often behaves in the same way. The vulgar, but realistic, cynicism of capitalists, who stand to lose their own money and not that of the taxpayers, is the perfect answer to technological snobbery.

Yet one great socialist was quite immune to these temptations: Mao Tsetung. It is easy to laugh and/or cry over many of his economic policies, but here at least he was quite right. Most notably, after the withdrawal of the Soviet experts in 1960 he stopped buying Soviet machines. The Central Committee of the Chinese Communist Party wrote to the Soviet Central Committee as follows: 'Did you think we wanted them for display?' Surely that was Mao's own personal style? In any case it was a paradigmatic attack on technological snobbery: no new technology without new knowhow.

Many technologies are very rigid, allowing no substitution between labour and other factors. This is particularly true for the advanced technologies. Let such a technology (call it I) be completely rigid, and yet the cheapest producer and therefore the one yielding most output. However, the only factor combination that it permits is likely to be very labour saving. An older technology II might be equally rigid, and only 10 per cent more expensive. However, if it employs 20 per cent more people

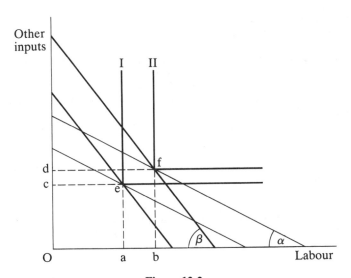

**Figure 12.2**

**Table 12.1** Investment allocation choices and their consequences

| | | Year 1[a] | Year 2 A | Year 2 B |
|---|---|---|---|---|
| 1 | Net national product $Q$ (thousand yuan) | 100 | 105[b] | 104[b] |
| 2 | Net[c] national savings and investment $S+I$ (thousand yuan) | 10 | 11.69[d] | 10.86[d] |
| 3 | Labour available (man-years) | 1,000 | 1,000 | 1,000 |
| 4 | Labour employed (man-years) | 600 | 615 | 620 |
| | *Net national income distributed* | | | |
| 5 | Wages (thousand yuan) | 70 | 71.8[e] | 72.0[f] |
| 6 | Non-wage value added[g] (thousand yuan) | 30 | 33.2[h] | 32.0[h] |
| 7 | Capital stock $K$ on 1 Jan. (thousand yuan) | 300 | 310[i] | 310[i] |
| 8 | $K/Q$ | 3 | 2.95 | 2.98 |
| 9 | Annual wage (yuan) | 116.67 | 116.85 | 116.13 |
| 10 | Savings[d] | 10 | 10.83 | 10.59 |
| 11 | Welfare[j] (%) | – | 6.5 | 6.8 |
| 12 | Factor productivity residual taking[k] $Q = K^{0.3} L^{0.7}$ (%) | – | 1.183 | 1.178 |

[a] Arbitrary base values.

[b] Reasonable growth rates.

[c] Replacement and repair have effects but do not appear. We need net investment for row 7.

[d] $S = 2\%$ of wages $+ 28.6\%$ of non-wage value added; both percentages are arbitrary, and in the base column they yield the (also arbitrary) 10.

[e] The 15 extra workers in row 4 receive 120 yuan each; compare row 9.

[f] The 20 workers taken on are also unskilled in view of the easier technology; they receive only 100 yuan.

[g] Mainly profits and taxes; this is used for all kinds of public purposes including investment and public consumption.

[h] Residual.

[i] $300 + 10$ in the base column. However, the extra 10 is spent on either technology accordingly.

[j] See text.

[k] The conventional exponents (or weights) 0.4 and 0.6 are shifted towards labour in view of the backwardness of the economy. If year 2 were a base we would have slightly different weights depending on whether we were on path A or path B, but year 1 is our base.

we face a real dilemma between output and employment.

In figure 12.2 we show two completely rigid technologies I and II, each of them capable of functioning only at points e and f where their curves make right-angled turns. Both curves represent the same single constant output throughout (I and II produce the same quantity of goods or services), and these turning points are their minimum cost points. At Oa/Oc I is cheaper than II, which is at Ob/Od. This is true whatever the relative price of the two inputs, which is tan $\alpha$ for a low wage and tan $\beta$ for a high wage. The shift from $\beta$ to $\alpha$ causes no substitution of labour for other things with either technology. The unthinking technological policy is to prefer Ie to IIf because it represents a smaller sum of money. However, this puts ab people out of work, and it may be a better policy to employ the extra ab, who therefore in a sense cost us nothing because they and 'we' prefer them to work, and the only cost is cd, which we decide to bear.

Thus, given a certain volume of resources we can set up say 10 enterprises like I or eight enterprises like II – the latter at a loss of 20 per cent of total output given that the input volumes are of the same quantity. However, the 20 per cent output loss has to be reckoned against the 33 per cent (ab/Oa) labour employment gain. Let us carry out this procedure with less startling numbers and using a nationwide model. Since there are so many absolute quantities and parameters, in a short chapter we can only use an arithmetical illustration. The economy is that of a socialist less-developed country in which the government disposes of all national income that is not wages, there is high unemployment, and two technologies are available, of which A (high technology) requires more capital per unit of labour and yields more output per combined unit of both, and vice versa for B (low technology). Looking ahead from year 1, what are the consequences of putting the national net savings of 10,000 yuan into either A or B?

Table 12.1 shows that if we choose B, we sacrifice output to employment. Any measure of the growth of welfare will of course be arbitrary. The figures given are the percentage growth of wages plus half the non-wage value added plus half the percentage growth of employment, where the halves are arbitrary relative weights. The factor productivity residual is, of course, lower with the less efficient technology. However, the less efficient technology also yields less savings and therefore less investment in subsequent years. This is a very serious argument against our proposed technology manipulation. Nevertheless, we believe it to be less serious than the balance-of-payments argument (see below), which cuts the other way, for domestic finance is less important than foreign finance.

The concept of this trade-off is anathema to the strict neoclassical economist and also to the less dogmatic Keynesian. The former holds that there is always some substitutability and therefore a wage low enough for more labour to be taken on; then, since labour must have a positive marginal product, it will always be possible to increase output. However, if the required factor proportion is completely rigid this is not the case. Even a negative wage may induce the enterprise to let people in, but the marginal product *must* be zero since no substitution is possible *ex hypothesi*. The extra workers are useless. Meanwhile the greater employment has to be subsidized, and the low level of the wage, which all workers of equal skill are eventually forced to accept, is demeaning, unhealthy etc. as discussed above. It also creates gross inequality, and so is incompatible with economic goal (d).

Keynesians are equally blind. They claim to increase employment cheaply by monetary means: stimulate demand and thus increase the use of productive capacity. They are completely optimistic about the concordance of output and employment, and our trade-off is again anathema. This is because, taking its origin in the world slump of the 1930s, the doctrine correctly diagnosed the troubles of the advanced capitalist world at that time as monetary. At that time there was also a deviant sect of, mainly American, economists, without formal education in the subject, who called themselves Technocrats. They held the slump to be due to technological unemployment: an absurd notion at that time. Moreover, to accept the importance of technological unemployment in other places and times is to assert that fuller employment is costly and difficult, demanding sacrifice.

Keynesians, then, are optimists. We shall now leave them aside as irrelevant to a planned economy unless the plan is so loose as to be quite ineffective and money, and hence aggregate monetary demand, is all that matters. There is now always enough demand; indeed, as China knows, there is far too much. Monetary stimulation is the opposite of what is wanted, and yet there is still unemployment.

The assumption of rigid technologies, incapable of substituting one input for another even when relative prices vary, must now be removed. As long as it is accepted, there exist definable workplaces and when these are empty there are vacancies. It is as if the enterprise had a wooden board with round or hexagonal holes in it, and was therefore seeking a certain number of round or hexagonal pegs to put into them. The marginal product of a hexagonal peg is zero if the empty hole is round and there are no hexagonal holes. This situation is not wholly dissimilar to an advanced technology, but even then it is always in fact possible to split up a 'task' (i.e. the skill definitions that determine the shape of the 'hole') between workers of different education and abilities, and so fill say two workplaces with three only slightly unsuitable people.

The consequence is that, if wages are low enough, a high-technology machine can after all be made to work by an ill-adapted labour force, and yield a profit. Indeed, only two types of machine come to mind that constitute a workplace for just one person with a closely defined qualification: the road vehicle and the typewriter![7] In any case, the rigidly defined workplace is an industrial concept. Perfect cases of substitutability, i.e. of undefined workplaces, are agriculture and administration. The service industries are also very flexible, as are the crafts and most of the simpler industrial technologies – however, the operation of road vehicles is one of these, and is the major exception.

Accordingly, we set out in figure 12.3 the extra complications brought about by the overwhelmingly more common case of substitutability between labour and other inputs. The enterprise, or planner, must first have confidence in the prices (tan $\alpha$, tan $\beta$ and the new tan $\gamma$) that he is using. It is well known that this state of affairs has not been achieved in China. The two input-substitution curves admit of many changes in input proportions, each within itself, let alone the possibility of switching technologies. Moreover, the curves intersect – a feature that could easily have been excluded in this figure or included in figure 12.2. Therefore there is a new price tan $\gamma$ at which we are indifferent between the two technologies, since the weighted sum of all the inputs is identical at x and y. This feature could also have been built into figure 12.2. However, above all the choice of technology is now far more price sensitive, and indeed prices dictate it. There are, for instance, w and z: they simply follow from $\beta$ and $\alpha$.

If we now pursue the labour-intensive policy B described above, we shall find ourselves creating, or preserving from the past, whole industries, scattered or regionally concentrated, using a low technology and incapable

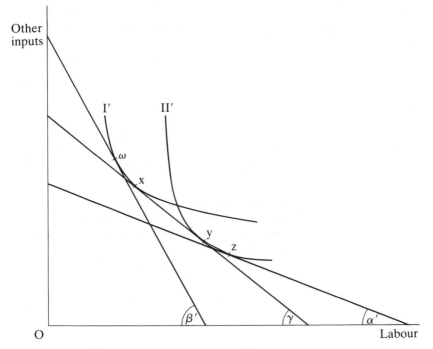

**Figure 12.3** Since I' and II' cut each other there are prices like $\beta'$ and $\alpha'$ that choose one or other of the two technologies, and $\gamma$ chooses some of each. However, I is superior to II (figure 12.2) at all prices. This has little to do with the contrast between the smoothness of this figure and the angularity of figure 12.2.

of price competition with possibly other domestic producers and certainly foreigners. Therefore, the policy stringently requires a form of protection after a certain time.

The prime practical case where our technological 'game-reserve' policy has been created is India, a country where the state of technology, the ability to invest and the level of wages are very similar to those in China. Eight million handloom weavers are kept in business by a system of quotas on power-loom cloth, on power-looms and on imports of both items. The quotas permit the power-looms existing in 1947, shortly after Independence, to continue to produce, to be replaced and to be repaired, but not to grow in numbers.

The system has achieved its aim of retaining many poor or rather poor people in work. It has not inhibited technical change in dyes, designs or the nature of yarn, which are unaffected by the technology controls. It has, of course, raised costs and prices, but not enough to deter the Indian buyer. Why does she buy? The answer is Gandhiite ideology, which is the basic weapon of the Indian handloom weaver. Gandhi entertained many of the ideas discussed here, under the name *swadeshi*, from protectionism through fuller employment by low technology to equality. His symbolic publicity portrait showed him spinning by hand, but this was so costly in comparison with power spindles that it had to be abandoned, together with the whole anti-industrial, anti-'progress' ideology. The hand-loom was left as a sentimental obeisance to the struggle for Independence and the great man who won it, and an apology for the nation's apostasy from *swadeshi*.

However, the hand-loom is not very inefficient, merely rather inefficient. The Indian middle-class woman happily buys expensive hand-woven saris, which come in all styles and qualities. She knows she is paying 'too much' (she also pays too much for power-woven saris, of course, since all saris compete with each other at these higher prices), and she does so for historical reasons and/or those poorer than herself. The Indian hand-loom is thus the paradigm of what I mean: what Mao Tsetung achieved in one way Gandhi achieved in another. In both cases, however, ideology fought alongside logic.

Naturally wages for the hand-loom workers are lower than in the power-loom sector. Whatever Keynes said, low wages are the first condition of fuller employment. Power-looms are not heavily taxed, but administratively restricted. This seems foolish, since the Ministry of Finance could do with the money. No doubt the rent accumulating in the hands of the power-loom owners and workers reconciles them wonderfully to the knowledge that they are not allowed to expand.

The special virtue of the protection of Indian hand-loom weavers is that the 'game preserve' within which they live and work is real, not a pretence. There is competition. There is bankruptcy, and so there is responsible management. There is a product which must be profitably sold. There is technical progress in all other aspects. Work is serious. No one is digging holes and filling them up again. Of course, the unskilled workers are very poor by all ordinary standards, but they have life and hope instead of death and despair – provided that they make an effort – for they have employment.

There are very many similar public sector jobs, of course. Indeed the Third World public sectors exist in large part to create 'unnecessary' jobs, and we must not forget that the classical Soviet-type economy is nearly all public sector and so is somewhat similar. However, these jobs, as we saw above, are too obviously unreal, demand too little effort and do too little to raise morale. Our Indian example, although it is rare, difficult to imitate and blessed by its unusual origin, is superior (Adhyaru et al. 1979: 43).

The Indian hand-loom weaver teaches us something else: to protect a technology is also to protect the country against imports. The argument goes as follows. We forbid a certain sector (the power-loom factories in Bombay) to grow, or we even abolish it. However, the hand-woven sari has a higher cost, and therefore a higher price is established. This invites traders to import, so as to replace the power-woven cloth, which *ex hypothesi* was selling at fractionally below the import price. Therefore this price remains well below the hand-woven price, and protection is an integral part of the programme. Free trade contradicts the proposed policy of protecting labour-intensive technology.

In a simultaneous development we diminish the demand for power-looms and raise that for hand-looms. However, in a less developed country it is virtually certain that the former are imported while the latter are manufactured in a traditional manner by craftsmen at home. Thus in every way our policy recommendation improves the balance of payments. A poor country seeking to develop will in fact always have serious balance-of-payments problems. We can go so far as to say that it should: otherwise it is not trying. This argument has been put briefly, but it is extremely important.

Fundamentally, however, the argument is moral. It is perhaps not completely obvious, at least to the foreign reader, how high Chinese unemployment is, even outside agriculture where everybody can find a little work because of the extreme flexibility of the 'workplace'.

This paragraph is addressed mainly to foreign readers, but plain speech about this tragedy is also useful in China itself. China pursues the humane and (up to a point) proper Soviet policy of compelling socialist sector enterprises to provide as many jobs as there are people of working age. It is indeed proper to give people uninteresting and rather unproductive jobs, which at least give them the status of a worker with its comradeship and (in this case diminished) sense of self-worth. However, there is a limit to this policy which China, even more than the USSR, has surely far exceeded. If the actual effort that workers are called on to supply is minimal, if workers perform less than that minimum and are not dismissed, if workers are frequently sent home (with pay, of course) as superfluous, if workers walk at snail's pace between particular tasks during the day, knowing full well that there will not be another task at the end of the one in hand and yet it is still morning, then the whole labour force is infected and soured. I feel passionately about this, while not relaxing scientific standards at least in my own opinion, because I recognized, on a fairly long visit to a single establishment, the symptoms of this condition. I was reminded of my days as a conscript in the British Army, although that was very slightly better: one always carried a box or a chair about, so as at least to appear to be working, otherwise the sergeant might allocate more unpleasant, although hardly more real, work. In China, however, this hypocrisy is often rejected.

This judgement is of course very subjective. It rests on a small amount of observation, but not on none at all, and on much frank conversation.

We now proceed to some non-industrial applications. What we have said about machines for factories must be extended to private consumption and housework. Housework is an industry,[8] but it is not held in much honour. It has not even a Ministry in Beijing to misdirect it, or at least to fight for its budgetary grant.

The consequence of this 'benign neglect' has been a remarkable self-adaptation of this enormous industry, whose labour force contributes about 30 per cent of all the person-years worked in China, to the brutal facts of technological choice. Nor is this surprising. The household is 'capitalist' in the purest form. Its budgetary constraint is very hard. It must take realistic account of the inputs available and their prices. It cannot afford snobbery, unless it is exceptionally rich. However, rich households 'consume' their equipment not only through wear and tear but also by extracting from them the pleasures of what Mao Tsetung condemned as 'display'.

The beauty and precision of these adaptations are perhaps less visible to the native than to the foreign traveller.

1   There is very little domestic plumbing, and so there are many buckets and jars, but any fool could think of that.
2   There is very little hot-water domestic plumbing, and so there are many very large, efficient and often picturesque thermos flasks. A whole courtyard can afford a permanent fire, which can also be used for cooking, but how can they afford the pump to send that hot water upstairs to every apartment? So, why install hot-water pipes?
3   Hotels are in the public sector. Hotels accept foreigners, and that raises questions of 'display'. Therefore they do have hot-water pipes. However, because of the absence of pumps and the low pressure of the local water supply there is no hot water – except in thermos flasks. The hotel management should have been less ostentatious. The 'display' of things that do not work is extremely counter-productive. Think of the expense: no fewer thermos flasks and no less labour to bring them upstairs, but the whole additional cost of empty pipes. If the builders of these hotels thought that they were saving money because it is cheapest to install pipes while hotels are being built, they must have been out of

their minds. No cost–benefit analysis will sanction a pipe that is not used for 30 years.
4  More obvious even than the thermos flask is of course the bicycle. It is so obvious, and so perfect an adaptation, that it need not be discussed. One surprising use of the bicycle, at least to a foreigner, is as a freight carrier and an ambulance.

We now move to similar sectors: local transport and business services.

5  Horse-drawn carts always have rubber tyres. Therefore the horse is made much more productive, while the country waits, as it must, a long time for small engines. The cheaper technical advance is made first.
6  Rickshaws are not allowed, on whatever type of wheel, and the population is deprived of the urban transportation that it certainly needs, and of the employment and earning power that it certainly needs. Bicycles do not suit the old and the disabled. It is difficult to follow the logic of the argument here. There is indeed something dehumanizing and reminiscent of slavery in a rickshaw, and so we put this aside as overwhelmingly a moral issue.
7  The abacus is still used in circumstances where the pocket calculator or cash register are used abroad. Shops are full of foreigners, and here is another major question of 'display'. However, the abacus develops mathematical, or at least arithmetical, ability that electronics does not. The inadequacy of mathematical knowledge is generally accepted as a prime reason why Western Europe replaced China as the scientific world leader in the sixteenth century, and its absence even among Chinese graduate students of today is rather surprising. Therefore China should perhaps be glad that the abacus, which cannot be used without mastering the technique, is still widespread. Modern substitutes teach their users very little and, in simple operations, are only slightly quicker. Above all they are more expensive in China – whereas abacuses are rare and costly objects in the United Kingdom!

Let us now try to summarize and avoid misunderstandings.

1  Consumption is good but work is also good. However, guaranteed work for all has a negative effect on production and thus on consumption. Therefore it is a question of an optimum mixture, not of a maximum and a minimum.
2  Technological choice should be governed by practicality, not sentiment. Whatever will not work, whether it is the snobbery of high technology (see above) or the nostalgia of backyard steel (see the appendix), must be firmly rejected.
3  Within these limits there remains a vast range of choice, and we should optimize as stated in 1.
4  A preference for labour intensity will reduce savings, but will also

reduce imports. It is the opposite of free trade.
5   Neither *laissez-faire* nor Keynesian economics is much help in solving
these problems.

I should perhaps also try to indicate my own position within a particular
stream of economic thought. Certainly this chapter owes little to Friedman, Keynes or Marx. It could be said that the principal intellectual
sources were Mao Tsetung and Gandhi. However, there have been many
less distinguished forerunners: critics of the Industrial Revolution in
various Western countries. The most systematic such critic, who made all
this kind of thinking respectable, was Schumacher (1973).

## Appendix   Why Pay Wages at All?

Marx's full communist vision denied the necessity of wages. Work was an
honour and a pleasure under communism, and so it was quite unnecessary
and also ideologically wrong to link it with direct reward: the people would
all draw an income. However, there was to be ultimate punishment for the
few who were unwilling:

He who does not work, neither shall he eat.

The kibbutz exemplifies this in practice, except that social ostracism
suffices as the punishment. Under the Great Leap Forward, every
People's Commune would have become a kibbutz. In prisons, monasteries
and armies commands and punishments replace social ostracism to a
greater or less degree, but again it is at least possible to mobilize everyone
for no pay. In each case there is strong ideological unity.

All these systems have the advantage that if labour is employed across
the whole nation or within the small community up to the point where its
marginal product is everywhere zero, the national product is maximized in
the short run. However, at whatever number of workers the zero point is
achieved, we should stop. Since employment is a good thing in itself, the
remainder should be given 'imaginary' work. The extra output from the
low producers just before the zero point raises community consumption,
not their own, since these workers, like all the others, receive no wage but
an income based on the general results of the community. Their employment hardly benefits them personally.

This completely different form of society is discussed in this appendix.
The rulers of such a society are strongly tempted to do what is for the first
time administratively possible: employ everybody, even on ridiculous
make-work projects. What kibbutzim very seldom do, because of their
democratic constitution, the People's Communes, even later under the
Cultural Revolution, did.

In a market economy, even in the real Soviet-type economy, the employers of these low contributors could not afford to pay them a living wage. It would eat deeply into the profits of the employing firms, and the burden would be shared by the economy as a whole. When we bear in mind that these marginal workers were alive anyway, somebody must have been subsidizing them already.

Labour is like, and also unlike, land. The comparison is most instructive. Both are produced by 'nature', that symbolic figure over whom we have no control. No government, no plan and no market can do much more than influence the supplies of labour and land, either in quantity or for that matter in quality: there are good and bad 'units', in great diversity. There is not, or at least there should not be, any practical or ideological obligation to extend full employment to land. If the Russians feel that they are obliged (by what? by whom?) to build towns on ice or if the Brazilians recognize a sacred duty to place their capital in the jungle, that is their error. China too has its deserts, and should take a strictly rational attitude to them, that is to say a grudging attitude concerned mostly with extracting minerals and preserving the environment. Where land is completely without use the market does not, and no one else should, spend one fen per hectare on it.

Labour is different, not in its virtually uncontrollable supply, but in the obligation of each human being to help another. Labour, being made up of human beings, has the right to live and (usually) the power to vote or at least riot. Human beings are very frequently 'worth only one fen per man-year', but nobody dares pay or otherwise spend only that sum on them. They are subsidized, not killed. We think here mainly of the disabled in body or mind.

However, like deserts, these are not a case for employment with very low-level technology. Rather, it is a wholly different group to whom we should give attention: the technologically unemployed, who bulk so large in the main text. Such labour can always be given an artificially low 'shadow price' on a diagram such as figure 12.3 simply by drawing the price line closer to the horizontal than, say, the line $\alpha$. Then profitability, equilibrium etc. indicate greater employment with more labour-intensive techniques, provided that someone subsidizes the labour so that it works at the lower wage. For shadow prices must be implemented by something concrete and non-shadowy, like a command or a subsidy. In the general case the marginal disutility of labour is nearly always such that the actual number working are satisfied to do so because of the wage they actually receive. Shadow rates are something that they do not understand and in any case do not receive! Therefore although their joining the labour force would raise the national product, and so the volume of consumption available to all, they will not voluntarily do so except for more than the current wage, not less. We cannot maximize employment without subsidies or commands.

The refusal to work is not always rational and is seldom patriotic. Work at a living wage is, as we have emphasized, a source of satisfaction and pride; mere work is not! There are many human reasons for refusing to work for low pay, and we have not felt bound to enumerate them all. The objective reasons come under the heading 'cost of employment'. For instance, let the worker be quietly unemployed at home. He or she will need extra food, possibly work clothes and money for the journey to work – which might be a very long one, even a seasonal one to a distant place. Therefore the marginal product of labour should always exceed zero by this 'cost of employment'.

However, that is not all. There are also subjective reasons that come directly under the heading disutility of labour. All human beings, for instance, must sleep. This truth had to be rediscovered during the Great Leap Forward, which among all epochs and countries came nearest to such a maximization of production. Housework must also be performed. Then there are administrative and moral difficulties, since some workers will refuse to work or commit acts of sabotage[9] out of bitter resentment of the fact that their labour is forced – for forced it would be.

Thus many planners faced with gross unemployment have written in very low shadow wages and planned new workplaces to be filled somehow at those rates. They allege that the family 'unnecessarily' supports the idle member, keeping him/her at home, where labour's marginal product is very low indeed, instead of making him work and so add to the national production, even at a wage far below average per capita family income. But where is the disutility of labour that these people feel? Why should they work at a lower wage than their present income? No persuasive reason can of course be given – only force. In general, a voluntary commune, such as an Israeli kibbutz, is a stable and worthwhile enterprise – or should we say way of life. However, a compulsory commune is different. It enables the institution to realize certain inefficient and inhuman features that are merely dormant in the voluntary model, which being democratic does not direct labour grossly against its will. In other words, it can revert to a still more capital-saving technology than the one in use for its marginal members, and compel them, at a vast cost in human dignity and exceedingly little gain to society, to spend many hours producing virtually nothing. It is not to such ugly extremes that we have proposed to guide China. The individual protection of each cotton flower from the frost, the backyard steel that is of too low a quality for ball-bearings, the dispatch of schoolchildren on a hunt for flies – this is not what we mean because we wish, naturally, to stay within the boundaries of commonsense.

Let us revert for a moment to a less strenuous state of society. While it is true from the point of view of production that the setting to work of unemployed labour (whether rural or urban) has no opportunity cost, this is not the case when we ask what the normal socialist state obtains from it. The family that has been maintaining the worker simply diverts what he was consuming to the other members, and cannot be prevented from doing so, while the newly employed person lives off his new wage. Therefore the state gains certain tax revenues from the expanded national consumption fund, and that is all – we assume that all these people are so poor that they neither save nor invest. It is mainly consumption that rises, and it is the duty of the state to feel very pleased about that!

It is the much more tightly organized full communist state (if we may use that phrase – or at any rate the kibbutz) that gains, for it does control family consumption, indeed it is the family. We have explained this above.

Finally, this chapter has used its own vocabulary, defined below, at many points.

1  *High technology* continually moves forward. It is at the cutting edge of humanity's knowledge, and so is nearly always imported, even in the United States.

2  *Traditional technology* is localized and not imported. However, it may be continuously undergoing self-development and even reacting to imports. It will do so very slowly, because traditionally it does not encourage R&D.

3  *Intermediate technology* is yesterday's high technology. It may also be imported, but is of course much cheaper since the R&D costs have long since been written off.

4  *Appropriate technology* is what we have recommended in this chapter. It will very seldom be high technology – perhaps only in weapons. It is not necessarily intermediate, since it might require inventing, and it may or may not be traditional. It tends, by definition, to labour intensity.

The bicycle and the thermos flask are old intermediate technology and were imported long ago. However, they have been adapted to China's needs. Acupuncture is traditional but self-developing. It is probably also at the cutting edge of humanity's knowledge, and so is high technology.

I have not used the term 'technical progress' at any point, only 'technical change'. This is because I fear for the environment, which has not until this last sentence received a single mention.

# Notes

1  The self-employed person's income is identical with a wage for our simple purpose here. A peasant is such a person. A housewife and mother also works, much harder than most people. She 'disposes of' most of the household income. All this gives her the same sort of status as an ordinary worker, although it is surely far too low considering the great importance of what she does. We simplify our argument by neglecting both these points!

2  Less-developed countries should concentrate on development (see later). In any case investment is from many points of view indistinguishable from R&D.

3  Strictly, a new high technology might demand instead a small number of well-paid experts and a slightly larger number of unskilled workers, resulting in

fewer employees as a whole and a lower average wage.

4 Note that a wage is not an expenditure in the sense meant here; i.e. final expenditure out of the national income used. In our sense, wages are part of national income produced.

5 In the appendix we show that under full communism, or in any other wageless system, there is usually no trade-off between employment and output, whatever technology is chosen.

6 Indeed in the field of supersonic civilian travel the United Kingdom and France lead the world, at the cost of an enormous subsidy every year.

7 Fighter aircraft and light civilian aircraft, and most musical instruments, also suggest themselves. It must not be forgotten, either, that shift work creates extra workplaces out of these rigid machines.

8 Indeed, in modern Marxist terms, housework should be defined as a productive service (cooking, clothes-mending, laundering, bedmaking), for all this activity either creates a finished material good from an unfinished one (cooking) or repairs a material good (mending and laundering). Perhaps only bedmaking is a true service, but is not that also repairing a material object? If retail trade is a productive service how can shopping not be one also?

9 Sabotage reduces the marginal product below zero.

# References

Adhyaru, P. H., Anubhai, P., Iyer, B. V., Mehta, P. C. and Parikh, J. G. (1979). In *Appropriate Industrial Technology for Textiles*. UNIDO, Vienna.

Schumacher, E. P. (1973) *Small is Beautiful*. London: Blond and Briggs.

# 13

# The Fiscal System

## Liu Hongru

For a long time China had a highly centralized system of economic management, based mainly on control of material supplies and mandatory planning, in which banks acted simply as accountants and paymasters. After 1978, during the reform of the economic management system, a start was made on expanding commodity and monetary relations and allowing the market to play a regulatory role. Increasingly, the regulatory role of banks, credit, rates of interest and rates of exchange has been taken seriously. Deng Xiaoping stated that banks should be run as genuine banks, acting as a mechanism to promote economic growth and technical renovation. Financial reform along these lines began in 1979. Eight years later, after feeling our way and experimenting, the following results have been achieved.

1    A central bank and several new financial institutions have been set up. Formerly, there was just one bank, the People's Bank of China, a currency-issuing bank which simultaneously performed a general banking function. On 17 September 1983 the State Council decreed that the People's Bank should function as a central bank, an organ directly representing the State Council, which guides and manages the state finances. It is the government's bank, the banks' bank and a currency-issuing bank. Industrial and commercial banks have also been restored or established, handling business in towns and cities, as well as agricultural banks, the Bank of China, which is responsible for foreign exchange business, the Construction Bank, which is responsible for long-term credit, the Investment Bank to handle World Bank loans, the International Trust Company and regional trust companies, and leasing and finance companies in various regions. At the same time credit cooperatives were set up throughout the country. From 1980 onwards, urban credit cooperatives were established to serve the collective and individual economy in the urban areas. In July 1986 the State Council decided to re-establish the domestic organizations of the Communication Bank, and transformed it into a composite bank dealing with both

domestic business and foreign currencies. This is a joint-stock enterprise and a pioneer in financial reform.

2   We have begun to use economic methods to increase deposits and attract funds. We have enlarged the scope of credit and made banks into important channels for raising funds for economic construction.

3   We have taken the first steps to change the monolithic system of bank credit and pressed ahead with the formation of a financial market. The expansion of commercial, consumer, share and private credit is leading away from the monolithic system. Financial mechanisms and forms of organizing capital funds have diversified: negotiable bills and financial and industrial bonds have developed to some extent, and have prompted the development of a financial market. At present this is mainly a discount market for enterprises in the same line of business, but in a small number of cities dealing in variable-price securities has begun.

4   We have changed the policy on interest rates and have begun to use this to regulate money supply and demand. We have increased the categories of interest rates and made their general level vary with the length of deposit, changing the old irrational system in which interest decreased over time. We have adopted floating interest rates that penalize enterprises which fail to repay loans or hoard goods.

5   The administrative system for loans and credit has been reformed, and we have begun to reform the supply system. For many years deposits had to be handed over, credit was according to quota and enterprises had to apply to higher authority for funds when needed. This led to many abuses. From 1985 the central bank implemented a system of planned divisions of funds among specialized banks, realistic deposits and loans, in which each bank caters for itself; the central bank does not guarantee the supply of funds to the specialized banks, and the specialized banks organize deposits or raise money on the financial market and seek their own balance. Necessary support is provided by the central bank, but it cannot be depended on for the supply of funds or the issue of credit.

6   The insurance system has been restored, together with a system of compensation. Insurance was abolished in China in 1959 and in theory the state became responsible for all losses. In fact the state could not do this, and the result was detrimental to economic stability and people's livelihood. Restoration of insurance began in 1980 and accelerated in the mid-1980s. In 1986 more than 100 types of insurance enterprise were set up, and insurance revenue reached more than 5,000 million yuan, an increase of 45 per cent compared with 1985. More than 2.5 million insurance claims were dealt with in 1986 and 1,230 million yuan were paid out, so that thousands of enterprises were able to continue production and thousands of individuals were assisted. International insurance business has also expanded.

7   China's isolated banking system has opened up and external

financial activity has considerably expanded. After 1979 financial relations and cooperation with other countries rapidly increased. In 1980 China regained its seat at the International Monetary Fund, and it formally joined the African Development Bank in May 1985 and the African Development Fund in March 1986. Chinese financial organizations have entered the international money market, issuing bonds and raising funds. As a bank specializing in foreign exchange, the Bank of China has expanded and increased the variety of its business, setting up overseas branches (over 184 in 1978 and 310 in 1985), and has established agency relations with 1,235 banks in 152 different countries or regions. The Chinese People's Insurance Corporation has reinsurance arrangements with more than 1,000 insurance companies in more than 100 countries and has joined international insurance activities in Asia and the Pacific region. Foreign financial organizations have set up several dozen agencies and branches in the special economic zones, which promote financial cooperation.

8   Progress is being made in developing the macromanagerial role of the central bank. Attention is being given to monetary policy, giving precedence to stable money and economic growth. The central bank has begun to use economic methods of regulation and control. For instance, we have begun to set up a system of reserve deposits, increased the rate of interest on credit to specialized banks and increased the grades of interest rates, encouraging funds to be raised publicly; we have begun to combine management of the renminbi with that of foreign currencies; we have started to exercise macroregulation and achieve monetary policy goals through foreign debt, foreign exchange and exchange rate management.

9   The bank's policy for internal unified revenue and expenditure management has been reformed. In some areas experiments are being made in changing primary-level banks into independent enterprises, with rights delegated from above and management autonomy; forms of the responsibility system and auditing methods are also being implemented throughout the country.

10   There has been a breakthrough in formulating financial law. The state has promulgated nine laws on such matters as bank management, foreign capital and the establishment of joint Sino-foreign banks in the special zones, bank borrowing and insurance. The People's Bank has also published regulations for urban credit cooperatives and for insurance and investment companies.

The direction of reform over the past eight years is correct, and satisfactory results have been achieved. The status of banks in the economy has changed markedly, and they have become the main channel for raising and distributing funds. In 1978, allocation by public finance departments made up 76 per cent of the total of fixed and circulating capital funds for expanded reproduction in enterprises (excluding capital raised by the enterprises themselves); bank loans accounted for just 23.4 per cent. By 1986 allocations were only 13.6 per cent, while bank loans had risen to 84 per cent. The role of banks in the national economy has changed substantially, and finance has become an important instrument of macro-management, although reform is still incomplete.

# A new framework for financial reform

Zhao Ziyang, in his report on the Seventh Five Year Plan pointed out that:

We must particularly strengthen the important function of banks in macroeconomic management and by means of reform of the financial structure establish a financial control and regulation system which is not only strong but also flexible and smooth, fully giving play to the financial system's function in raising funds, and directing the flow of capital, raising the efficiency in the use of funds and its function as a regulator of society's demands.

He noted that the Chinese People's Bank – as the central bank – is one of the most important regulating bodies, whose status and independence should be enhanced. In his Report on the Work of the Government to the People's Congress in 1987, he proposed increasing the pace of financial reform, the establishment of specialized banks at sub-provincial level, turning insurance companies and other financial organizations into enterprises, and the encouragement of appropriate competition between financial organizations. This is a clear indication of the direction of future reform. Now that ideas about the road to take are fairly clear, we can sketch the outlines of a new financial framework.

The mainstays of such a framework would be as follows.

1   A powerful yet flexible system of macroeconomic regulation and control should be established at different administrative levels to promote the efficient assembly and use of the nation's capital funds, to maintain the overall balance of supply and demand and basic price stability, and to promote the growth of economic coordination and the rationalization of the economic system.
2   A credit system based on bank credit, which would be multichannel, multiform and use a wide variety of financial instruments for the concentration and circulation of capital, should be established; financial centres of different sizes should be set up at various levels around central towns and cities, and adapted to Chinese conditions.
3   A socialist financial system with the central bank at its head, based on multifunctional and specialized banks in which insurance and other financial organizations coexist and cooperate, should be set up. The central bank's function should be progressively strengthened. Banks and financial organizations should all be gradually transformed into enterprises. This will ensure the smooth implementation of financial

policies and allow financial enterprises to raise and use capital. It will link rights, responsibilities, risks and profits, and will increase management vigour through competitive pressure.

4  A financial management system with a modern scientific base and better qualified personnel should be established. A group of high-ranking financial administrators should be trained. Computers and other modern technologies should be used so as to create a banking service with scientific management – a sensitive information system which will provide better financial services for clients and produce good economic results.

The establishment and integration of the above four systems will gradually be achieved in the process of reforming the whole financial structure. Apart from modern equipment and training, there are three main elements of reform itself: growth of the financial market, the establishment of specialized banks operating as enterprises and the perfection of a generally indirect system of macroeconomic regulation and control. The central link in financial reform is the formation of a financial market. It must be based on the invigoration of financial organizations, especially on the specialized banks operating as enterprises because, if financial organizations do not act as genuine enterprises, relations between specialist banks and the central bank, between banks and enterprises, and between specialist banks at different levels will not be smooth, and the problems of financial supply and 'all eating out of the same pot' will not be solved. Successful formation of a financial market and transformation of specialized banks into enterprises will invigorate the microeconomy. However, this must be linked with the completion of the macroeconomic regulation and control system. If invigoration by opening up on the microeconomic level causes inflation, then the aims of reform will not have been achieved. Control and relaxation of control are complementary and symbiotic; with each step forward in reform they can be combined in a new way. Microeconomic invigoration must be subordinate to macroeconomic administration; however, a well-timed transformation from direct to indirect control in macroeconomic administration is the essential precondition for the formation of a financial market and for turning specialist banks into enterprises.

## Some measures for extending reform

Specific measures are required to realize the basic concept of financial reform and to create a new structural framework. Certain measures need to be taken if we are to extend reform and reduce the length of the transitional period between the old and the new methods.

# Strengthening the macroregulation function of the central bank

All money in circulation (including money on deposit) is injected through the credit mechanism. Hence, it is crucial to macroeconomic financial administration that the central bank keeps a firm grip on the credit valve. This is the key to effective regulation of supply and demand. The following important problems in macroeconomic administration must be dealt with.

**Limiting the money supply by social tolerance**   The basic function of money in circulation is to express the value of commodities. Social tolerance means controlling the money supply needed by the total value of commodities produced (as measured by total price) over a certain period (usually a year) so as to keep price increases to a tolerable level, given a normal velocity of circulation. At the level of microeconomic equilibrium, this principle requires that increases in capital accumulation should not exceed the growth of output of capital goods; the increase in the consumption fund should not exceed the growth of output of consumer goods, and a suitable ratio between them should be maintained. In the last three years both accumulation and consumption have far exceeded the rate of increase of national income. The problem of excessive demand will have to be solved by all the economic departments working together.

**Maintenance of relative stability in monetary policy**   Excessive fluctuation in money supply can cause economic instability. Money supply has always been a matter for state monetary policy in any given period; its ultimate aim is to maintain stable prices, to promote economic coordination and to balance international payments. The central bank achieves these aims mainly by regulating the money supply; a moderate increase has always been an effective instrument for controlling inflation. A relatively stable monetary policy is conditional upon determining the rate of growth of money supply according to changes in the economic growth rate, the planned (i.e. socially tolerable) rate of price inflation and variations in the rate of circulation. The source of funds and the overall scale of borrowing should be determined in accordance with the scale of increase in the money supply, and demands for funds should be restrained by the availability of funds, and not the other way round. The level of money supply is an index of economic growth, to which it is very sensitive. This, of course, applies to rational growth and is not the case if growth is excessively rapid. In the process of commoditization and monetization there is indeed a slowing down in the velocity of circulation, but this is not immutable and this factor cannot always be taken for granted in considering the rate of increase in money supply.

**Flexible use of regulatory methods**   A socialist economy is a planned commodity economy. The market is guided both by direct and indirect planning, and gradually exercises an influence on enterprises. After macroeconomic targets have been determined there should be a gradual shift from direct to indirect methods of economic regulation and control. The central bank does this by adjusting the monetary base directly under its control to regulate the money supply and the scale of borrowing. As long as the central bank properly regulates the amount of credit to specialist banks it can indirectly regulate the money supply throughout the country. The central bank should gradually stop being responsible for the supply of funds to specialized banks, who should themselves organize deposits or raise money by entering the market and issuing bonds, and move towards being responsible for their own balance so that they have more resources available for borrowers. The monetary base should be under the tight centralized control of the central bank; in order to achieve macroeconomic goals funds should be supplied monthly and quarterly to the various financial organizations according to the state of the money market, prices and the rate of interest. The main function of the central bank should be to circulate funds via economic methods, regulating the volume and structure of borrowing through flexible use of its own volume of borrowing and rate of interest, and through the rediscount volume and rate of interest. As the financial market develops, the amount of funds distributed through the market should be increased and funds made to flow towards uses with high returns.

**Combining the macroadministration of Chinese and foreign currencies** Implementation of the policy of opening up has resulted in an increase in economic exchange with foreign countries so that changes in international market prices and exchange rates increasingly affect China's foreign exchange receipts and disbursements; this in turn has a major influence on China's own finance, investment and prices, and initially on the scale of credit and the supply and stability of money. Goods for export are paid for in renminbi; foreign currency must be exchanged for renminbi; foreign capital which is used requires corresponding renminbi. If China has foreign exchange reserves, then foreign payments can be guaranteed, and they can also be used to import material to support production or to withdraw domestic currency from circulation. Consequently, overseeing the balance of payments is an important task for the central bank: it must administer foreign exchange as well as renminbi. It is important that we reform the system of administering foreign exchange and foreign loans. International balance-of-payments planning must be strengthened so as to achieve comprehensive balance in renminbi. The unified administration of foreign currency must be strengthened and the system of proportionate retention of foreign exchange earnings reformed. We need to improve exchange rate policy, implement a controlled floating exchange rate, stabilize foreign exchange reserves, establish a foreign exchange fund at the central bank, and strengthen foreign debt administration by determining suitable levels, time limits, rates of interest, currencies and a sound monitoring system. We also need to understand how to use the limited foreign exchange market and make the best use of foreign exchange.

## Establishment and expansion of the money market

The immediate task is to deal effectively with short-term funding. This includes the borrowing market, the bill market and the short-term debenture market. The borrowing market is a means of circulating funds among financial organizations in order to correct shortfalls in money supply turnover. The free flow of funds between financial organizations assists the formation of an interlocking vertical and horizontal distribution of funds. Even more important, it means using spatial and temporal transfer of funds to satisfy urgent needs and increase returns without increasing the money supply. We need to promote financial activity which operates beyond sectoral or provincial boundaries, creating a financial network at different levels across the whole country, with the main cities as focal points. The bill market is mainly for the use and negotiation of commercial bills, and involves both financial bodies and enterprises. If commercial or bank credit is not conducted on the basis of paper claims, it is not a complete credit system, in which case the movement of funds can become separated from the circulation of goods and materials, causing credit inflation. Using debentures to conduct the movement of funds between financial bodies and enterprises, and between enterprises, is a fundamental financial reform.

In China the shortage of capital funds for construction will be a long-term problem. At present, in view of the large increase in extra-budgetary funds and insufficient guidance in the use of self-generated funds for capital construction, the development of a market in long-term funds, i.e. a capital market, is an effective means of controlling the scale of investment, regulating the structure and increasing the returns from investment. Currently, only joint enterprises and, with permission, a small number of collective-ownership enterprises can issue shares, and so any market development would be a bond market which would include treasury bonds, major construction bonds, financial bonds, enterprise bonds and so on. In the long run, growth of a long-term capital market must be combined with reform of the investment system. Apart from major state construction projects, basic facilities and public enterprises, in which the government invests directly, the main responsibility for investment in ordinary industrial and commercial projects should be transferred to the enterprise or to financial organizations. This should be done by entering the market, raising and circulating funds, issuing bonds, and being responsible themselves for decision-making, risks and relating the cost of raising funds to the returns from the project. This will reduce the financial burden on the state. The market mechanism and the cost of raising funds will regulate the structure of investment, which will facilitate the flow of funds towards construction projects with high economic returns. With the increase in financial assets a market can be developed which gives more choice to investors and operators, and further improves long-term funding. Simultaneously, insurance must be developed, particularly life insurance, pension insurance and other such contractual savings organizations in order to provide a long-term stable source of funds.

## Extension of the reform of specialist state banks

There are some outstanding problems with specialist state banks: they cannot assume responsibility for their own profit and loss, their own interests are separated from their business results, and their investment is directed towards risk-free activities. This makes it difficult to use high-efficiency methods for mobilizing funds, and diverts the allocation of funds from enterprises and construction projects with high returns. It is important that we turn these banks into genuine enterprises.

The reform of specialized banks should concentrate on improving urban banks (rural banks are county branch banks), because central towns and cities are linked with industrial centres and economic regions, relying on them for the collection and distribution of goods, materials and funds; they are the pillars of the economic regions. Urban banks should be invigorated so that they circulate funds and establish remittance networks based on urban centres. This will increase the pivotal role of towns; it will also help to end the dual control system and to create production and commercial areas. The basic requirement of a specialized banking enterprise is that rights, responsibilities and profits are linked. A specialized bank must be an economic entity, which is managed autonomously and is responsible for its own profit and loss, for risks and for balancing its funding. It must have a self-regulating mechanism and be responsive to change. The first step in achieving this is to make a grant to the basic operating units of specialized banks as their 'capital' and leave the management to them, so that all transfers of funds, vertical or horizontal, become credit relations. Secondly, their rights, like those of state enterprises, should be extended; they should be given the necessary autonomy of operation to extend credit, to float rates of interest and to allocate after-tax profit, as well as the right to appoint, dismiss, reward and penalize staff, and the right to set up internal organizations. Thirdly, rights and responsibilities, risk and profit must not be separated. Systems of economic responsibility and credit risk assessment must be established. The principles of risk and profit must be used to restrain the loan activities of financial enterprises and to encourage them to decide investment on the basis of the reputation of an enterprise, its results and its ability to repay in order to protect their interests. Fourthly, the system whereby all payments at every level are made with central bank approval, which in fact is a survival of unified revenue and expenditure, must be changed. Fifthly, socialist financial organizations cannot take profit-making as their sole aim. They exist in order to invigorate financing and the economy, but when microeconomic and social benefits coincide they should be permitted to seek profitability. Hence, with the banks as enterprises, a system of assessment norms based on profitability should be developed. Otherwise the linkage of rights, responsibilities, risks and profit will not be realized. Sixthly, new forms of financial organization should be developed with overlapping spheres of business. In the past few years many urban and rural collective organizations and non-bank financial organizations responsible for their own profit and loss have been set up, and the forces of market competition have begun to penetrate their activities. In addition, state specialized banks have gradually extended the scope of their business. They have become more competitive so that they operate less monopolistically and come under more business pressure. Finally, financial organizations should also experiment with separation of ownership from management rights. The introduction of the responsibility system in savings banks in some regions is an excellent beginning and should be tried out more widely.

## External relations of the financial system

There are major difficulties in reforming the financial system, and its effects are widespread. It must be coordinated with reform of the whole economic system, and relations with the economy outside the financial sphere need to be handled well. The independence of the central bank *vis-à-vis* the planning system should be strengthened, to allow it to implement monetary policies, and the specialized banks should have the right to deal in funds independently. There should be coordination with public finance departments in order to control inflation and guarantee steady expansion. If public finance is in deficit, the state should attempt to restore balance by issuing bonds to enterprises, units and individuals, to which the central bank should not subscribe. Legal forms should be employed to regulate relations between banks and public finance departments.

The abolition of the system whereby banks are responsible for the money supply of enterprises is an important means of furthering reform; if enterprises cannot succeed in borrowing money they should go to the market. However, the cost of raising funds by an enterprise which is responsible for its own profit and loss is a severe test of its profitability. In this way, the financial requirements of enterprises can be depressed by internal mechanisms. Financial enterprises will also provide a whole range of financial tools in order to improve efficiency and the quality of service. in the process of competition banks will be able to select enterprises, and enterprises to select banks: they will both assist and restrain each other, and promote reform together.

# 14

# The Investment System

## Wang Jiye

In China the term 'investment' refers specifically to investment in fixed assets, comprising capital construction and investment in replacement and renewal. Such investment is the starting point for growth in socialist economies, directly affecting the national economy, science and technology, and both long- and short-term social development. The scale, structure and returns from investment largely reflect a country's strength and the efficiency of its economic system. Where there is public ownership of the means of production, investment is crucial to planning, and consequently is an important factor in the reform of the economic system.

## Progress and results in investment reform

The investment system which evolved in the 1950s showed increasingly serious shortcomings as the economy developed. Its centralized administration and rejection of the concept of value and of the market mechanism seriously repressed the initiative of localities and enterprises. Moreover, it gave rise to a distorted, unscientific assessment of investment returns as well as softening budget constraints on enterprises. At the same time, the feedback of a large amount of information of an administrative nature prevented policy-makers from clearly observing the investment process. Resource allocation on the basis of the productive capacity in one product (such as steel), or of several products, led to an irrational investment structure and a lopsided production structure, as well as causing considerable long-term imbalance in the relative growth of agriculture and industry, and of heavy and light industry. This system of resource distribution independent of market forces created a high degree of internal accumulation by means of price and income policies, and accelerated the development of heavy industry. However, it also led to serious dualism in industry and agriculture, and extreme difficulty in the rational adjustment of the industrial structure. Backed by disbursements from public finance departments, funds were used without having to be repaid, and this blurred the distinction between ownership and management, and weakened the responsibility of those involved in the process of investment. This system, which was dependent on large-scale input from central government, led to low efficiency in resource use, low competitiveness of products, self-circulation in heavy industry and difficulty in exporting, which in turn resulted in a steadily increasing burden on public finance. This is the main reason why, over a long period, growth in China was unable to move from a primarily extensive to a primarily intensive form. The direction of investment dictated by these factors and the overall system of allocation of funds, goods, material and labour lies at the heart of the lack of vitality and elasticity in industry and in the national economy.

This weakness in the investment system is not something which has only just been diagnosed. From the 1950s to the 1970s there was a great deal of debate (and some practical experiment) on whether investment should be centralized or the responsibility of local authorities, i.e. whether it should be mainly administered by departments or by local government. The matter was brought to a conclusion when the central government took over control of investment. Since the Third Plenum of the 11th Congress and the beginning of the reform of the agricultural structure, which was extended later to overall reform of the whole urban economic system, the highly centralized system of investment has come under vigorous attack. Many people have been forced to the conclusion that the fundamental reason why reform of the investment system always encountered obstacles was the failure to give proper authority to enterprises as commodity producers, and because relations between central and local governments was still dominated by conventional ideas about administrative authority. Reform of the investment system started with the following main objectives.

## Reform of the system of investment planning and administration

Reform of investment planning and administration started rather late and only began to have an effect after 1984. First, the roles of the state, the ministries and local government with respect to responsibility for investment were clarified according to the source of funds. Secondly, authority to approve investment in basic construction and for replacement and renewal was devolved. More precisely, state budget investments in the form of credit rather than allocations were made part of credit for capital construction in the state credit plan. In the case of capital construction using funds from international financial organizations, or loans from foreign governments, the state is responsible for equilibrium and employs mandatory planning. This part of investment is mainly used for meeting national needs in energy, communications, raw materials, crucial machine and electronic industries, key science and technology projects, basic research projects and national defence. In cases where government departments and local authorities raise their own funds for investment, where the state borrows but local governments are responsible for repayment and when departments and local governments themselves borrow and repay funds for capital construction, they are also responsible for maintaining equilibrium. This type of investment is mainly used for development of local energy and communications, raw materials, rural water conservancy, textiles, food production industries, science and education, urban facilities, public utilities, etc. In order to control the total amount of investment and influence the way in which it is used, the funds have to be deposited in the Construction Bank for six months before they can be drawn on. All investment other than that in energy (including energy saving), construction, transport and communications, schools and educational facilities is subject to the construction tax (Wang and Zhu 1987: 56).

Productive construction projects are classified according to the amount of investment: those over 30 million yuan (previously 10 million yuan) have to be approved by the State Planning Committee. If funding, energy, materials and equipment can be arranged for non-productive projects, then in principle the department, province, autonomous region or municipality can give approval, but the investment involved is included in the overall figure for investment in capital construction (Wang and Zhu 1987: 57).

In line with the decentralization of authority for capital construction, there have been corresponding reforms in the planning and administration of investment for technical improvement. This is controlled by mandatory planning, with the state making allocations from the budget or using foreign capital. Credit for this is included in the state credit plan and is controlled by the People's Bank. Mandatory planning is also enforced where technical improvement is financed by investments raised by departments, local government or enterprises. The scope of technical improvement projects which can be approved by local government and government departments has also been widened (Wang and Zhu 1987: 57).

## Shift from government allocation to bank credit

In China investment in fixed assets has always been made by direct financial allocation by the state to government departments or local authorities for use by construction units. These allocations do not have to be repaid. This is the typical form of mandatory planning in a barter economy. With the expansion of state investment, economic relations have become increasingly complicated and abuse of the system of non-reimbursable funds has become more and more flagrant. In order to resolve this contradiction, early in 1979 a small number of industries and regions experimented with the replacement of state allocation for capital construction by credit from the Construction Bank. Trials in light industry, textiles and travel were made in Beijing, Shanghai and Guangdong, as a result of which, from 1981 onwards, credit for capital construction, with appropriate interest rates and terms of repayment established for different sectors, replaced allocations in all enterprises with independent accounting and repayment abilities.

## Investment contracting

Investment contracting takes several different forms, of which the most important are investment contracts between specialized departments, such as metallurgy, railways, petroleum or the non-ferrous metal corporation, and the state. In some cases the constructing unit makes investment contracts with the regulatory department (as in the case of the first-stage construction of the Baoshan Iron and Steel Corporation or the Shanghai Central Petrochemical Company). In other cases the contract is between the unit in charge of construction and the constructing unit, and even sometimes between different divisions within the unit in charge of construction. All these forms of contract have two characteristics: first, the unit issuing the contract guarantees the funds, equipment, materials and external conditions, and the contracting unit guarantees the investment, the duration of construction, the quality of the product, the consumption of primary material and overall productivity.

## Increased autonomy of investment in enterprises

Under the old system enterprises owned by the whole people handed over to the state the greater part of the total depreciation fund, which seriously impaired their capacity to expand and even made it difficult to meet running costs. After 1980, in order to resolve this problem, the state gradually raised the depreciation rate for fixed assets in industrial and communications enterprises, and left 70 per cent of the depreciation charge for the use of the enterprise; the remaining 30 per cent was used by the regulatory department as a reimbursable regulator for borrowing and repayment. Small-scale enterprises with fixed assets with an original value of less than 1 million yuan were able to keep the whole depreciation charge for their own use (Resolution of the State Council; see Wang and Zhu 1987: 124). In 1985 the government decided that industrial and communications enterprises should keep the whole depreciation charge for their own use and no longer hand it in. This, and the increase in their own funds, gradually began to correct the unsatisfactory system in which enterprises had very little or no investment capacity, and increased their enthusiasm for investment and their capacity to expand. As a further measure for stimulating investment the government decided that enterprises using their own funds for the provision of living quarters, for extensive repairs to equipment, for the purchase of individual pieces of equipment or for projects requiring an investment of less than 50,000 yuan need not be included in the state investment plan. At present the profit retained by Chinese enterprises after tax, depreciations, funds for major repairs and bank credit amounts to a total of 100,000 million yuan – equal to one-third of annual national investment. This has a great invigorating effect on enterprises.

There has been a corresponding increase in autonomy in the construction industry with the institution of a system of tendering, surveying and designing units operating as enterprises, the establishment of contracting companies and subcontracting of construction work of below 100 yuan in wage content or of work with a small surface area.

These measures have encouraged the development of the commodity economy and have increased the returns on investment. There has already been a marked change in China's investment system, with the development of a multilevel pluralistic system.

First, there has been a move away from the centralized single-track state investment policy, and the evolution of a multilevel system. Table 14.1 shows that from 1981 to 1983 about 70 per cent of investment was in the public sector; since 1984 this has fallen to about 66 per cent. Investment in the collective ownership sector, except for certain years in which there was a slight increase, maintained a level of about 12.13 per cent. Private investment has seen a more marked increase, and stands at about 21 per cent of total investment. As reform proceeds these two forms of investment will increase.

Secondly, the structure of investment for capital construction, replacement and renewal in the public sector has changed. Prior to reform, the greater part of investment was for capital construction, and very little was for replacement and renewal – 3.8 per cent of total investment during the First Five Year Plan, 7.7 per cent during the Second Five Year Plan, 15.5 per cent between 1963 and 1965, 19.3 per cent during the Third Five Year Plan, 22.5 per cent during the Fourth Five Year Plan and 26.5 per cent during the Fifth Five Year Plan. Although investment for replacement and renewal increased between the First and the Fifth Five Year Plans, it has still been too low – showing that socialist growth has not yet come to depend mainly on technical transformation. The use of national funds for investment for technical improvement in existing enterprises shows a saving of over one-third in funds, raw materials and equipment in comparison with the cost of establishing new enterprises by investing in capital construction. The time required for construction can be reduced by half, which also increases investment returns. Since reform, there has been an increase in the proportion of fixed investment used for technical improvements in the public sector.

Table 14.2 shows that in 1986 investment for replacement and renewal was already more than 30 per cent of total investment, and was more than 40 per cent when 'other' fixed investment is included. This represents a marked change in the structure of investment. Finally, although the urban share of collective and individual investment has increased, the rural share is still the largest. Table 14.3 shows that the urban share rose by 10 per cent from 27.4 per cent in 1981 to 37.4 per cent in 1986, while rural collective investment fell from 72.6 to 62.6 per cent. The rural share of private investment maintained its high level of 90 per cent. Table 14.4 shows that the rural share of both collective and private investment has remained

**Table 14.1** The structure of total investment in fixed assets

| | 1981 | | 1982 | | 1983 | | 1984 | | 1985 | | 1986 | |
|---|---|---|---|---|---|---|---|---|---|---|---|---|
| | Investment (100 million yuan (%)) | | | | | | | | | | | |
| Total | 961.01 | (100.0) | 1200.40 | (100.0) | 1369.06 | (100.0) | 1832.87 | (100.0) | 2543.19 | (100.0) | 3019.62 | (100.0) |
| Ownership by the whole people | 667.51 | (69.5) | 845.31 | (70.4) | 951.96 | (69.5) | 1185.18 | (64.7) | 1680.51 | (66.1) | 1978.50 | (65.5) |
| Collective ownership | 115.24 | (12.0) | 174.28 | (14.5) | 156.33 | (11.4) | 238.69 | (13.0) | 327.46 | (12.9) | 391.74 | (13.0) |
| Private investment | 178.26 | (18.5) | 180.81 | (15.1) | 260.77 | (19.1) | 409.00 | (22.3) | 535.22 | (21.0) | 649.38 | (21.5) |

*Source: ZTN 1982–7*

**Table 14.2** The structure of investments in fixed assets in the public sector

|  | Investment (100 million yuan (%)) | | | | | | | | | | | |
|---|---|---|---|---|---|---|---|---|---|---|---|---|
|  | 1981 | | 1982 | | 1983 | | 1984 | | 1985 | | 1986 | |
| Total | 667.51 | (100.0) | 845.31 | (100.0) | 951.96 | (100.0) | 1185.18 | (100.0) | 1680.51 | (100.0) | 1978.50 | (100.0) |
| Basic construction | 442.91 | (66.3) | 555.53 | (65.7) | 594.13 | (62.4) | 743.15 | (62.7) | 1074.37 | (64.0) | 1176.11 | (59.4) |
| Replacement and renewal | 195.30 | (29.3) | 250.37 | (29.6) | 291.13 | (30.6) | 309.28 | (26.1) | 449.14 | (26.7) | 619.21 | (31.3) |
| Other[a] | 29.30 | (4.4) | 39.41 | (4.7) | 66.70 | (7.0) | 132.75 | (11.2) | 157.00 | (9.3) | 183.18 | (9.3) |

[a] This includes investment in maintenance, development of oil wells etc.
*Source:* ZTN 1982–7

**Table 14.3** The structure of investments in fixed assets in the collective sector

| | Investment (100 million yuan (%)) | | | | | | | | | | | |
|---|---|---|---|---|---|---|---|---|---|---|---|---|
| | *1981* | | *1982* | | *1983* | | *1984* | | *1985* | | *1986* | |
| Total | 115.24 | (100.0) | 174.28 | (100.0) | 156.33 | (100.0) | 238.69 | (100.0) | 327.46 | (100.0) | 391.74 | (100.0) |
| Urban | 31.57 | (27.4) | 42.89 | (24.6) | 45.65 | (29.2) | 63.86 | (26.8) | 128.23 | (39.2) | 146.39 | (37.4) |
| Rural | 83.67 | (72.6) | 131.39 | (75.4) | 110.68 | (70.8) | 174.83 | (73.2) | 199.23 | (60.8) | 245.35 | (62.6) |

*Source:* ZTN 1982–7

**Table 14.4** The structure of private investment

| | Investment (100 million yuan (%)) | | | | | |
| | 1981 | 1982 | 1983 | 1984 | 1985 | 1986 |
|---|---|---|---|---|---|---|
| Total | 178.26 (100.0) | 180.81 (100.0) | 260.77 (100.0) | 409.00 (100.0) | 535.22 (100.0) | 649.38 (100.0) |
| Urban | 11.92 (6.7) | 12.28 (6.8) | 16.72 (6.4) | 29.89 (7.3) | 56.79 (10.6) | 74.56 (11.5) |
| Rural | 166.34 (93.3) | 168.53 (93.2) | 244.05 (93.6) | 379.11 (92.7) | 478.43 (89.4) | 574.82 (88.5) |

Source: ZTN 1982–7

relatively high, and this has played a role in encouraging the progressive increase in agricultural production and the development of rural and urban industry. It has also helped to resolve the problem of labour force transfer.

# Ideas for further reform

As mentioned above, with the complete opening up of reform of the whole economic system, a whole series of reforms have been implemented and certain results have been achieved initiating new methods of funding, the use of reimbursable investment, the simplification and devolution of authority to approve investment, and the institution of tendering and the contract responsibility system. Clearly these reforms are only a beginning and several fundamental problems remain.

1   Too many investments still have to be approved by the central government, and its control is too detailed. Moreover, extra-budgetary investment cannot be controlled. The direction of investment lacks guidance. New construction projects are launched without sufficient thought and duplication is a serious problem.

2   In major construction the state takes too much on its own shoulders. The investment controlled by the central government is insufficient for the large number of major projects, and the source of funds is unstable. Because too much consideration is given to short-term returns, a large proportion of investment outside the budget and of bank credit investment has been used for non-productive construction, such as general processing and hotel development. At the same time deficiencies in the supply and delivery of energy and raw materials have become increasingly severe.

3   Administrative methods for investment allocation still depend on departmental or local subordinancy. Rights, responsibilities and benefits are divorced from one another, and the investing body does not have to bear the risks involved. Both self-restraining mechanisms and outside pressure are lacking, and competition for investment, and projects to invest in, without regard for the returns is common.

4   In planning and construction no proper system for inviting and submitting tenders has been developed; damage, waste and 'all eating from the same big pot' are rife. If these abuses are not corrected at the organizational level, the chronic complaint of overinflated investment will not be cured. There will be no efficient regulation and control of the investment structure, and it will continue to deteriorate. Nor can investment returns and the health of the economy in general be significantly improved. Consequently, as reform of the economic system develops, reform of the investment system must be resolutely pursued and a new administrative system set up which meets the needs of a planned commodity economy.

With the experience of reform of the investment system over the last few years in mind, further reform should aim primarily at raising the efficiency of resource allocation. The investment system must be reformed in such a way that there is an organic link between reform and growth. Each reform measure must help to solve the problem of overinvestment, improve the overall balance of supply and demand, and advance the long-term growth and stability of the national economy. Reform must facilitate the concentration of the finance and resources necessary to strengthen major construction, improve the investment structure, promote rationalization and quality in industry, and raise the level of investment returns and economic returns in general.

Investment in fixed assets has a bearing on the long-term distribution of productive forces and the realization of economic strategy, and must be subordinate to the state's industrial policy. Investment in non-major construction can be determined by the enterprise in question and the market. In the case of investment for commercial and industrial construction, the practice of reimbursable investment must be maintained and a strict responsibility system set up to regulate use, repayment and appreciation. Non-commercial and industrial construction should still be dealt with under the plan and given allocations from public finance departments. However, in general the focal point for the next stage of reform should be the progressive devolution of investment decision-making, the establishment of a responsibility system in which rights, responsibilities and benefits are linked, and the initiation of an efficient system of regulation and control. The main characteristics of such a system are as follows.

1 Long-term investment must be managed at different levels and the responsibility of local government for major construction projects must be increased. Although decisions regarding important long-term investments affecting the whole country should still be taken by central government, ordinary regional long-term investment can be left to local government. In accordance with this principle, an appropriate division of investment responsibility between central and local government should be made. This will necessitate the transfer of certain projects, especially major construction projects, from central to local government.

2 The rights of enterprises to make decisions about investment should be increased so that they become the main beneficiaries of short-term loans. At present enterprises provide their own investment for technical renewal projects and main welfare facilities. Well-funded enterprises should also undertake capital construction projects and increase their scale of production. As regards forms of investment, enterprises should be encouraged to organize group investment in order to guarantee a suitable scale of production. Greater investment authority should be given to enterprises, according to their investment role, with respect to

depreciation funds, ordinary technical replacement and essential expanded development.

3 A basic construction fund system should be set up to guarantee a stable source of funds. Basic industries and installations and certain large-scale items of social development usually need heavy investment and take a long time to build. Under the present system of financial allocation they are strongly affected by the prevailing state of public finance, lack a stable source of investment and can only keep to a suitable construction schedule if there is guaranteed funding – this requires a basic construction fund. Funds for productive construction are mainly used for major construction projects within the plan; funds for non-productive construction are for those which have no economic revenue. These funds should be separated from budgetary expenses and used as a special circulating fund, so that special categories have their special uses, and are placed clearly into the 'income' and 'expenditure' parts of the government budget.

4 Specialized investment corporations and investment development banks should be set up for various industries such as energy, raw materials, transport, agriculture and processing (or possibly the Construction Bank might assume this function). Economic methods should be used to manage investment, changing the present administrative relationship into an economic relationship. Investment corporations should be responsible for providing the funds and materials needed for major construction projects, and by means of inviting and submitting tenders and contracts between enterprises and groups of enterprises, guarantee them reimbursable investment. The investment corporations would also be responsible for the regular payment of principal and interest, and should also provide investment information. The state investment development bank is a financial organ of government whose main aim is not profit-making but the implementation of state policy.

5 A system of tendering should be set up to bring the competitive mechanism of the market fully into play. Planning and construction units should become progressively detached from ministries and local government and become autonomous enterprises, responsible for their own profit and loss, and their own good name. Rights, responsibilities and benefits should be linked. These enterprises should use tendering to encourage competition and to conduct their business.

6 Self-restraining mechanisms in investing bodies should be strengthened and the macroeconomic control system improved. In joint investment projects a board of directors may be used for this purpose; in projects funded solely by the state a management committee should perhaps be responsible for all the risks involved in the preliminary period until the enterprise in question goes into production. All projects should employ the contract responsibility system, where investment, duration of construction, increased production capacity, quantity and benefits are all contracted for and investment is reimbursable. On the macroecono-

mic level, the state should direct the use of total bank credit for fixed assets and, according to economic change, tighten or loosen the money market and flexibly control the strength of regulation and control to ensure the healthy operation of investment in line with the coordinated development of the national economy.

The above suggestions may be the basic framework for a new investment system, but to make them compatible with reality requires detailed preparatory work and preliminary experiments before they can be realized.

# References

Wang Jiye and Zhu Yuanzhen (eds) (1987) *Handbook on Reform of the Economic System.*

ZTN [*Chinese Statistical Yearbook (Zhongguo Tongji Nianjian)*] (1982–7). Beijing: Zhongguo Tongji Chubanshe.

# 15

# Energy Policy

## Austin Robinson

I can make no claim to specialist first-hand knowledge of energy conditions in China, but during the past 25 years I have been involved in conducting energy surveys in Europe, India, Bangladesh and Taiwan. This experience of other rather similar countries makes me wish to ask certain questions regarding energy policy in China.

At present, the Chinese hope to quadruple the 1980 output of agriculture and industry by the year 2000, representing an average annual growth rate of 7.2 per cent. Since in almost all developing countries the average annual rate of growth of services and other activities is greater than that of agriculture and industry taken together, this figure can be taken as a slight underestimate of the implied growth of gross domestic product (GDP) as normally defined. It is a high figure, but not impossible, and is not higher than has been achieved in a number of other Asian countries.

It is the present expectation to increase the total supply of commercial energy, mainly in the form of coal, to a little over twice the 1980 supply (table 15.1). This growth of energy supply is not the result of deliberate planning but the outcome of disappointments regarding possible discoveries of new oil supplies. It is necessary to ask whether these two elements of economic policy are mutually consistent and what is likely to happen if they are inconsistent.

The GDP policy requires an average annual growth rate of about 7.2 per cent per annum. The policy for commercial energy requires an average annual growth rate of 3.6 per cent per annum. What is generally called the energy elasticity – the ratio of the growth rate of use of primary energy to the growth rate of GDP – is 0.5, which is very far below the more typical

My interest in this subject was initially aroused by a paper presented to a seminar in Cambridge by Dr Elspeth Thomson, Fellow of the Contemporary China Institute in London. The data that I have used relating to China are wholly derived from her work. She is not responsible for the use or misuse that I have made of them. The data relating to India and Taiwan are taken from official publications of the two countries.

**Table 15.1**  Present target supplies of energy in China

|  | 1980 (% of total supply in 1980) | Target in 2000 (% of output in 1980) |
|---|---|---|
| Coal | 69.4 | 193.5 |
| Oil | 23.8 | 188.7 |
| Gas | 3.0 | 174.8 |
| Hydroelectricity | 3.8 | 344.7 |
| Nuclear power | 0.0 | [a] |
| Total | 100.0 | 204.0 |

[a] The target for nuclear power in 2000 is equivalent to half the target for hydroelectricity.

value of 1.0. Is this a realistic assumption? In my view it is almost certainly not. It is contrary to the experience of all the similar developing countries for which data are available.

Consider first the example of India. In India, as in China, a very large proportion of energy consumption is in the form of non-commercial energy – firewood, agricultural waste, dung cakes. This is particularly true of household consumption for cooking and similar purposes. It is estimated that 67.6 per cent of all energy consumption in India in 1953–4 was of non-commercial energy, principally in the form of firewood, which accounted for 44.1 per cent of all energy consumption. By 1975–6 the share of all non-commercial energy had fallen to 43.5 per cent and that of firewood (which was in danger of denuding India of its trees) had fallen to 28.3 per cent of the total.

This shift from non-commercial to commercial energy has been of considerable importance because it has implied that the demand for commercial energy has reflected not only the consequences of economic growth but also the consequences of a change in the pattern of consumption and an increasing shortage of firewood and other non-commercial fuel. In consequence, the proportion of all energy that is derived from commercial energy is estimated to have risen from 32.4 per cent in 1953–4 to 56.5 per cent in 1975–6. It would be relevant to any attempt to analyse the energy problems of China to consider how far, with similar problems of increased urbanization and local shortages of non-commercial energy, it may be necessary to make provision for a significant shift towards commercial forms of energy similar, although possibly on a smaller scale, to that which has taken place in India.

However, the shift of household consumption in India has not been a dominating factor influencing the total consumption of commercial energy.

In fact, household consumption now represents a smaller proportion of total consumption than it did in 1953–4. Surprisingly to anyone who does not know India, it is agriculture in the form of electrification of water-pumping which has most significantly increased its share of the total use of commercial energy. Energy elasticity in India has consistently been above 1.0, although it has declined slightly in recent years. However, the long-period elasticity from 1953–4 to 1982–3 is as high as 1.7 (table 15.2).

Because of the discovery of new offshore sources of oil, which has greatly increased indigenous supplies and offset the decline of earlier supplies in Assam, India has been under less pressure than most other countries to modify its pattern of energy sources in the light of the OPEC monopoly of oil supplies and the consequent increase in the relative price of crude oil. Between 1971 and 1985 Indian production of crude oil increased by 320 per cent, an annual average of 10.8 per cent, while Indian production of coal increased by 109 per cent, an annual average of 5.4 per cent. The changing pattern of the Indian final consumption of energy is shown in table 15.3 which emphasizes the shift towards consumption in the form of electricity. Between 1971 and 1985 the annual generation of electricity increased by 176 per cent, an annual average increase of 7.5 per cent and a specific energy elasticity of over 2.0. The inferences that can be

**Table 15.2**   Energy elasticities in India

| | Average annual growth rate of GDP at constant prices (%) | Average annual growth rate of internal use of commercial energy (%) | Energy elasticity[a] |
|---|---|---|---|
| 1953–4 to 1965–6 | 3.4 | 6.2 | 1.8 |
| 1965–6 to 1975–6 | 4.0 | 5.6 | 1.4 |
| 1975–6 to 1982–3 | 3.6 | 4.3 | 1.2 |
| 1953–4 to 1982–3 | 3.6 | 6.1 | 1.7 |

[a] Defined in text.

**Table 15.3**   India: forms of final consumption of commercial energy

| | 1953–4 | 1965–6 | 1982–3 |
|---|---|---|---|
| Coal (%) | 47.5 | 35.3 | 22.0 |
| Oil (%) | 39.9 | 44.2 | 47.5 |
| Electricity (%) | 12.6 | 20.5 | 30.5 |
| Total (%) | 100.0 | 100.0 | 100.0 |

drawn from the experience of India suggest that the overall energy elasticity in a country not unlike China in its present dependence on agriculture and its rapidly increasing urbanization may be appreciably over 1.0 and that the trend towards electricity may be of the order of twice the growth of the GDP.

We now consider evidence from Taiwan. This is of special relevance for two reasons. First, Taiwan has in some respects special analogies for China, as it illustrates what a largely Chinese-born population can achieve. Second, Taiwan has faced the need to make drastic energy economies on two occasions. First we examine the energy elasticities. Table 15.4 shows the elasticities over short periods, some as short as four years, as well as over the period of 23 years from 1963 to 1986. It can be seen that over the period 1963–86 the energy elasticity was slightly in excess of 1.0. From 1955 to 1973 it was consistently about 1.05.

The periods 1972–6, 1979–83 and 1982–6 have been separated out because they represent two very interesting phases which may have possible lessons for China. Up to 1973 Taiwan was an oil-based economy. Of all sources of primary energy, oil and petroleum products together made up 72 per cent, and almost all of this was imported. Thus the OPEC price rise hit Taiwan very severely. Above all it created problems of inflation that had been almost absent in previous years. The increases in oil prices came to Taiwan, as to other countries, predominantly in two instalments. In 1973–4 the price of crude oil was increased by a factor of about 3.5. In 1979–80 the price was raised again to about 10 times the pre-1973 price. On the first occasion the government of Taiwan rode out the crisis. There was a short period of two years of acute fall in the rate of growth of GDP. This was primarily an industrial depression. Energy consumption outside industry was less affected and grew faster than GDP.

**Table 15.4**   Energy elasticities in Taiwan

|  | Average annual growth rate of GDP at constant prices (%) | Average annual growth rate of internal use of commercial energy (%) | Energy elasticity |
|---|---|---|---|
| 1955–63 | 7.2 | 7.8 | 1.08 |
| 1963–73 | 11.1 | 11.7 | 1.05 |
| 1972–6 | 7.9 | 8.3 | 1.05 |
| 1976–9 | 10.6 | 11.6 | 1.09 |
| 1979–83 | 6.0 | 3.8 | 0.56 |
| 1982–6 | 7.8 | 7.7 | 0.99 |
| 1963–86 | 9.1 | 9.4 | 1.03 |

By 1975 the rate of energy consumption was close to pre-1973 levels. The economy continued to be predominantly oil-based, and oil-intensive industries, although less profitable than pre-1973, continued to be developed. The second oil price rise was very different. The effect on consumer prices was much greater and the government of Taiwan reacted vigorously. First, it initiated a very severe economy drive to cut down all energy consumption. Second, it undertook a very thorough review of energy policy, including an energy survey in which I took part.

The economy drive was so severe that some industrial experts thought that in some respects, such as workshop lighting, it was self-frustrating. The overall effects are shown in table 15.5. In the year 1981 there was a reduction of about 11 per cent below the level that would ordinarily have been expected. This and other measures consequent on the balance-of-payments effects resulted in a substantial reduction in the growth of GDP in 1982. By the time that normal growth was restored in 1983 annual energy consumption was about 11 per cent lower than it would have been before the economy drive. The most interesting lesson from the experience of Taiwan is that of the years 1982–6. It can be seen from table 15.5 that,

**Table 15.5**  Taiwan: years 1972–1976, 1979–1983 and 1982–1986

| | Growth of constant price GDP over previous year (%) | Projected growth of use of commercial energy on basis of previous trend (%) | Actual growth of commercial energy (%) | Change from previous trend (%) |
|---|---|---|---|---|
| 1972–3 | 12.9 | 13.5 | 11.7 | −1.8 |
| 1973–4 | 1.1 | 1.1 | 0.6 | −0.5 |
| 1974–5 | 4.6 | 4.8 | 10.9 | +6.1 |
| 1975–6 | 13.8 | 14.5 | 19.6 | +5.1 |
| 1972–6 (4 years) | 35.5 | 37.3 | 49.0 | +11.7 |
| 1979–80 | 7.3 | 7.7 | 6.5 | −1.2 |
| 1980–1 | 6.1 | 6.4 | −4.4 | −10.8 |
| 1981–2 | 2.7 | 2.8 | 1.9 | −0.9 |
| 1982–3 | 7.7 | 8.1 | 9.1 | +1.0 |
| 1979–83 (4 years) | 26.1 | 27.4 | 16.1 | −11.3 |
| 1982–3 | 7.7 | 8.1 | 10.9 | +2.8 |
| 1983–4 | 9.5 | 10.0 | 6.7 | −3.3 |
| 1984–5 | 4.3 | 4.5 | 10.8 | +6.3 |
| 1985–6 | 9.9 | 10.4 | 3.2 | −7.2 |
| 1982–6 (4 years) | 35.2 | 37.0 | 34.6 | −2.4 |

after achieving by 1982 the lowest level of energy consumption associated with any given GDP, the consumption of commercial energy has grown at almost the same rate as the GDP, i.e. the current energy elasticity is almost exactly 1.0.

The lessons of the experience of Taiwan emphasize three things. First, they confirm the evidence from India that energy elasticities are normally very close to 1.0. Secondly, and of particular importance for China, the elasticity that can be achieved once and for all over a short period cannot be projected over a long period. It is just conceivable that savings of 25 per cent could be achieved over a period of a year. However, this does not mean that a further saving of 25 per cent can be obtained in the following year. Economies are exhaustible and the economy will quickly revert, as did the Taiwan economy, to the normal energy elasticity at a lower level. Third, a very severe economy drive in Taiwan reduced energy consumption by only 11 per cent. If the economy is to continue to operate and grow there are limits below which transportation, domestic consumption, industrial inputs and the other main uses of energy cannot be reduced.

We now return, with some diffidence, to the problems facing China, and first make a general point. All progress in excess of population growth is ordinarily energy intensive. It is the result of adding more efficient technology and more energy to human input. If technology and human input were constant, growth could come only from the energy input growing and representing a larger proportion of all inputs. Thus an energy elasticity no greater than 1.0 – an energy growth equal to that of output – already assumes that there is appreciable steady progress in energy-saving technology. In other words an *ex post* calculation of energy elasticity inevitably includes the energy economies which have been achieved during the period concerned. A projection of that elasticity over future years implicitly assumes that economies will continue to be made at a similar rate. Embodied in an energy elasticity for 1960–80 are all the technical economies of 1960–80.

If we assume (what we would regard as the upper limit of practicable possibility) a once and for all saving of 25 per cent in energy consumption per unit of output combined with an average annual growth of energy supply of 3.6 per cent and an energy elasticity of 1.0 starting from the consequent lower level, the currently envisaged energy supplies would be consistent with an average annual growth rate of GDP of 5.1 per cent compared with the planned rate of 7.2 per cent. If, stretching imagination far beyond anything that has ever been achieved anywhere in the past, we assume that a saving of one-third of present consumption of commercial energy can be achieved and that thereafter consumption will grow proportionately with output, the resultant energy supply will be consistent with a GDP growth rate of the order of 5.7 per cent.

What is likely to happen in such circumstances? If we return to the Indian experience, what was happening at the time of the first Indian energy survey was that industrial development, and particularly small-scale industrial development, was being held back by an inability to obtain connection to electricity supplies, and the greatly needed expansion of agricultural output was held back by an inability to supply energy to villages and to pump water. In effect, energy supply limited production growth.

If energy supply is not made consistent with production plans the same may happen in China. At this point it is of importance to see how Taiwan adjusted the pattern of its energy supplies to permit most economically an average annual growth rate of GDP during 1982–6 of 7.8. It will be seen in table 15.6 that the required energy increased by a factor of 2.3 between the pre-OPEC pattern of 1973 and 1986. During that period the proportionate contributions of all energy sources except two declined. The two exceptions were imported coal and nuclear power. The total proportion of crude oil and petroleum products has been reduced from 71 to 53 per cent with a very considerable increase of local refining. Nuclear power provides almost 17 per cent of all energy.

If I am right about the limits of possible economies and the order of magnitude of the underlying energy elasticity and if the Chinese authorities want (as I would expect) to stick to their 7.2 per cent growth rate, I would calculate that they need the equivalent of an increase of energy supplies by a factor of 3 instead of the present factor of 2.04. In other words they would need to increase the average annual growth of energy supplies over the period from the present 3.6 per cent to 5.6 per cent. This would imply, if it were to be achieved completely by an increase in coal supplies (at

**Table 15.6**  Taiwan: sources of commercial energy

|  | 1973 | 1986 | Volume in 1986 as percentage of 1973 |
|---|---|---|---|
| Coal |  |  |  |
| Local (%) | 13.4 | 3.0 | 51.8 |
| Imported (%) | 0.7 | 19.5 | 6,606.7 |
| Crude oil |  |  |  |
| Local (%) | 1.0 | 0.3 | 62.7 |
| Imported (%) | 60.1 | 47.6 | 182.7 |
| Petroleum products: Imported (%) | 11.0 | 5.0 | 105.4 |
| Natural gas: local (%) | 8.8 | 3.0 | 80.3 |
| Hydroelectric power: local (%) | 5.0 | 4.7 | 213.9 |
| Nuclear power: imported[a] (%) | 0.0 | 16.9 | – |
| Total (%) | 100.0 | 100.0 | 231.0 |
| Local sources (%) | 28.2 | 10.4 | 90.0 |
| Imported (%) | 71.8 | 89.6 | 286.2 |

[a] Imported only in the limited sense that the basic fuel is imported.

present they represent about 70 per cent of the total), an increase of the coal supplies in the year 2000 from the estimated 1,200 million tons to slightly more than 2,000 million tons – an increase of 800 million tons – both as compared with a 1980 output of 620 million tons and a 1986 production of 870 million tons.

These figures are so immense compared with total world supplies that one hesitates to say what is possible or impossible. Total world supplies outside China in 1986 were no more than 2,760 million tons, of which 630 million tons were produced in the USSR. Thus it is far more certain that it would be physically possible for China to solve her problems as Taiwan has done by large imports of cheap coal from the thick seams of Australia, the west coast of the United States and one or two other low-cost suppliers. An estimate made in 1982 of possible increases of supplies in 2000 from these low-cost sources put the highest growth believed practicable as about 600 million tons, as part of a possible total world increase of coal exports to 730 million tons, but it was expected that normal growth of consumption in countries other than China would require some 560 million tons or possibly more. It is most unlikely that China, with its immense economy, could solve problems on the scale that I am envisaging wholly by imports of coal, even if the consequent balance-of-payments problems could be solved.

Thus if the orders of magnitude of the energy requirements for a quadrupling of the GDP proposed in this chapter are correct, there will have to be a much greater expansion of the internal energy resources of China, principally in the form of coal, than is at present planned. Whether that increase and its transportation is physically possible, I do not know. If it is not, my expectation is that energy supply will prove a bottleneck and that a quadrupling of national production will not be achieved.

# 16

# Foreign Trade

## Zhou Xiaochuan

China's economic reform is closely connected with changes in habits of thought, which to a great extent determine the rate of progress of reform, both in China and in other socialist countries. The level of understanding differs widely in so large a population. Whether reform can progress depends primarily on the ideas of China's leaders and the economists who advise them. It also depends on whether cadres at all levels accept the new theories of reform and are convinced by the results. This is not always appreciated by Western economists.

Two important factors from pre-1978 promoted ideological liberation among Chinese economists. The first was the bitter experience of the Cultural Revolution, which led many people to become deeply suspicious of accepted theories and the established system of planned economy. The second was Deng Xiaoping's insistence that 'practice is the only criterion for judging the truth', which did a great deal to counteract dogmatism among cadres, economists and the people in general. Once they were able to compare economic growth and economic systems elsewhere in the world, after the 'opening up' of China, they developed an intense hope in reform.

This ideological change stimulated foreign trade reform. If we are to understand this reform, the concepts which lay behind it and the deficiencies in understanding which led to partial setbacks, we need to know the views of leading economists, which of these views hindered reform and how the process of reform itself gradually changed people's views. Rather than focusing on the achievements, or on what should be done next, in this chapter we shall focus on economic thinking which was the background to reform. The ideas which determined policies, including those which ought perhaps to have been chosen and were not, are examined.

## Ideological liberation and changing perceptions

The early period of ideological liberation began around the time of Deng Xiaoping's return to office after the Cultural Revolution, and ended with the resolution on reform made by the Third Plenum of the 12th Congress in 1984. During this period ideological bonds were continually being broken. All sorts of novel ideas and reforms emerged, but did not crystallize into a coherent reform model. Research began on the economic systems and the experience of some other countries, but not on a global scale. What was common to all reformist economists was that they were highly critical of the dogmatic economic theories of the past. In a new stage after 1984, economists turned their attention to the theory of reform. Different schools of thought appeared, so that policy-makers had a wider field of choice.

Certain changes in economic thinking, although strictly speaking outside the realm of foreign trade, were nevertheless of great importance.

1 There was a debate on the purpose of production under socialism. It rejected the model of self-perpetuating development of heavy industry under socialism, and affirmed that production is for the purpose of the maximum satisfaction of people's material and cultural needs. However, there was a failure to identify what kind of information system and what system of resource allocation might fulfil this requirement. (Of course, these questions had a bearing on the distribution of foreign exchange and the structure of foreign trade.)

2 Distribution according to labour and the principle of material incentives were affirmed, although there was still no clear concept of optimal resource allocation or remuneration for labour and other factors of production.

3 The importance of a rational system of commodity prices was recognized, but the necessity for market supply and demand to determine prices and the connection with Marx's theory of production price were not explained. No satisfactory explanation was forthcoming of why microeconomic behaviour is sometimes in conflict with the economic interests of society as a whole.

4 While there was some understanding of the difficulty of centralized planning and the advantages of regulation by market forces, many naive illusions existed about the possibility of a happy marriage between plan and market. Some people thought that all problems could be solved merely by the decentralization of planning and regulatory powers.

5 The need to give autonomy to enterprises was recognized. However, no one could explain what kind of governmental management system and market environment would simultaneously guarantee tight financial restraints on enterprises and allow them autonomy. Who should have the right to employ the 'economic lever' and several other related questions remained unsolved.

6 The advantages of competition were recognized, but its preconditions, as well as the possibility of market failure (such as the cobweb effect, monopoly and externalities) were not understood.

It was not until after 1984 that some economists began to address these questions in a thoroughgoing and systematic way. The effects of inadequate theories on previous reform and economic policies had become obvious by then. At the time of writing, in the late 1980s, the USSR and certain East European countries are passing through a similar stage. Perspicacious economists can see the importance of these problems of understanding and their effect on the early period of reform of China's foreign trade system. Ideological liberation had a marked effect on this, and on foreign trade policy. However, it still left much to be desired.

1   The excessive emphasis on self-sufficiency in the old central planning system was gradually put aside. The idea that foreign trade was merely a regulator of surpluses and shortages gave place to a recognition that earning foreign exchange through exports led to a marked increase in imports and exports in the early period of reform. However, the advantages to the economy of participating in the international division of labour and introducing international competition has not yet been fully appreciated.

2   We began to realize that highly centralized import–export planning and management, and the financial system of 'all eating out of the same pot', impeded the expansion of foreign trade; there should be decentralization of power in the management of foreign trade (especially exports) in order to stimulate activity. However, we are not yet clear as to whether power should be delegated to local government or to enterprises, industrial enterprises or just foreign trade organizations. We have not yet solved the problem of reconciling microeconomic import–export practices with macroeconomic aspirations, given the present distortions in the price system. Nor have we found a way of strengthening financial restraints on import and export enterprises.

3   We moved away from blanket rejection of the theory of comparative advantage in international trade, from the idea that it was entirely dominated by advanced capitalist countries, and began to realize that, in order to expand exports despite limited financial backing, it is necessary to make the most of China's latent advantages, especially that of cheap labour. However, we have not yet analysed the pattern and dynamics of comparative advantage on a world scale. For instance, before 1984 very few people raised the question of the relationship between the changes in China's export structure and the newly industrialized countries. We have not yet created the policies or the environment which will allow the microeconomy to assess its own comparative advantage.

4   We understood that to attract foreign capital and encourage foreign businessmen to invest directly can be of mutual advantage, and can promote technical and managerial progress. On the theoretical level, although at first still influenced by the belief that 'foreign capital and foreign businessmen exploit us', we have begun to welcome such

exploitation if it is mutually beneficial. We do not understand clearly how to assess the economic benefits of different forms of foreign investment projects. Indeed we have no effective method of assessment on which to base rational differentiated policies.

5 In a country as large as China it is difficult to summon up sufficient determination to undertake overall reform, although we realized the value of setting up special economic areas and pilot areas which can be popularized and expanded once experience of reform and 'opening up' has given people confidence. However, insufficient thought was given to the form of the special economic zones and the possibility of their proliferation; the strategy and goals were not clear before they were started. Consequently there have been complaints that transferring reforms made there to other parts of the economy leaves much to be desired. The structure of the special economic zones has been adjusted during their operation and as understanding has improved, but vested interests make regulation difficult.

6 We recognized the need to link industry and technology to foreign trade, and the importance of improving the export structure. However, we have not adequately analysed the basic causes of dislocation between foreign trade and industry. Moreover, the lack of direct contact between our industrial enterprises and the international market has held back progress in this area.

7 We realized that the price system and the exchange rate should be rationalized, and the policy of discriminating against exports has been abandoned. However, we have not yet understood the connection between international market prices and our own price rationalization. There is still some resistance to international market prices; in imports, in particular, we have not sufficiently analysed our excessively protectionist policy and the discrimination which exists against exports.

In short, there was a great deal of ideological liberation and a remarkable change in attitudes without the emergence of a reasonably coherent theoretical system. Insufficient attention was given to the interconnections between reform theory in different sectors and logical economic analysis. There was too much reliance on experimental projects and 'playing it by ·ear'. It was often thought that the experience of reform in agriculture could be applied to industry. Sometimes novel systems were enthusiastically created without proper evidence as to their practical applicability. To some extent a certain immaturity was inevitable in the early stages of ideological liberation and, although it caused errors and setbacks, there was considerable progress in the reform. Whether it can continue depends to a large extent on our ability to learn from experience.

# The ideological challenge of foreign trade reform

There has been a whole series of measures in the reform of the foreign trade system since 1978. In this section a few examples which particularly reflect the theoretical background and the level of understanding are selected.

In about 1978 it was decided to revise our development strategy, end China's isolation, open up to the outside world, increase exports and raise the status of exporting industries. We were able to uncover the hidden export potential of Chinese products, and as a result trade doubled between 1978 and 1980 alone. The 'substitute coal for oil' project is an example. Before 1978 large quantities of crude oil were used for fuel, but with the change in development strategy great efforts were made to persuade enterprises to shift to coal, so that the oil could be exported. Of course, even when the exportability of Chinese goods had been identified, it was another matter actually to expand their export.

About this time, we began to give up our misplaced pride in the fact that China had no foreign debt. Loans were negotiated and foreign business-men were encouraged to participate in joint-investment enterprises in China. The Shenzhen special economic zone was established. The scale of borrowing by the government itself is modest, but an effective supervisory and management system was not promptly set up when the right to borrow and admit foreign investment was decentralized. The policy of attracting direct foreign investment and the laws relating to it were only carried through by finding loopholes in the web of restrictions inherent in state policies and prevalent attitudes – a process sometimes called 'finding a way out through the seams'. In retrospect, this policy was unsatisfactory, with over-reliance on tax concessions to attract foreign businessmen, and too much stress on the self-balancing of foreign exchange. There was too much use of administrative methods to support foreign investment enterprises, rather than relying on the market, and there was a lack of discrimination in selecting such enterprises. However, at the time these things were not easy to achieve. Some people feel that, on the basis of this start, policy and foreign investment should have developed and improved far more but were hampered by economic thinking and present-day policies in China. The achievements and experience of Shenzhen and the other special economic zones have attracted much attention and have had a considerable effect on ideological liberation. They have even attracted interest in the USSR and Eastern Europe. However, the aims of and policies towards the special economic zones have not been sufficiently rigorously thought through, and too many illusions exist about their function. They have been called 'four windows and two sides of a fan' – the four 'windows' are technology, management, knowledge and foreign policy, while a fan opens outwards and reflects light inwards. In a country as large as China such things were not easy to achieve. Unrealistic expectations and unclear policy have sometimes led to unfair competition with the special zones 'getting blood transfusions from the hinterland', and have also led to imappropriate attempts at imitation. We need to consider carefully whether this is indeed the best way to promote the smooth progress of reform in China.

As mandatory planning has become increasingly inadequate for export growth we have now begun to employ economic levers, including the right to retain a proportion of foreign exchange earnings and a special internal foreign exchange rate. The purchasing power of the retained portion of foreign exchange earnings is greater than that of foreign exchange at the official rate, and has the unique non-monetary advantage of permitting the import of up-to-date technology and equipment. This has helped to overcome the longstanding discrimination against exports. Price distortions and discrimination against different products varies, while the degree of reliance on important raw materials is different between one product and another. Consequently, some people advocate rights to retain a different proportion of foreign exchange earnings in different export industries. Others favour rights to retain a different proportion of foreign exchange earnings depending on the conditions in different regions: they argue that in minority and backward areas, for instance, it should be greater. In fact this amounts to using the retention of a proportion of foreign exchange earnings as an instrument for regulating income distribution. In practice, when adjustments are being considered, this is often the main influence on the outcome.

At the end of 1980 it was decided to set an internal exchange rate for foreign trade accounting, i.e. a dual exchange rate was adopted (the internal rate was 2.80 yuan to the dollar and the official rate was 1.53 yuan to the dollar, which was constantly raised). This helped to improve our balance of payments, and in the space of three years the government's foreign exchange reserve increased sixfold to sevenfold, not of course all due to the effects of this lever. Although in 1981 and 1982 world trade as a whole was far from booming, exports continued to rise. At that time there was a certain amount of inflation and the fixed internal exchange rate gradually ceased to have an impact. By 1984 it was clear that the value of the RMB was too high. Thus in 1985 the dual exchange rate was abolished and the official rate was readjusted twice. There have always been different views about the function of the exchange rate, and in some of them we can still see the influence of the old Soviet model. After 1984 we began to study the use of economic levers. We also paid more attention to international practice and the degree to which trading partners could accept Chinese policies.

The decentralization of foreign trade and the problems encountered is a topic as important as it is complex. Prior to reform, China had less than ten specialized foreign trade companies, but no general companies with local branches. Provincial foreign trade management organizations generally took orders from central foreign trade departments. Decentralization took three forms.

1   Authorization was given for the special economic zones and for the establishment of foreign trade companies in Guangdong and Fujian provinces, initially for export only and later for import as well.
2   Permission was given for setting up several export companies more closely linked with industry. Later, a small number of industries were allowed to run their own foreign trade, although in practice it was not very common for productive enterprises to obtain such rights. Indeed, there is still mutual resentment between industry and foreign trade organizations, with the latter complaining that industry provides them with substandard goods. Industrial enterprises tend to reply that without direct contact with the international market they lack both knowledge and incentives.
3   Local governments gradually acquired increased rights and incentives, and set up their own foreign trade companies. The former single vertical dependence of local foreign trade administration began to give way to dual dependence (although there is regional variation), and to some extent local branches of specialized foreign trade companies also moved towards dual dependence. Local interests and the administrative intervention of local governments are often not in harmony with the aims of the national industrial structure, market carve-ups exist and there is resistance against enterprises acquiring rights of operation.

By 1983 the devolution of foreign trade operation was in obvious collision with China's distorted price system. The prices of some primary products and simple processed goods had always been very low, and this was criticized as 'buying at high prices, cutting prices for export, so that the milk and honey flows abroad'. Some economists consider that the introduction of international market prices through imports and exports is positive and beneficial, since it helps to reduce price distortion in China. Unfortunately the government did not recognize the possibility of linking the two sets of prices, and losses resulted for certain types of goods. Nor did the government impose a resource tax on goods falling into this category, which led to the excessive export of such goods with most of the profit accruing to a few companies and individuals. The government could have made effective use of such price conflicts by means of reform. Many people are reluctant to acknowledge that there is anything wrong with China's price system and that the price conflicts resulting from decentralization have had damaging results. They consider that the problems should be resolved by recentralization of control rather than price reform, and, indeed, at the end of 1983 the decentralization of operation rights was severely limited.

This, of course, acted as a damper on the vitality of enterprises, and so a new round of decentralization was discussed very rapidly and initiated around the end of 1984. It was intended to formulate an export policy on the basis of different exchange rates for different categories of exports.

However, the economic management departments were unqualified to implement a differential policy of this kind. There was a shortage of expertise, the information system was inadequate and the administrative structure was unsuited to such a task. The immediate result was maladjustment and chaos, and there was a return to the system of giving differential financial treatment to foreign trade companies according to the nature of their specialization. However, the decentralization of operation rights and the rapid proliferation of commodity types meant that it was increasingly difficult to define the limits of trade companies' specialization. Unfair competition and price conflicts persisted, and the government responded by tightening up management through permits and quotas. At first, this unfair competition originated in financial conditions (including proportionate retention of foreign exchange), but problems of financial control in certain foreign trade companies rapidly became evident, especially in those responsible for implementing the state's plan for the accumulation of foreign exchange. When their task under the plan conflicted with the principle (under certain financial conditions) of enterprises being responsible for their own profit and loss, and, based on past experience, companies hoped that the department which controlled them would relax its financial regulations, they sometimes indulged in unfair competition and ignored budget constraints. Therefore, in 1987 the government tightened up financial discipline and hardened budget constraints on enterprises, which were also urged to institute a contract responsibility system in which they were responsible for their own profit and loss. Economists familiar with the reforms in Hungary and other socialist countries will be aware that in order to tighten budget constraints effectively a whole series of related reforms are necessary (including the abolition of mandatory planning, the separation of government and enterprise, the adoption of indirect regulation, the development of proper markets on which enterprises can rely, and reform of the system of public ownership). There is no evidence that a fundamental solution to this problem will be found in China in the near future.

The process of reform has made people change their attitudes and think about new questions. On the whole, more and more people favour further opening up (including the establishment of special zones and the employment of foreign investment). There is increasing support for an indirect system of economic adjustment, the break-up of monopolies, devolution of operating rights, responsibility for profit and loss, and further structural reform of foreign trade and its coordination with general economic reform. There is bound to be further reform of the foreign trade system. However, because reform of the whole economic system has not yet formed an integrated trajectory, and because the difficulties of achieving macroeconomic balance have led to slow progress in key aspects of reform, foreign trade reform is likely to face some difficulties in the short term: (a) a certain amount of unfair competition still exists; (b) making enterprises responsible for their own profit and loss and tightening budget constraints will take a long time, and bargaining between government and enterprise is still very common; (c) devolution of operation rights to enterprises is still proceeding slowly; (d) it is difficult to carry through the complicated task of rectifying price distortions; (e) there is little room for manoeuvre in the adjustment of policies respecting special economic zones and foreign investment.

## Further reform of the foreign trade system

As a result of the experience of several years of reform, economists in general have improved the scope and quality of their research. Different schools of thought have emerged on the subject of further reform. Some consider that as long as an appropriate overall level of supply and demand is maintained, interlinked reform of enterprises, the market and macromanagement should be pursued nationwide. Others believe that the key to future reform should be transformation of the economic mechanism and the ownership system. Some advocate a strategy of overall regional reform based on pilot areas. The government now has more theories and draft plans from which to select its future strategy, but the choice has become extremely difficult. It remains to be seen whether coordination of all the different aspects of reform can be achieved.

Relatively few economists are investigating the future development of the foreign trade system (which is partly because the relevant information is not very accessible to the public) and there are few coherent plans. Choice is also limited by what is internationally acceptable. One relatively well-known plan of this kind envisages the following.

1   Mandatory export plans should be abolished, government and enterprise should be separated and a regulatory system which makes enterprises entirely responsible for their own profit and loss should be established. This new system would include the following: (a) rationalization of the exchange rate (by adjustment or by increasing the proportion of foreign exchange earnings retained and by the creation of a foreign exchange market of importers and exporters); (b) complete remission of indirect taxes on exported goods and of customs duties on inputs (including indirect taxes on inputs), and, before a value-added tax can be generally implemented, certain products should be subject to a refund of a stipulated proportion of their tax payments; (c) credit support for industries producing superior quality exports; (d) improvement of the efficiency of customs, simplification of procedures and reduction of duty differentials; (e) the introduction of a system of annual tenders for the necessary permits and quotas for imports and exports; (f) legislation to reduce to a minimum direct interference in foreign trade by administrative departments, so that operational rights really belong to enterprises.

2   Enterprises should become autonomous and responsible for their profit

and loss. Restrictions on the scope of operations, both in industrial and foreign trade enterprises, should be reduced, including restrictions on division of labour by specialization, and between internal and foreign trade. The long-standing excessively monopolistic system should be changed, and efforts should be made to encourage medium and large industrial enterprises to handle their own foreign trade. They should be given freedom to import and engage in competition, which should be regulated by import and export chambers of commerce set up for the purpose. The organizational form of future foreign trade enterprises should not be determined by government departments, but decided by the enterprises themselves in the process of competition and in accordance with the actual situation. In other words, there may still be specialized enterprises as well as comprehensive trading associations.

3   The strategy for foreign trade development and interrelated reforms in other spheres prevent China from adopting an excessively impetuous overall reform programme. A new system for the import and export of manufactured goods can be implemented fairly rapidly, and followed by a similar system for primary products.

To a certain extent these views have already been accepted by foreign trade departments, and attempts have been made to incorporate them in plans for reform. However, such measures require close coordination with other reforms in planning, prices, finance, industry and so on; since the concept of coordination is lacking in China's overall planning of reform, the development of foreign trade is unlikely to be straightforward. Several problems are likely to have an influence:

1   some people are suspicious of coordinated reform and deny that it is necessary, preferring to continue the method of separate break-throughs in each sphere;
2   some reject the possibility of overall balance of supply and demand in a socialist country, considering that it is impossible in a shortage economy to have markets which clear and opposing reforms which depend on the market mechanism;
3   there is serious disagreement on the theory of prices and inflation, and analyses of the contemporary economic situation are very different, with many people advocating extensive use of price control in order to reduce inflation;
4   the abolition of mandatory planning causes some people anxiety;
5   some believe that, in a country as large as China, the central government cannot formulate regulations for economic adjustment and that this task should be left to various levels of local government;
6   given the influence of the model which gives priority to quantitative growth and the demand that reform should not dampen growth, it will be difficult to concentrate reform on the key issue of low economic returns;

7   some doubt the possibility of developing the market mechanism under a system of public ownership, and advocate the postponment of this until the question of privatization has been solved;

8   some industrial enterprises, used to taking responsibility only in conditions in which there are no risks, demand that foreign trade enterprises should bear all the risks.

These are problems both of practical coordination and theoretical understanding. They will have a major influence on the future reform of the foreign trade system. Undoubtedly, it will continue to develop and accelerate, but whether the path will be smooth and the goals will be achieved will depend on the development of economic theory in China, on the changes in understanding which we have discussed and on the acceptance of forward-looking ideas.

# 17

# The Regional Economy

## Chen Dongsheng

In China, with its vast territory and wide range of resources, natural geography and human geography, the rational spatial allocation of resources and the improvement of local economic structures is an important factor conditioning the growth of the national economy. The reform of the spatial distribution of the economy and its operating mechanism and the creation of a system of self-regulation in the local economic structure have therefore become important in the reform of the economic system as a whole.

## The present situation and its problems

In the highly centralized mandatory planning economy which existed for many years in China the spatial distribution and creation of local economic structures depended mainly on the planned distribution of state investment and local responsibility for construction projects. This system of administrative regulation played a positive role in the early days of New China. Administrative mobilization and concentration of limited resources, laying the foundation for industrialization and guaranteeing economies of scale, reversed the former concentration of industry in the coastal areas and rapidly extended the framework of local economic distribution. In 1949, 71.5 per cent of Chinese industry was concentrated in the coastal areas, and only 28.5 per cent in inland regions. The northwest and southwest regions, comprising 56 per cent of the land area, had only 5.5 per cent of railway mileage. Seven provinces, mostly in the west, had no railways at all. By 1985, the inland share in industry had increased to 38.8 per cent (Chen 1987). West China had 24.6 per cent of the total railway mileage, and all the provinces, cities and autonomous regions, with the exception of Tibet, had railways. A high price was paid for all this and it created many problems. With economic development both the intraregional and local economic structures became increasingly complicated.

## Inefficiency in spatial economic distribution and local economic structure

The system of centralized direction depressed the initiative of localities, enterprises and individuals. The local economy lacked the capacity for self-regulation; there was vertical distribution of factors of production, but no flexible horizontal movement. There was no information structure. China's territory is large, and the level of transport and communication facilities is still low. Transmission of information is slow, and under the present hierarchical system of administration the upward and downward channels of communication are narrow. The long-term antagonism to the market mechanism allowed productive resources from the land, the mines and the sea to be provided as free goods. Under the unified national wage system, intraregional differences in labour costs were concealed, so that the real local costs of production in different industrial systems were impossible to determine. This led to errors in spatial distribution policy and inefficient resource allocation. Further, once decisions had been made and enforced by administrative directive, information feedback was slow. For instance, between the 1950s and the 1970s, the principle of 'equal allocation', which controlled economic distribution in China, was intended, by means of the widespread creation of industry throughout the country, to reduce regional differences in economic development. The cost of this was reduced growth and efficiency. However, for a long time this was considered to be an immutable principle of socialist distribution, and some people still hold this view today. In so far as it rapidly laid the foundations of a national industrial system, the pre-1957 policy of equal allocation, with China regarded as a single great chessboard, was relatively successful. (During the First Five Year Plan (1953–7) 694 major industrial projects were put in hand in the coastal areas and in the interior.) However, in 1958 it was decided that regions should establish independent industrial systems. First districts and then provinces should set up more or less independent and complete industrial systems, after which the various regions, all at different stages of development, should create their own industrial structures based on the same model. All provinces, municipalities and autonomous regions, despite their great differences in natural resources, existing forces of production, and social and cultural conditions were instructed to set up complete local industrial and economic systems, taking the production of steel and grain as the 'key link'. The opportunity to take advantage of a favourable situation was thrown away.

Forests and pastures were put to the plough, and land was reclaimed from lakes. To stop the transport of coal from north to south, funds for development in coal-rich northern areas such as Shanxi, where the returns from capital construction were high, were substantially reduced, and exploration and mine construction were concentrated in South China (in nine provinces and one municipality) where coal was scarce and returns on investment low. In Shanxi and other provinces great efforts were made to develop light industry and textiles, in which they were deficient, while in South China, where the opposite was true, the development of these industries was held back. All provinces but one set up steel plants, although some lacked both coal and iron ore and transport facilities were primitive, with the result that production costs were several times higher than the selling price. This attempt to make regions self-sufficient by seeking to make productive sectors completely self-supporting was incompatible with efficient resource allocation. It caused damage to the economic structure of the regions and reduced economic returns. From the mid-1960s onwards there was a large-scale westward movement in China's economic distribution – the theory of the 'third line construction'.[1] In the Third Five Year Plan (1966–70) investment for construction in inland regions was 66.8 per cent of the total, of which 52.7 per cent was in the 'third line' region. In the eastern provinces and cities the output coefficient for investment in basic construction (i.e. the net increase in industrial value produced per yuan invested) was between 1.7 and 6.69, whereas the highest figure for the 'third line' region was no more than 0.89 (Shanxi Province), with the lowest being 0.15–0.25 (Guizhou and Quinghai). The efficiency of resource allocation with respect to spatial distribution and regional economic organization was extremely low. Non-economic considerations were dominant.

## Man-made fragmentation and ossified distribution of factors of production

In order to exercise unified leadership over several hundred thousand enterprises, the central and local government at various levels set up innumerable administrative organs to be responsible for them. This fragmented the internal links in the economy, and hence each vertical organization made its own allocations in the same region, often without sufficient coordination, so that 'productive links' and synchronization were difficult to achieve. For instance, a generating station might be in production before the railway serving it was finished. Enterprises under local government administration were even more indisciplined and failed to consult each other. Apart from their vertical links they constituted closed or semi-closed systems in which, once factors of production were allocated and installed, they became the property of the locality or the department and quickly became frozen. Productive capacity lay idle while there was shortage. It frequently happened that in one region or one system a certain type of productive capacity was seriously under-utilized, whereas elsewhere there was large-scale investment in the same type of productive capacity.

## Absence of self-organizing capacity in local economies

Apart from the period 1958–70, when the policy of downward delegation of power was practised, for most of the time the management system employed was a combination of centralized administrative and economic power. Enterprises were subordinate to administrative organs and the economic rights of local government were severely limited, so that they were unable to organize the local economy. In the relatively developed areas and major cities of the eastern coastal region, the profits created by the older enterprises and even their basic depreciation funds were generally appropriated by central public finance departments, and used for investment in new areas. Such methods as 'whipping the willing ox' and 'taking from the fat to pad the lean' decreased the vitality of the regions and large cities where the economy was relatively developed, so that output and technology stagnated. These undesirable results became increasingly evident in the late 1970s and early 1980s.

Some modern industrial enterprises, particularly heavy industrial projects, were installed with central government finance in backward areas with mainly agricultural or pastoral economies. Such enterprises had no internal economic, technical or organizational integration with the local economy, and the localities were unable to provide the missing link in the chain of production. Self-sufficient agriculture and stock raising, in which traditional methods predominated, and modern industry, in which extra-regional relations predominated, each developed their own independent circulation system. This had a deleterious effect on the economic structure and slowed down the transformation from a dual to a unified structure.

In some very backward regions (mainly in the border areas west of longitude 104°E) economic construction was totally dependent on central government subsidies and investment. Although this allowed relatively rapid economic growth, many enterprises became too reliant on subsidies and showed very little competitiveness. The local economy's own power of accumulation atrophied. Local government was entirely dependent on constant external support, and one injection of funds often led to more. In order to keep up the treatment it was necessary to 'whip the willing ox' at the expense of the more developed areas.

In a country with such regional variation, the attention of those in centralized economic management who are responsible for local economic decision-making is inevitably focused on major projects, while the development of related industry is often neglected. Such problems were noted as early as 1956, after the First Five Year Plan, and Mao Tsetung spoke of those who 'only pay attention to the bones and ignore the flesh, 'factories and buildings have been put up, and other equipment installed, without municipal construction and service facilities to go with them; this will become a big problem in the future' (Mao 1977: 333). As Mao foresaw, many problems of imbalance between main and related industries, and basic installations, remained unsolved.

Under the old system, local economic development took the form of the presentation of a long list of items and investment to the central government by local governments. The total needs and demands of all localities put together was far beyond what the government could afford. Incessant bargaining followed and in the end the government gave a little to everyone.

Until the end of the 1970s the inter-regional structure was broadly as follows: the inland regions sent raw materials and all types of primary products from agriculture and mining to the coastal regions and major cities, where they were processed and returned to the interior. The inland regions provided goods and materials at low prices, which allowed high manufacturing profits for the coastal regions. Thus most of the profit went to the state, and was invested in new capital construction projects and used for subsidizing backward regions.

# Choices in reform

In 1978, after the overall plan for reform had been put forward at the Third Plenum, thus opening up and invigorating the economy, there was a great change in the situation. Opening up meant opening up to the outside world but also opening provincial, regional and municipal doors. Factors of production which had previously been clogged began to flow across regional and departmental boundaries. In this process of 'horizontal economic linkage' the flow and reorganization of factors of production, at first limited to the regulation and exchange of surplus and scarce goods and materials, was extended to goods and materials in general, and to technology, funds and labour. For example, in Shanghai, China's largest city, 80 per cent of raw materials used in factories was formerly allocated by the state; now 80 per cent is purchased by Shanghai itself. This has led the city to invest a total of 900 million yuan in areas rich in raw materials and to cooperate in the development and supply of raw materials and energy, as well as supplying technical expertise and personnel (*Renmin Ribao*, 21 September 1987, 15 October 1987).

With the beginning of market penetration and the recognition of local interests, more attention has been paid to the exploitation of comparative advantage, and economic returns have increased in some localities. This can be seen from the increased rate of development in Guangdong, Fujian and Jiangsu over the last eight years, and from the changes in such provinces as Yunnan, Guizhou and Inner Mongolia, which were formerly at the bottom of China's economic ladder (*Renmin Ribao* 21 September 1987, 15 October 1987). Before 1978 the average taxes on profits from capital in the latter provinces were 11.59 per cent, 7.69 per cent and 5.88 per cent respectively; by 1985 these figures had risen to 22.28 per cent, 15.01 per cent and 10.64 per cent. In the countryside, where reform began rather earlier with the introduction of the family responsibility system, there was an increasingly obvious labour surplus. Some was absorbed by the expansion of local enterprises, but many people migrated to towns, or from poor and underdeveloped regions to more developed areas, looking for work. At the same time, some technical personnel and those with special skills moved from towns and developed regions to the countryside and backward regions, bringing knowledge, technology and the new concept of a commodity economy, knocking on the long closed doors of the poor villages. This quiet change attracts little attention, but has made clear the difference in inter-regional labour costs and has stimulated the mobility of labour. With the passage of time it will produce profound changes in the structure and distribution of industry in the regions. However, these positive changes have been accompanied by a variety of difficulties and problems.

First, there is a lack of variety in local industry. In the early 1980s the provinces, cities and autonomous regions all rushed to set up factories making bicycles, sewing machines, watches, cigarettes and so on, most of which did not reach the minimum economic size. This wave had not entirely subsided when a new one began, with the production of colour television sets, washing machines, refrigerators, tape recorders, electronic organs and other such consumer goods. By the end of 1985 a large number of production and assembly lines for these products had been imported – more than a hundred of each – so that nearly all provinces had several. While the regions have been developing profitable manufacturing industries, basic industries and services have stagnated elsewhere, creating national disequilibrium.

Secondly, this uniformity in regional economic structure has exacerbated market friction, so that tariff barriers and market carve-ups have appeared. The 'trade war' over wool and tobacco is an example. In order to profit from the higher value of processed goods, all the areas producing wool and tobacco set about establishing wool-spinning and cigarette factories to process their goods on the spot. The productive capacity of small wool-spinning factories increased by a factor of 14 in the six years after 1980 (Yu 1987), and, in order to increase local output value and their own financial revenue, local governments adopted a policy of protecting these enterprises. When the old wool-processing bases and large wool-spinning factories starting buying wool at higher prices, the local governments used administrative measures to raise tariff barriers. Long dominated by planned buying and allocation, now that the country was opened up, the wool market was once again carved up and monopolized by some local governments. Other agricultural products also suffered the same fate to some extent.

The reasons for this are complicated. A fundamental reason is that, with the coexistence of the old and new systems, there is a lack of healthy competition in the growth period of the commodity market. The immediate causes are are as follows. First, there is a serious distortion in relative prices: the interests of regions selling raw materials are neglected so that they have little incentive to develop their own manufacturing industry from which the revenue is higher than that obtained from the direct sale of primary products, although from a macroeconomic point of view the benefits are few. Secondly, the government administrative function is mixed up with its managerial function. The socialist government is both the organ of state power and the representative of 'ownership by the whole people', as well as having a management function. The two functions have long been confused. With a high degree of centralization this system maintains some order, even if it is inefficient, but when power is divided the result is chaos. Decentralization in 1958 and 1970, rapidly followed by recentralization are examples of this. After the introduction in 1980 of a new financial system with contracts between different levels and a clear distinction between revenue and expenditure, regional interests were strengthened. In order to increase regional revenue there was competition for the most profitable projects, for scarce resources and even for the use of administrative power for local protectionism and carving up the market. In order to use the market to ensure efficient resource allocation, the administrative and management functions of government must be separated. Management of enterprises 'owned by the whole people' can only be the function of the enterprises or the group of enterprises or investors' companies; government at whatever level, as administrators of publicly owned enterprises, should only have a controlling and regulatory role. Only this can guarantee that factors of production can flow freely into regions where the returns are highest and that industries can establish themselves in areas where costs are lowest, in order to achieve efficient resource allocation and improvement of the local economic structures. To establish this kind of economic environment it is necessary for all factors of production (including land, mining, environmental resources etc.) to become commoditized, and that there should be a unified market embracing all factors of production which is sensitive to shortages. Regional price variations should reflect the relative costs, supply and demand in the different areas. The state should simultaneously control and regulate the market in accordance with socialist goals.

State regulation and control of the market through economic levers should be based on clear policies with regard to the regions, and to the regional distribution of production, including the following.

1   A policy of appropriate bias in economic distribution should be established. For the remainder of this century there should be no major change in spatial economic layout. The emphasis should be on consolidation, completion and improvement of the region east of the line between Lanzhou, Chengdu and Kunming, where an economic framework is already in place. There should be rational reorganization of the capital stock through the allocation of new investment, and the efficiency with which funds are used should be increased. The focus for

new construction should be on the eastern seaboard and in the central and adjacent western regions Shanxi, Shaanxi, West Henan, Inner Mongolia and the large raw material and energy base of the Hongshui River and the present medium-sized and large cities). A concentrated effort should first be made to develop the economy in these areas, so that the shortages of funds, technology and energy (all vital to the growth of the national economy) can be solved.

2   A strategy for regional development, putting into effect a regional policy for the distribution of production, should be drawn up, and plans and preparations made for sequential development of production in different areas. Favourable sites should be selected for those industries which require special locations, and preferential treatment given as a matter of policy to allow such industries to establish a number of national centres. Leading industries should be encouraged according to the specific strengths of a particular region, surrounded by linked industries and basic facilities which are independent, highly efficient and form composite local economic entities with their own special characteristics. There should be a rational division of labour between regions according to their resources and to the market, and a vertical division of labour according to levels of industrial development. We should promote the regular steady progress of local industrial structures. In accordance with changing local advantages, we need to regulate the spatial transfer of industries between developed, less-developed and underdeveloped regions. This will enable the creation of a dynamically regulated intra-regional industrial structure, allowing regions at different levels of development and with different conditions to develop their strong points and advance together. We should encourage competition but not allow it to be excessive.

3   A pattern of point and axle development which encourages regions to develop their own specialities, raises their capacity and promotes regional growth should be adopted. Modern transport and communications networks should be used to join points into zones. We should create production and urban zones, and make horizontally interlocking industrial belts.

4   We must aid poor and backward areas. Aid in the past has always been in the form of relief funds, resulting in 'annual relief and perennial poverty'. In future this should be changed to a system whereby the state establishes a special repayable revolving fund with public tenders and contracts for development to support economic bodies whose specific purpose is to aid the poor areas and create employment opportunities. Financial assistance should be mainly used to improve operation and investment, so as to allow participation in local competition on more or less equal terms. In the end state aid must result in a capacity for local self-generation.

# Note

1 In the mid-1960s, for the purpose of national defence, China was divided into three 'fronts' (*xian*): the third 'front' was the area south of the Yangize, north of Shaoguan, east of Wuxiaoling, and west of the Beijing–Guangdong railway line, which includes most of Sichuan, Guizhou, Yunnan, Shaanxi and Gansu, the western parts of Henan, Hebei, Hunan, Hubei and Guangxi, eastern Qinghai and northern Guangdong.

# References

Chen Dongsheng (1987) Zouxiang 2000 niande Zhongguo jingji bujn duice (Economic distribution in China in the year 2000). *Gongye Jishu Jingji*, no. 2.

Mao Tsetung (1977) *Selected Works*, vol. 5 (English edn). Beijing: Foreign Languages Press.

Yu Huijin (1987) Yangmao dazhan heshi liao, langfei zhi duoshao (The battle over wool: when will it end? Who knows how much waste?). *Jingji Cankao*, September, 4, 5, 7, 8.

# Index